READINGS IN
CALIFORNIA CIVILIZATION

California Redwood Country (Courtesy of Alan Kirshner)

READINGS IN
CALIFORNIA CIVILIZATION

Interpretative Issues
Fourth Edition

Howard A. DeWitt
Ohlone College
Fremont, California

KENDALL/HUNT PUBLISHING COMPANY
4050 Westmark Drive   Dubuque, Iowa 52002

Copyright © 1981, 1989, 1994, 1998 by Kendall/Hunt Publishing Company

ISBN 0-7872-5093-7

Printed in the United States of America
10 9 8 7 6 5 4 3

CONTENTS

PREFACE AND ACKNOWLEDGMENTS

The fourth edition of **Readings in California Civilization** is a revision with a new perspective and fresh readings. The addition of material on the emergence of the Chinese American during World War II, a new essay on Senator William Gwin and the politics of prejudice, a series of contemporary documents on the late nineteenth century debate over the railroad add a great deal to this edition. The emphasis remains on women, multicultural activity and ethnic differences. The purpose of **Readings in California Civilization: Interpretative Issues** is to provide a wide variety of viewpoints and to stimulate discussion on key issues.

Many of the suggestions for revision comes from the comments of students and letters from professors who have used this book. They have suggested some contemporary observations, which have been added to issue 6, and they wanted more emphasis on multicultural contributions. There were new questions, new readings and a new direction. The numerous suggestions received during the last few years since the last revision are appreciated.

Professor John C. Chen was helpful in refocusing some of the issues on Asians in California. Professors Daniel Gonzalez and Alex S. Fabbros of San Francisco State University were helpful in the selection of materials as were Jerry Stanley, Rudolph Lapp, Richard Peterson, Harvey Schwartz, Jim Kluger, Ingrid Scobie, Earl Pomeroy, Richard King, Bradford Luckingham, Leonard Pitt, Richard Dillon, W. Turrentine Jackson, David Williams and Alan Rosenus. The eight issues included in this fourth edition would have been impossible without their help.

My brother, Dennis DeWitt, criticized all portions of the manuscript and provided some light and popular touches to the otherwise trenchant academic writing. Chuck Borgquist handled the editorial part with his usual care, diligence and above all patience. My wife, Carolyn, and my two children, Melanie and Darin, were highly supportive. Jeanne MacDonald and Connie Karasek provided morning coffee at my local specialty shop and they also criticized the manuscript. At Ohlone College Dr. Alan Kirshner, Professors L. Stacy Cole and Sheldon Nagel offered advice and encouragement. The late Hans Larson, Chuck Reed and Walt Halland all offered excellent advice. My tutors Vernon Lucas and Ralph DeUnomuno provided important suggestions. My former professors at Western Washington State University August Radke and Keith Murray are owed my thanks for putting up with four years of silly questions. At WWSU Dave Page was a constant historical companion. He remains the finest thinking historian that I have ever met. Warren Johansen was another undergraduate who influenced my historical thinking and Mr. Johansen remains the best read non professional historian in America. Professor Geoffrey Hirsch, the man with funny ties, helped to formulate the recent material on California. Professor Hirsch is a veteran of the civil rights movement and it was due to him that I included a reading on W. Byron Rumford. My dean, Dr. Ron Quinta, helped facilitate a schedule to complete my various projects, including this one.

Professor Earl Pomeroy of the University of Oregon directed by M.A. Thesis and provided much of my early professional focus. I can only say thanks for spending the time helping me get my career off the ground. At the University of California, Davis the late Jim Shideler was an important influence. After studying agricultural history with Professor Shideler, I moved into ethnic history and he gave me the first insights into this field. Although I never took a class from W. Turrentine Jackson at UC, Davis, he was a strong influence upon my career. His work ethic and sound scholarship was an important catalyst to my career. At the University of Arizona the late Herman Bateman saw my Ph.d. dissertation through to completion in a tale that now goes back almost thirty years. I owe a great deal of my professional life to these former professors. B. Lee Cooper, dean of instruction at the College of Great Falls, was an important source for reading selections and I thank Dr. Cooper for his imput. Adam Eterovich and Bob Reed published my earliest materials on ethnic history and I can only say thank you for the help. At Cochise College more than thirty years ago Joe Gilliland encouraged my writing and I remain grateful to him. The Bancroft Library made pictures and research materials available. After seventeen years all I can say is thank you to the dozens of schools that have adopted this reader. Enjoy it.

Howard A. DeWitt
Ohlone College
Fremont, California

A Mojave Mother and Son

The Two Worlds of Native Americans and the California Missions

READINGS: THEODORA KROEBER *"ISHI IN TWO WORLDS"* JEFF JONES, *"NOMLAKI LIFE: AN ORAL HISTORY"* JERRY STANLEY, *"JUNIPERO SERRA V. THE CALIFORNIA INDIANS"*

California's Indian population of 300,000 made it the densest populated Indian settlement in North America. Generally, however, the ancient past of California's earliest settlers is shrouded in mystery. The predominantly Catholic Spanish settlers could not believe that the Christian Bible failed to mention the Native Americans' history. This resulted in a skepticism about the place of the California Indian in the greater framework of the Spanish empire.

When the Missions were set up as twenty-one settlements connecting Spanish California from San Diego to Solano a "Christian siege" mentality prompted the Franciscan Friars and the military to view the Indian population as primitive. As a result the California missions were the heart of the social-economic success of Spanish California. The Franciscan Friars, aided by eager soldiers, coerced much of the coastal population of California Indians into the missions. While baptizing 54,000 Indians the Franciscans reduced Native Californians to a pliable work force. In the process California Indian civilization was destroyed. The justification for this cultural castration was a simple one. The Indians needed civilizing and christianizing.

Once the Spanish settled San Diego in 1769, the Franciscan order brought the cross into California to accompany the sword. At least this was the view of Juan Bautista de Anza, one of the earliest and most capable Spanish military leaders. What made Anza a ferocious Indian fighter was a family tradition which saw his grandfather and father fight on the Spanish American frontier. When Spanish soldiers, like Anza, met the California Indians they were overly militaristic, and the cost of this wholesale transformation saw the Indian population between San Francisco and San Diego decline from 72,000 to 18,000.

The Spanish scarcely noticed this decline as they zealously planned their settlement assault on California. In January, 1774 Father Francisco Garces guided Anza and thirty four men from Tubac in northern Mexico into Southern California. This was the first large migration of Spanish settlers through the San Jacinto Mountains. On March 22, 1774 Anza's party arrived at Mission San Gabriel. After a brief rest Anza moved on to Monterey and secured the Spanish California frontier. The significance of Anza's expedition is that it provided the first land link to California settlement. The next expedition which Anza led founded San Francisco.

By 1775 Spanish authorities planned to send another party of settlers from Sinaloa and Sonora. On October 23, 1775 more than two hundred men, women and children left Tubac with Anza in command to settle in Spanish California. When they arrived in California some colonists remained in Southern California at the Mission San Gabriel while others traveled north to settle in Monterey and the remainder settled in what is now San Francisco.

The formal dedication of the presidio of San Francisco de Asis on September 17, 1776 and the founding of the Mission Delores on October 9 made Spanish California a permanent civilization. It also doomed Native Americans. The Spaniard envisioned California as a laboratory to civilize the Indians and Father Junipero Serra and others viewed as "primitive" and in "need of Spanish civilization."

Jack Forbes' book **Native Americans: California And Nevada** argues that "the Native Americans responded initially in a friendly albeit sometimes shy, manner towards the Spanish intruders." Forbes suggests that the naive manner of the Native Californians helped to shackle them to Spanish institutions.

The primary instrument of civilization in the Spanish colonial era was the mission system. The construction of a roadway known as the El Camino Real (the King's Highway) linked twenty-one missions from San Diego to Sonoma. Since each mission was a one day journey, the El Camino Real formed a transportation network for local settlers. There were other mission functions which guaranteed California a permanent future. The Spanish-California missions were the basic source of food, livestock, craft goods and cultural activity as well as the social focus of local life. As a result, the missions provided the key elements in civilizing California's countryside.

The California missions controlled large landed estates, enormous livestock herds and a craft industry which was highly prosperous. The Neophytes (a term used by race conscious Spaniards) were forced to live in primitive surroundings while they toiled as skilled blacksmiths, brick makers, farmers, shepherds and weavers. At its peak the mission herds numbered more than 400,000 cattle, 60,000 horses and 300,000 sheep and goats.

The Indians did not grant this labor freely. It was a forced labor and it destroyed the last remnants of Native California culture. The old traditions died as Spanish soldiers publicly whipped Indians for the slightest indiscretion. Punishment of Native Americans led to a high death rate.

But the California Indian still had ways to preserve their culture. The use of Coyote Tales by the California Indian was a means of communicating their culture. Coyote told stories of creation, puberty rites, agricultural production, child bearing and rearing and most other aspects of daily life. To the Spanish military and clergy these tales appeared "childlike" and "primitive." The punishment for repeating Coyote Tales was a beating. The stage was set for a clash of cultures which led to open resistance by the Native Californian.

As early as 1775 there was significant Indian opposition to the Spanish and their various systems of colonization. Pedro Fages reported that "the Indians of the numerous villages . . . are habitually restless and commit hostile acts. . . ." Spanish military and religious leaders downplayed Native California discontent and suggested that the mission system was establishing civilization. The Franciscans Friars, notably Father Junipero Serra, kept self serving diaries that eloquently detailed the challenges of frontier life. As Professor Alfred Kroeber wrote: "The Franciscans were saving souls only at the inevitable cost of lives."

In the rough frontier atmosphere the Catholic church believed that it provided a civilized buffer between the Indians and Spanish settlers. The Franciscans had a vision that the Indian could be integrated into the mainstream of California life. As a Utopian visionary, Father Serra hoped to establish a model Christian community which would provide the Indian with the necessary education and vocational training to become Spaniards.

The initial plan for educating the California Indian placed a ten year limit upon the apprenticeship period. If a Native Californian remained longer than ten years on a mission he or she was eligible to enter the free population. This was a noble plan but it failed. The average mission Indian spent almost forty years under the guidance of the Franciscans. The missions were wealthy and powerful in California, and this prompted Spanish officials to ignore the New Laws of 1542. This edict by the Spanish King granted Native Californians a parcel of land and citizenship within a decade. The royal proclamation was never enforced.

Unfortunately, the missions failed to bring the Indian into the mainstream of California life. There are many reasons for this failure. The most significant one is that the Franciscans were unable to understand Native American culture. A key to understanding the California Indian is demonstrated in the career of Ishi.

In August, 1911, a middle-aged Yahi Indian, wandered down from the foothills surrounding Mount Lassen and walked into a ranch near Oroville. He was gaunt, tired and defeated by years of isolated living. As the last surviving member of the Yahi civilization, this lone Indian represented an important link to the past. The Yahis had once thrived in the Mill Creek region south of Mount Lassen. Since the 1850s gold miners, hunters and settlers had pushed the Yahis into hiding. Most people believed that the Yahis were extinct. When Ishi was discovered, he challenged the stereotype that the California Indians were diggers. To live alone in the mountains, Ishi had to master a variety of survival techniques. The perseverance, intelligence and adaptability necessary to survive in the wilderness was a testimony to Ishi's intelligence. By the time that Ishi was discovered the "Digger Indian" myth was a widely held scientific view.

The term "Digger Indian" originated with race conscious Americans who encountered California Indians in the mid-nineteenth century and were struck by the Native-Californians lack of civilized qualities. This was a value judgment based on a lack of understanding of Native-American culture. Not only did the "Digger Indian" stereotype suggest that the Indian population was primitive, but they were described as a people without culture or history. As a result of this view many popular books and school textbooks distorted the role of the California Indian. The use of such terms as "primitive," "Stone Age creatures," and "savage" revealed a lack of historical understanding about the California Indian.

Many early academics also viewed the California Indian as primitive, because they used a criteria suited to American society. Among the strongest academic charges were that the Digger Indian failed to practice permanent agriculture, lacked the rudiments of modern technology, didn't collect war instruments and shunned political-economic activity. There were other means used to re-enforce the Digger Indian myth. Some historians pointed to the lack of knowledge about the wheel, the inability to use metals, the unwilling-ness to engage in systematic writing, and the indifference to aggrandizing material goods. There was also a spiritual base to this stereotype. The lack of creation tales among Indian tribes, some academics argued, indicated that the California Indians' religious beliefs excluded a well defined system of Gods.

The list of exceptions to the Digger Indian are important in exploding the myths behind this vicious racist stereotype. Since most Indian tribes had a story about their origins, there was a religious base. The Ohlone Indians, for example, believed that on a small island, Coyote, the only living thing in the world, saw a feather float onto his island. Suddenly the feather turned into an eagle, and a small hummingbird swooped down from the sky. This strange trinity of animal-gods created a new race of people. For hundreds of years this Ohlone story of creation passed from one generation to another and it serves as an excellent example of religion's influence upon California Indians.

For years historians have neglected California Indian culture. This rich and varied culture centered around the temescal. This structure was a mud and stick thatched building with a small hole in the ceiling to let out the steam from the hot rocks that were sprinkled with boiling water. It was much like a sauna and the Indian males met there to plan celebrations, plan food foraging expeditions and discuss changes in their lives. This careful organization serves as an example of Indian political and economic institutions.

There are many examples that contradict the Digger Indian stereotype. The strongest challenge resulted from Ishi's years living at the University of California museum. In his daily life Ishi was the most civilized man that Alfred L. Kroeber and Thomas Waterman had ever encountered. As Kroeber remarked Ishi had a "stoic quality" and a sense of his destiny. With Ishi's help Professors Kroeber and Waterman learned a great deal about the Yahi people and their culture. Ishi's sensitivity to his new surroundings gave him the opportunity to educate Kroeber and Waterman in the Yahi way of life. A brief camping trip to Mount Lassen allowed Ishi to demonstrate to the professors the manner in which the Yahi adjusted to mountain life. As he acclimated himself to his former environment, Ishi made a salmon harpoon, killed a deer with an arrow and shaped a piece of juniper wood into a hunting bow. As Ishi swam in the familiar creeks, he used a kissing sound to call rabbits. During this trip Ishi demonstrated the Yahi's ability to cope with nature.

Equally impressive was Ishi's grasp of California life. Although he was caught between two cultures, Ishi managed to learn about 600 English words. He mingled well with local people and was described as a kind, sensitive person with inordinate patience. As thousands of tourists wandered through the University of California Museum, public interest failed to divert Ishi from his daily tasks. He had a strong personality. One that allowed Ishi to ignore the inquisitive Californians who intruded upon his past.

In San Francisco Ishi's life was surrounded by modern technology. He marveled at the white mans' matches and glue, and he considered these useful devices. Plumbing fixtures, automobiles and furniture brought a sly smile to Ishi's face. He believed the white man practiced inventive folly.

It is Ishi's relationship with women that offers important insights into his personality. He was friendly, yet reserved, and he was a charming dinner companion. For a time Ishi lived with Professor Thomas Waterman, and he observed the practice of never initiating a discussion with a woman. Yet, when a woman spoke to Ishi, he was courteous and animated in conversation. There was a quiet dignity and sense of order in Ishi's life.

Much like the Japanese, Ishi viewed orderliness as a prerequisite to happiness. As a result Ishi's clothing, toilet articles, tools, books and other possessions were arranged in a careful, calculated manner. Whether Ishi was at the University Museum or camping with the professors at Mill Creek, he maintained a clean and clutter free environment. A small tarp was spread when he chipped wood at the Museum. When he cooked for Kroeber and Waterman during the camping trip, Ishi cleaned the fish and butchered the deer with a skill and ingenuity that belied his sense of nature. Ishi's tools were carefully cleaned and preserved due to their level of importance.

It was in his social life that Ishi was able to relax. He loved to smoke, go to dinner parties and attend the theater. In Ishi's culture tobacco was part of the "sacred pipe," and he believed that tobacco was a right for the tribal elders. Ishi, a careful listener and interesting dinner companion, even received a marriage proposal. Due to his civilized qualities, Ishi was the darling of San Francisco society.

Theodora Kroeber's book **Ishi in Two Worlds** is an exceptional argument defending Ishi and his culture. Ishi was caught between two cultures once he began living in San Francisco, but he had the strength of character and intelligence to transcend the white man's world. This reading is a valuable insight into California Indian life as well as a resounding answer to the Digger Indian stereotype.

A less famous but equally significant California Indian, Jeff Jones, took time to record his reminiscences. In 1936 the seventy year old Nomlaki Indian provided ethnographers a glimpse into his life. The Nomlaki were one of several tribes who occupied the region from the Sacramento River Valley to the Coast Range in present-day Tehama and Glenn Counties. At one time the Nomlaki numbered about 2000, but the ravages of time and the white man's civilization reduced the Nomlaki population to a few survivors.

What is interesting about Jeff Jones is that his mother was Nomlaki and his father white. Although he was raised in the Nomlaki ways, Jones' mixed ancestry provides a glimpse into two cultures. Jones offers positive comments about Indian attitudes towards war, childcare, women, divorce, business enterprise and property. Jones' memoirs reveal that the Nomlaki held highly sophisticated concepts of civilization.

The reminiscences of Ishi and Jones offer excellent insights into twentieth century California Indians. It is much more difficult to analyze Native-Americans in the Spanish period. Once the Franciscan missions were constructed local Indians found their way of life radically altered. There are numerous accounts of California Indians adjusting to the mission system. Since there is no general agreement, historians tend to be overly critical or inordinately praiseworthy of Father Junipero Serra and the Franciscan mission system. The Spanish believed that close associations with the Franciscan friars would civilize the Indians. The example set by Father Serra and his followers would bring the Indian into the mainstream of Spanish civilization. Not only did the Franciscans have a positive dream for the Indians, but they were zealous in their attempts to educate and christianize. In theory, each mission was designed to educate the Indian and provide them with the means to earn a living. In ten years the Indian would be set free to become a functioning member of Spanish society. It was an ideal but impractical dream as Native-Americans became virtual prisoners of the mission system.

Despite the charges of cruelty against the Franciscan missionaries they were impressive leaders. For instance, the legendary Father Junipero Serra devised the mission system and personally supervised the construction of the first nine sites. Always a man of action, the five foot two inch Serra possessed a mammoth ego and a physical constitution which amazed his colleagues. He had a capacity for work which allegedly brought 5000 Indians to the Catholic church. Although he was a testy and ego centered leader, Serra was a highly skilled administrator who possessed the totalitarian traits necessary to make the mission system successful.

In his personal life Serra was a charismatic figure. While walking from Vera Cruz to Mexico City, as a manifestation of his religious purity, Serra suffered an insect bite. His foot and leg were not properly treated and for the rest of his life he suffered ill health. Serra delighted in holding out his ulcerous foot as a sign of his strong faith. He also suggested that it was a testimony to God's power and protection.

The theatrics associated with Serra's sermons are legendary. Often in the midst of a fiery sermon, Serra would beat himself with a chain or burn his chest with a candle. In the sleeping quarters at the Carmel Mission, Serra kept a long tong of sharp-pointed irons near his bedside to expel evil thoughts. There is no doubt that Serra's integrity and commitment to the Franciscan order were unquestioned, but he was often inconsistent, controversial and abusive to the Indians. These traits have created a heated debate about his place in history.

Despite his personality quirks, Father Serra was a natural leader. He convinced the Spanish Viceroy to deploy married troops to California. Local Spanish military authorities and later Governor Felipe de Neve complained that Father Serra meddled in lay affairs. Serra responded that Indian wars would result if the unmarried soldiers continued to abuse Indian women. It was the Spanish governors who were the subject of the Franciscans strongest criticism. Father Serra was critical of Governor de Neve's Reglamento of 1779 which expanded the rights of all Spanish-Californians, because he saw it as another means of cutting into church authority. In time Father Serra demanded that Governor de Neve be replaced and his successor, Pedro Fages, also felt the wrath of the Franciscan's demands.

When Father Serra died, he was replaced by Fray Fermin Francisco de Lasuen. An energetic worker with a public relations type personality, Father Lasuen was the perfect successor to Serra. He completed nine missions, broadened the base of the California economy and encouraged foreign traders. In 1797 the seventy-seven year old Lasuen consecrated four new missions and toured every Alta California mission. By 1800, however, Spanish bureaucrats were disenchanted with the Franciscan missions. When Padre Antonio de la Concepcion Horra was sent back to Mexico City because of suspected insanity, Father Lasuen provided an in-depth report of the mission system. While Lasuen's report defended the mission system, there was little doubt that its future was limited.

The Franciscan's inability to place the Indian into the mainstream of Spanish life doomed the mission system. The growing power of the rancheros, the military officials and the governmental appointees did not bode well for the future of the mission system. Perhaps the best way to understand the relationship between the California Indian and the Franciscan is to examine the Ohlone Indians.

The Ohlone Indians' reacted positively to the Spanish mission system. By nature the Ohlone's were a trusting and altruistic people. There was a part of the Franciscan belief which attracted the Ohlone civilization. The Franciscans "were Utopian visionaries who had come to the New World to set up the perfect Christian community of which the Indians were to be the beneficiaries." The Ohlone's approved of this direction. While this vision never materialized, the Franciscans did establish six missions in Ohlone territory. The conflict between the Franciscan concept of civilization and the Ohlone way of life was evident.

What is intriguing about the Ohlone lifestyle is that it continued to prosper during the Mexican and early American periods. As Michael Galvan, a local Catholic priest and a descendant of the Ohlone Indians suggested, "They have become accustomed to being ignored." Historians defending Father Serra suggest that he had the best interests of California Indians as the basis for his mission plan.

Many historians feel that earlier historians have romanticized Father Serra and the Franciscans, but this criticism ignores the strong feeling that Serra had for the Indians. In his diary Serra talked about the need for strict rules, and he suggested that in the future the Native Californian would be better off because of this discipline.

After more than two centuries of controversy over the Digger Indian stereotype, the stage was set for the canonization of Father Serra. In the summer of 1943 Father Serra's remains were dug up in the graveyard at the Carmel Mission and Father Eric O'Brien verified them. By 1989 Serra's sainthood was guaranteed. Scholars have continued to debate his role in California. Professor Gerald Stanley of California State University, Bakersfield, has written a paper which suggests that Father Serra was a negative influence upon California. Not only does Professor Stanley make a strong case against Serra and the Mission system but he accuses Serra of "deceit and trickery." The church, according to Stanley, urged Father Serra to do whatever was necessary to bring the Indians to Catholicism. Historians, Stanley argues, have ignored the negative influences of the mission system.

In a strongly worded concluding essay, Professor Stanley blames the decline of the Native American population upon an ill advised mission system. Serra's lack of leadership set up the California missions to bring salvation and the civilization to the Indians, Stanley writes, but the end result was "starvation, disease, punishment and sexual abuse."

In examining the Native-American population and the Franciscan mission system there are a number of important questions to consider. Did the conflict between the Franciscan friars and Spanish military authorities prevent assimilation of the Indians? Did Fathers Serra and Lasuen understand the nature of the Indian culture and lifestyle? Finally, was Spanish civilization not suited to the Native Americans? The reminiscences by Ishi and Jones provide some speculative answers to these questions.

The accomplishments of the Franciscan order were remarkable despite the continued historical debate over their intentions. Each mission was staffed by one or two Franciscans and they dealt with a large California Indian population. By 1810 twenty thousand Indians were converted to Catholicism. No more than 30 Franciscans oversaw the education and training of local Indians. The courage, skill and dedication of the Franciscan order is beyond question. As a buffer between the Spanish military, governmental authorities and the civilian population, the Franciscans were the chief force of permanent California civilization.

Ishi in Two Worlds
by Theodora Kroeber

In 1911 Ishi was discovered in Oroville, California. He provided an important link to nineteenth century Indian life. The following selection from Theodora Kroeber's, Ishi in Two Worlds *is an excellent analysis of the character and personality of the Yahi Indian. This excerpt also offers a glimpse of a way of life and thinking that is no longer part of California's heritage.*

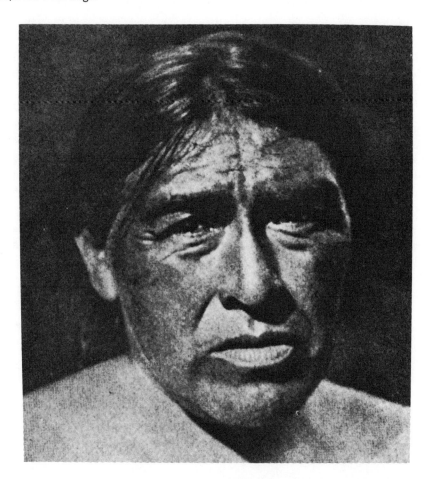

Ishi (Courtesy of the Bancroft Library)

Theodora Kroeber, ISHI IN TWO WORLDS. Reprinted by permission of the University of California Press.

Ishi was a man of middle stature, five feet eight inches tall, presumably born between 1860 and 1862, hence fifty-two to fifty-four years old in 1914. Pope could find no evidence of childhood disease, and Ishi did not remember having had any. Neither was there evidence of smallpox or chicken pox; no glandular abnormality, no scars from boils or burns or injury.

Skin—*light reddish bronze which darkened with sun exposure, fine in texture.* Hair—*black and straight, worn long over the ears, tied in a single brush down the back.* Musculature—*well developed with even distribution of subcutaneous fat.* Teeth—*all present, strong, no evidence of decay or pyorrhea. Molars much worn but in good condition.* Eyes—*set straight, lids Caucasian in contour. (Eye and lid contour in many California Indians suggests a more Mongoloid form.)* Breath—*sweet and free from foetor, an Indian trait noted also by Stephen Powers when he traveled amongst and wrote about California Indians in 1877.* Body odor—*faintly musty. (Non-acid.)* Noae—*strong and wide.* Chest—*full, normal.* Thighs and legs—*well-formed. Spring and leg action not that of one who in his youth had been a sprinter. Both habit and build made for endurance rather than speed. A tireless walker.* Hands—*medium small. Size 8 glove. Palms soft and pliable, fingers tapered, fingernails ovaloid in outline, texture excellent.* Feet—*broad and strong, toes straight and unspoiled, longitudinal and transverse arches perfect. Skin of sole thick but not rough. Toenails round in outline, strong, and short.*

Pope preached a sermon about feet to each of his classes in medical school after he had examined Ishi's feet and taken casts of them. Indian scouts, hunters, and ethnographers who have traveled and lived with Indians in forest, desert, or plains have commented on how quietly they walk, without the snapping of twigs underfoot and the disturbance of dirt or sand and pebbles which happens when white men walk. Pope observed and described how Ishi actually walked:

He (Ishi) springs from the great toe which is wonderfully strong in its plantar flexion and abduction. His method of locomotion is that of rather short steps, each foot sliding along the ground as it touches. Neither the heel nor the ball of the foot seems to receive the jar of the step. The foot is placed in position cautiously, not slammed or jammed down. He progresses rather pigeon-toed, and approximates crossing the line of his progress each step.

Ishi had no history of venereal infection. He knew, in a vague and general way, that there were such diseases. He was free from sex perversion of any sort. Kroeber found that Ishi was reticent about any discussion of sex, blushing furiously if the subject came up. He did not question him about his personal sex life at all. Pope did, using a doctor's opportunity and privilege. Ishi had had very little if any actual experience in sex function; perhaps a little when he was barely pubescent. There were no women left in the tiny band whom he could have married or with whom he might have had a passing relation by the time he was grown. There was only one young woman, and she was a sister or a cousin. In any case, she stood in a sister relation to him. He was much attached to her in what seems to have been a brother-sister bond made closer by their own youth, and the older ages of the other three in the group.

There was certainly fondness and tenderness in their feeling for one another; there is not the slightest evidence for construing sex interest or experience to have been a part of it.

Toward all white women whom he met during his museum years, Ishi was friendly but reserved. He was a guest for dinner and overnight many times in his friends' homes, and he lived with the Watermans for three months. During these visits he never initiated conversation with his hostess, her daughters, mother, mother-in-law, or any women guests. When a woman spoke to him he answered courteously but without looking directly at her. This behavior, it must not be forgotten, was correct Yana etiquette, a proper showing of respect. How much of it was something more than that—a shyness born of sex starvation in a person who was reserved but not shy, generally speaking—it is impossible to say. Having accustomed himself to living without any sex life during his young years, there was, no doubt, little urge to change his ways in his late forties or early fifties, particularly among strangers.

Continuing old Yana custom, Ishi bathed daily, and daily he plucked out any beard hairs which had sprouted overnight, using tweezers of split wood. No one ever saw him at this operation except by coming on him while he was engaged in his toilet in private. Daily he brushed and combed his long hair. He washed it frequently, drying it by a filliping and beating, using a flat basket paddle. In the hills, he would have put grease on it. Pope offered him bay rum, as a city substitute, but he declined it. In the hills, his bath would have been a sweat bath. The Yana used a solution made by heating the leaves and nuts of the bay tree until they were reduced to a semisolid state, and rubbed this solution on the body after a sweat bath. It acted as a soporific, "like whisky-tee" said Ishi. Ishi kept in his clothes box a bar of scented soap and a can of talcum powder, "lady powder" he called it. These were gifts that he treasured but never used.

Ishi was orderly by nature probably, and by old habit, certainly. His clothes, toilet articles, tools, treasures, all his possessions, stood neatly on shelves in his small room, or were folded in exact arrangements, or were wrapped in paper and stored in drawers. He worked wherever he chose to in the museum, and his was the sort of work to make chips or flakes or scraps and to create disorder. But he spread newspapers or a tarpaulin to work on, cleaning everything up when he was finished. In camp, his friends found that he cleaned fish or butchered a rabbit or a deer with deftness, leaving no messy and fly-attracting scraps about, and that his cooking and dishwashing were done more quickly and neatly than their own.

This easy competence and pleasure in well-ordered arrangements of the tools and possessions of living suggests the Japanese flair for raising mere orderliness to an aesthetic of orderliness. There is a temperamental and possibly a kinaesthetic something in this trait not to be explained by poverty in the variety of things owned, or difficulty of replacement and consequent need to take good care of them. Poverty the world over does not, *per se*, make for orderliness or aesthetic satisfaction, nor for cleanliness nor pride nor even for care in handling the little one has. The aesthetic of order and arrangement would seem to be rather something inborn, deep-seated in the individual psyche. Some cultures turn this preference and capacity into an approved value: thus the Yana and the Japanese. We do not, nor do the Mohave, to name two different value systems.

Ishi enjoyed smoking, but was not a regular or confirmed smoker, going without tobacco for weeks sometimes. Tobacco was no novelty to him, the sacred pipe being a part of ritual and ceremony and prayer with his people. The no-smoking rule which held both in the museum and the hospital he regarded as reasonable: he may well have assumed that the taboo covered more esoteric hazards than those of fire. He believed tobacco to be bad for the young, not so much for reasons of health as of propriety. Amongst his acquaintances in the museum and adjoining buildings were a few who chewed tobacco. He enjoyed this pastime with the copious spitting which is part of it, but only when he was alone with one of his tobacco-chewing companions, and always out of doors. It would have seemed to Ishi a nest-fouling performance to engage in inside a house or shelter.

Ishi liked doing all kinds of things with other people. The young internes and medical students and orderlies at the hospital drew him into their games, some of which Pope knew of only afterward. None of them could match Ishi's skill in rope climbing, nor did any of them venture onto an upper window ledge of the hospital as Ishi occasionally did. Teetering there above them, laughing, and pretending to be about to accept their "dare" to jump, he clung with his bare feet to the man-made ledge as securely as he used to cling to the high ledges in Deer Creek cañon. He was not so good as the least good of his young friends at any sort of ball game, for he was not able to throw as far or with as much accuracy as they. To be good at throwing and catching, one must have learned it early in life. Although innocent of technique, Ishi had a respectable showing in informal boxing and wrestling, and he found a friendly scuffle great fun. He was expert in certain styles of swimming, using the side stroke except in rough water, where he changed to a modified breast stroke. He knew no overhand or other fancy strokes, and, unlike the Yurok Indians, he did not dive. He was accustomed to slipping into a river at water level, but he could swim underwater with great skill and for long distances. He would walk, hunt, fish, or practice archery without fatigue all day. And he was a tireless and interested partner in any sort of work at all within his range, although Pope quaintly remarks that "Ishi was indifferent to the beauty of labor as an abstract concept. He never fully exerted himself, but apparently had unlimited endurance."

Whether it was play or work, Ishi preferred company to solitude; but not in order to compete or to excel or to demonstrate his own strength or skill. The impulse to any sort of exhibitionism was totally absent in him. He might well have found in Pope's "beauty of labor," as in the white man's strenuousness and competitiveness and wish to be first, some of the seeds of the display motive which he so shunned. This reticence may have accounted also for his strong distaste for acrobatics and tumbling, whether as participant or as audience.

Ishi was normally calm and equable of disposition, never vehement nor given to bursts of anger. He showed displeasure and on occasion some excitement when an unauthorized person touched or misplaced his belongings. He was scrupulous in never touching anything which was not his, and so watchful of museum property that he reproved Popey for picking up and putting into his pocket a museum pencil. On the other hand, nothing made him happier than to be able to give something. He would give away his arrow and spear points, even a bow which had taken many patient hours to make, or anything else from his little hoard. During the camping trip he enjoyed the role of host, cooking, ladling out, and sharing his bounty from a successful day's fishing or hunting.

Ishi was religious, his mysticism as spontaneous and unstrained as his smile. He believed according to Yana formula in the making and peopling of the world by gods and demigods, and in the *taboos* laid down by these Old Ones. He also believed in a Land of the Dead where the souls of Yana live out their shadow community existence. Christian doctrine interested him, and seemed to him to be for the most part reasonable and understandable. He held to the conviction that the White God would not care to have Indians in His home, for all Loudy told him to the contrary. It may have occurred to him that the souls of white men would fit but poorly into a round dance of Yana dead. If so, he was too polite to say so.

Perhaps it was as well Loudy did not become a missionary—he left Ishi with certain misconceptions about the story and teachings of the New Testament. When Ishi saw the cinema of the Passion Play, which moved him and which he found beautiful, he assumed that Christ was the "bad man" whose crucifixion was justified.

At ease with his friends, Ishi loved to joke, to be teased amiably and to tease in return. And he loved to talk. In telling a story, if it were long or involved or of

considerable affect, he would perspire with the effort, his voice rising toward a falsetto of excitement.

Needless to say, Ishi did not learn to read beyond recognition of no smoking and electric and billboard signs which were constants of San Francisco; the letters and numbers which identified the streetcars which he rode; newspaper titles; and his reading of a clock, however that was done by him. He enjoyed funny pictures, and had no difficulty in getting their "point." Perhaps funny pictures of forty years ago were more simply comic and less narrative than most of those today, less dependent upon words for communicating their meaning.

Ishi's "broken English" was much commented upon during his life at the museum—too much, perhaps. Kroeber says that none of the staff except Sapir, whose genius was for language and who knew Northern and Central Yana, pronounced Yahi as well, or used it as indiomatically, as Ishi used English; and he estimates that by 1914 Ishi commanded an English vocabulary of at least five or six hundred words. He of course understood many words which he did not himself use. Many Yana words end on a vowel sound like Italian words. The consonantal endings of English were sometimes troublesome to Ishi as they are to Italians, and he tended to naturalize them to the sound and speech pattern familiar to him as do Italians when speaking English. "How much?" for example under Italian and Yana vowel end preference may become *How mucha?*

Before giving any further approximations of Ishi's English pronunciation, it should be said that there is risk of a misconstrual of the person in such quotations—they tend to make Ishi sound quaint or childlike, whereas he was neither. A European refugee of Ishi's age and with no previous knowledge of English will in all likelihood attain a good mastery of English usage and vocabulary after four years here. Ishi's English vocabulary by comparison remained small and his usage relatively pidgin. But it should be understood that Ishi was simultaneously confronted with unfamiliar objects, activities, meanings, and concepts, as well as with a strange language. Book, bank, and dishpan are not difficult words to learn, you may say. But what of their difficulty if your long experience had not included the concept of writing so that you did not know what were the significances of marks on the pages of a book, much less their meaning, or if you did not know what money was, or what the purpose of a dishpan?

Ishi's *Hullo*, or if the occasion was formal, *Howdado*, were cordially said and accompanied usually with a warm smile. He retained a reluctance to the use of words of farewell. His preferred phrase was a casual, *You go?* or, alternatively, *You stay. I go.* He would add a *Goodboy* when he felt it was expected of him but his heart was not in it. For whatever personal or custom-ingrained reasons, there attached to parting a significance best not accorded recognition in words.

Besides his friends, a Sioux Indian once passed judgment on Ishi. It happened in this way. Pope and Ishi were attending a Buffalo Bill Wild West Show, of which they both were fond. There were a number of Plains Indians in the show. One of them, a tall, dignified man decked out in paint and feather war bonnet, came up to Pope and Ishi. The two Indians looked at each other in silence for several moments. The Sioux then asked in perfect English "What tribe of Indian is this?" Pope answered, "Yana, from Northern California." The Sioux then gently picked up a bit of Ishi's hair, rolled it between his fingers, looked critically into his face, and said, "He is a very high grade of Indian." When he had gone, Pope asked Ishi what he thought of the Sioux. "Him's big chiep," was Ishi's enthusiastic reply.

Ishi was not given to volunteering criticism of white man's ways. But he was observant and analytic, and, when pressed, would pass a judgment somewhat as follows. He approved of the "conveniences" and variety of the white man's world—neither Ishi nor any people who have lived a life of hardship and deprivation underrate an amelioration of those severities or scope for some comforts and even some luxuries. He considered the white man to be fortunate, inventive, and very, very clever; but childlike and lacking in a desirable reserve, and in a true understanding of Nature—her mystic face; her terrible and her benign power.

Asked how he would, today, characterize Ishi, Kroeber says, "He was the most patient man I ever knew. I mean he had mastered the philosophy of patience, without trace either of self-pity, or of bitterness to dull the purity of his cheerful enduringness." His friends all testify to cheerfulness as a trait basic to Ishi's temperament—a cheerfulness which passed, given half a chance, into a gentle hilarity. His way was the way of contentment, the Middle Way, to be pursued quietly, working a little, playing a little, and surrounded by friends.

The figure of Ishi stands, part of it in the sun, varicolored and idiosyncratic and achieved; part in deep shadow, darkened by the extent of our own ignorance and by its own disadvantagements. A biography should include something at least of the nature of these shadows, the unrealized potential, the promise unfulfilled, even in that brightest year of his life, 1914. He had only one name, not the usual two or three. He had only a museum address, although it was in very truth home to him. There was no living person with whom he could, from time to time, revel in a rapid and idiomatic exchange in the childhood tongue. Affectionate and uncorrupt, he was denied the fulfillment of wife and children, or of any sex life whatsoever. Then there was the total lack of immunity to diseases of the modern world, which had been disastrous to thousands of other Indians, and which brought to Ishi illness and untimely death.

He was unique, a last man, the last man of his world, and his experience of sudden, lonely, and unmitiated changeover from the Stone Age to the Steel Age was also unique. He was, further, a living affirmation of the credo of the anthropologists that modern man—*homo sapiens*—whether contemporary American Indian or Athenian Greek of Phidias' time, is quite simply and wholly human in his biology, in his capacity to learn new skills and new ways as a changed environment exposes him to them, in his power of abstract thought, and in his moral and ethical discriminations.

With little room for choosing, Ishi made choices as courageous and enlightened as the scope of his opportunities permitted. In the Oroville jail he chose life with a strange white man, rejecting the alternative of joining subjugated members of his own race; later he chose the dignity of an earned salary and independence, rejecting government wardship; and when "civilization" bestowed upon him the gift of tuberculosis he chose to fight it according to Popey's instructions and to accept defeat with grace, his concern being to make himself as little a burden as might be to those who cared for him.

Nomlaki Life: An Oral History
by Jeff Jones

This reading selection is an oral history of the Nomlaki Indians by Jeff Jones. In 1936 Jones was seventy years old as he recalled his tribes history. Despite his age Jones was a vigorous man with a large mustache and sparkling eyes. His alert mind and fond memories provide a window into the Native-American past that is both interesting and informative.

The Nomlaki View of Warfare

Nomlaki Indians fight at close range. They let their fastest runner use the elkhide. He runs up close and then crouches down. The men come and stand behind this shield. The enemy can't hit the Huta [secret society] members because they dodge the arrows and are good fighters. If a warrior wastes his ten arrows without any results, he doesn't fight any more. They never shoot back the enemies' arrows, but they might save them. A man who is being held at bay may shoot back an enemy arrow, however. They quit fighting just at sunset. The peacemaker will yell, "Quit, the sun is down."

It is against the rules to throw rocks at an enemy who is being held at bay hiding under a bush. They won't shoot arrows at such a person unless they actually see him. It is too wasteful of arrows.

They never talk about wars except among themselves, and then only in a whisper. They don't brag about what they have done except at the place where they killed the man. . . .

Killing a common man isn't important, but they like to get a man with a lot of tattooing because he will be a "big man." They don't take every scalp—just those of certain people, such as the headman or a person close to him. The brother of a chief would be satisfactory. They like to kill some "big man" and take his scalp.

The Nomlaki View of Childcare

They have an extra basket for a child when it is born; an aunt might have given an old one, or a grandmother might have made one especially. They roll the inside bark of red or white willow (rich people use maple bark) into soft balls that they use as diapers. Layers of it are put in the baby's basket, and the baby is laid on it. The diaper material is changed; it might be washed once or twice but, if possible, clean material is used. They are always very particular to keep these things nice and clean. When the baby is first put into the basket, they have a peculiarly shaped rock as a pillow for the head. They keep it there for about a week to [flatten the back of the head, a mark of beauty], and then take it away. The baby stays in the basket until he is old enough to crawl and sometimes he crawls with the basket still on.

Malcolm Margolin, HOW WE LIVED: REMINISCENSES AND STORIES OF CALIFORNIA INDIANS, 1981. Reprinted with permission of the author and Heyday Books.

The Nomlaki View of Women

"Women are troublemakers." An old woman said that to me when I was young. Out of my four women, only one got along with me nicely. Indian women are jealous. Children will get you into trouble. The older people teach us not to get in the habit of fussing with our wives, and if one starts complaining, to walk away if you can. A woman is more jealous than a man. A man isn't after a woman for nothing.

As a rule, a poor man has more children, but I guess he lies around and has more babies. A man of importance isn't around the house very much. Such a person hardly ever jokes with his wife. He may only be around in the evening. He may lie down alone for a while and then come to her to get warm. There are some men who like to be around their women all the time. They get to hating each other bitterly after a little while because the more love-making they do, the less time the marriage will get. There are some men who will stick with their women, and women with their men. They always go around together; she'll go along carrying wood, he'll go gather berries. Such a marriage may last. That kind of people are said to "hang together." There are families that stay together, and perhaps none of them ever get married. They say that in such a family the baby girl is often as wild as can be. Often that will happen in Indian families.

The Nomlaki View of Divorce

Divorce: A couple can decide to separate by agreement. If a woman who is a basketmaker wants to leave a man, she will make him a real nice basket, mad and pouting all the time. This may take her from six months to a year. She will remain there and work for him and talk to him, but the two will simply not be getting along very well. When she finishes the basket she will hand it to him, saying that she is leaving. He gives it to his mother and tells her what has happened. Now the man's parents have to give her parents something. That is a friendly separation.

The Nomlaki View of Business Enterprise

Traders: Once there were two fellows who roamed around from place to place to trade. The folks kind of got after them. "Why do you go around to trade; why don't you let them come here?" they would ask. "If I stay home," they answered, "I won't learn anything. By going from place to place, I learn more, I learn other people's ways and how they act and treat each other. If I stay here, I don't see anything and can't learn anything. By traveling around I learn more of different things, of talking." Probably this man was a good speaker, but he learnt how to act and carry himself and to treat things differently.

"By going around I trade for things that I don't want, but I take them to the next place and trade for something else. When I get something that I care for or that would be handy to me, I keep it. I'm stingy with that."

The people could not do anything with these traders. . . . That was long before the whites came into the country. They always got by; they got along. There were only three or four who could go any place and travel around. They were wise and would travel and were good speakers. They would go to the house of some good speaker first, have something to drink [soup], and say what they had come for. They would smoke and talk and joke. The next morning the hosts would give them some food to get to the next place on. They would go on for three or four days. The old people objected, but these men insisted that they could be treated no better by their own people. They learned quite a bit and picked up a lot. They got so that people would invite them from a great distance.

The Nomlaki Concept of Property

Property: The land does not [generally] belong to individuals. Dominic's grandfather [a chief], by being such a big and good man, was favored. He was left a big valley. He owned one big oak tree of a special kind. It was a singular tree called *nuis*. There was a rancheria nearby, but old Dominic's grandfather owned that tree and got all the acorns from it. He also owned a valley of about 2,000 acres of open land. It was two or three miles away from his home. This valley was staked off—each different division [kin group] got a different part of the valley for themselves. They had poles to mark the different persons' territories. . . .

Where there is a tree of small acorns, some family owns that tree. He will lean a stick against the tree on the side toward which he lives. Thus the people know what family owns it. He may set up too many and will give away the others to his relatives. This person kind of owns the tree—like you would a fruit tree. In those days the families owned them. They own trees in the mountains, too. They maintain border lines, but if you are friendly with them they may give you a tree in time of need.

Junipero Serra v. the California Indians

by Jerry Stanley

The role of Father Serra as a founder of Spanish-California civilization is a controversial topic. Although Serra planned 21 missions, built the El Camino Real highway connecting the mission and christianized thousands of Indians, there is a dark side to the Franciscan missionaries story. As Jerry Stanley's article suggests, the Franciscan missions attempted to bring salvation and civilization to the Indians, but the end result was more often starvation, disease, punishment and sexual abuse. In an original essay written for this volume, Professor Stanley of California State University, Bakersfield, asks whether Father Serra was a Saint or a Sinner?

Not only does Professor Stanley question the methods and motivations of Father Serra, but he provides convincing evidence that the Franciscan missions were less than successful. This does not necessarily diminish Father Serra's contribution to Spanish-California, but it argues for a much-needed revisionist concept of the Franciscan's impact upon the Native American.

On a still summer day in 1943 in Monterey, California, two hired hands entered the graveyard at Mission Carmel and started to dig. The men were surrounded by the graves of thousands of Costanoan Indians who had died in this mission centuries ago, but the men were being paid to dig at the base of the largest stone marker and to exhume the remains of Junipero Serra, a Franciscan priest, founder of the mission, and "Father" to California's "uncivilized, un-Christian" population. Described as "gentle, courageous and heroic," Father Serra had established 9 of California's 21 missions, which operated from 1769 to 1834 to bring salvation to the savage and to teach him the best of western civilization. As a Spanish institution run by Franciscan priests, the mission system succeeded in converting approximately 22% of the state's native population to Catholicism.

Serra, called the "First Citizen of California," made this possible. And so, 140 years after his death, Serra was being disinterred by Franciscan priests for the avowed purpose of making him a saint.

After the workers unearthed the coffin, Father Eric O'Brien opened it and looked inside to verify that Serra was still in it, a prerequisite to canonization. Then O'Brien, Father Noel Moholy, and other Franciscan priests set about the most difficult task in modern Catholicism, the making of a saint. In 1948 they presented the documentary life of Serra to the Bishop's Court in Fresno whose duty it was to determine if Serra had lived "a life of heroic virtue." The Court said that he had. Next, a *summarium*, a glowing biography of the candidate's life in the form of a lengthy legal brief, was submitted to Rome where the Congregation for the Causes of Saints was asked to decide if

Jerry Stanley, JUNIPERO SERRA AND THE CALIFORNIA INDIANS. Reprinted by permission of the author.

Serra's life exemplified the Seven Holy Virtues: "Faith, Hope, Charity, Prudence, Justice, Fortitude and Temperance." The Congregation said that it did.

The bishops based their decision on three events described in the *summarium* that occurred while Serra was setting up the missions from 1769 until his death in 1784. First, Serra prevented Spanish soldiers from seeking revenge on a band of Indians who had murdered a missionary. Later, he became a champion for Indian rights in California. In 1773 Pedro Fages, the military commander of Alta California, refused to help Serra establish a new mission, and soldiers under Fages' command sometimes raped Indian women and made others their personal servants. So Serra obtained a decree from Mexican Governor Antonio Maria de Bucareli granting the Franciscans exclusive control over the education and training of all missionized Indians. This decree, which the *summarium* calls an "Indian Bill of Rights," is at the core of Serra's case for sainthood, for it demonstrates, the *summarium* says, that Serra "transcended his times." Also emphasized is the fact that Serra performed his duties in poor health and without complaint and that he frequently lashed himself during prayer until he bled.

In 1985 Pope John Paul II declared Junipero Serra "venerable," the first of three steps needed for sainthood. Two years later, on his trip to America, the Pope stood over the closed grave of Father Serra at Mission Carmel and conducted a "bearifying ceremony," called Serra "a shining example of Christian virtue and the missionary spirit." Then, at an open-air mass in St. Peter's Square in 1988 Pope Paul granted Serra the title "blessed," elevating him to the rank of "beati-

fied," one step shy of full canonization. Authorities on church policy say it's a safe bet that Serra will be awarded a halo within the next five years.

The Pope's trip to America and Serra's swift march to divinity have received much media attention. The publicity has not hurt Serra's cause. But there is another side to the story, less publicized but no less true. Professional historians, those who teach about missions, write about Indians, and rely on mission records for facts say the priest was more like an angel of death. They point out that the native population of California was 350,000 when Serra set up the mission system and 100,000 when it ended. Missionization had something to do with this population collapse. Many scholars describe the system as a form of slavery in which Indians were tricked into entering the missions, exploited for their labor, abused sexually, and whipped into submission and death. "The brute upshot of missionization" the noted anthropologist A. L. Kroeber once wrote, "was only one thing: death." The case against the sainting of Serra illustrates a basic truth in history: that history relies upon memory and memory relies upon will. What Serra's *summarium* ignores may be more important than what it says—at least to surviving Indians and to the Costanoans at rest in Carmel.

When the Spanish arrived in California there were at least 350,000 Indians in the state, perhaps as many as 400,000. This population represented the largest concentration of Native Americans in North America. Following the migration of the great ice-age animals in the Pleistocene period—enormous bison and mastodon much larger than the elephants of today—the nomads from Asia wound their way through the tricky mountain passes of the Klamath, Cascade, and Sierra Nevada ranges and began to trickle into California as early as 8,000 B.C. By the time of Christ they had populated most of the state and it has been said of them that they were "the luckiest Indians in North America"—before 1492.

The natural bounty of California—salmon, acorns, a variety of edible plants and small game—made subsistence easy. A hostile desert, forbidding mountains, and the Pacific Ocean meant isolation from other Indian groups, which meant the absence of warfare, no new diseases, and the development of a unique culture. Farming was unnecessary and required too much work, yet starvation was unknown in the state. Religion, government, social structure were simple because living seemed simple. The typical California Indian lived in a hamlet community of about 500 people and had little contact with the crowd living 50 miles down the road. There was no need for a larger view of the world, no need for a written language, no need for a new god, no need for plunder, no need for change. The population of the California Indians and their life expectancy had been on the rise for over 9,000 years. It is not inaccurate to say that before the Spanish arrived the California Indians mostly ate, slept, and made love.

This historic pattern of life changed with the arrival of Junipero Serra, good luck turned to bad. However, the result of mission life for the Indians should not be confused with the motives of the Franciscans. Father Serra's religious order did not believe that "the only good Indian is a dead Indian," the Franciscans did not deliberately enact policies that led to genocide, and Serra, in spite of what went on

behind mission walls, is not accurately described as a "sadist" and a "fanatic," as has been the case. The motives of the Franciscans were honorable: to make the Indians good Spaniards and Christians. That they failed to do this is a matter of historical importance, but *not* why they tried. That much is understandable for the time.

The case against Serra and the missions starts with deceit and trickery. Church superiors ordered the Franciscans to do anything they had to get the Indians into the missions—they ordered the priests to treat the Indians "as children." They did. They cloaked themselves with the vestments of Catholicism, with brightly colored chasubles and ornate copes, and conducted spectacular ceremonies in Indian villages. Accompanied by polyphonic music and waving banners of silk and richly embroidered cloth, the Franciscans led grand Rosary Processions to capture the interest of the natives. Afterwards, the priests distributed baskets of food to the onlookers, promising more if the Indians followed them to the missions. And the missionaries told stories, fables and parables to lure the natives away from home. The point of this "instruction" was to convince the non-Christians that the Franciscans were in immediate and continuous contact with God and only through them could the natives enter the afterworld. No one knows how many Indians entered the missions because of these activities, but the number was certainly less than half of the total mission population. For the general practice in the early years of a mission was to send out Spanish soldiers to capture the first converts.

By whatever means, once an Indian entered a mission the door slammed shut behind him and he was not allowed to leave. The Franciscans did not consider this incarceration. In theory the mission system was to last for no more than 10 years. By then, the priests figured, all Indians would be converted and released and the missions would be secularized. In reality the process of missionizing Indians went on for 65 years (1769 to 1834) and involuntary confinement was the rule. The proof for this is found in the runaway rate.

Mission records show that at least 10% of all missionized Indians escaped permanently and another 20 to 30% ran away at least once, were caught and returned. The runaway rate was high in the beginning of the period and escalated towards the end. It is generally believed that the mission system would have ended of its own accord due to the high escape rate, the high death rate, and a lack of new recruits. Indians who had avoided missionization tended to move away from the coastal missions into the interior valleys beyond the reach of the soldiers. When the Franciscans closed shop in 1834 there were only 15,000 Indians left in the 21 missions.

Simple arithmetic suggests mission life meant death for Indians. Altogether, 81,000 natives were baptized in the missions while 60,600 died within the adobe walls, not counting, of course, the permanent fugitives. At Mission Santa Barbara 4,771 Chumash accepted Catholicism; today the graveyard at Mission Santa Barbara contains the bodies of about 5,000 Chumash. At Mission Dolores, approximately 3,000 Coast Miwok, the entire tribe, were placed under the tutelage of Franciscans; today, a handful of Miwok live, the rest died in Dolores. But Indian depopulation in the missions is more complex than these figures imply. It was not simply a matter of accepting Catholicism then dropping dead on the spot, though it often seems that way.

Demographers tell us that the population curve for *all* California Indians continued to rise rapidly during the mission period, then it leveled off and started to decline towards the end of the period. But this was not the case for the Indians in the missions. From the day the doors swung shut, the population curve for missionized Indians plummeted. Why?

A lower birthrate in the missions figured into this decline. The sexes were separated until holy matrimony, locked up at night to preserve virginity, protect chastity and avoid sin. And almost from the beginning there was a growing sexual imbalance within the missions due to the fact that males had a far greater tendency to run away and elude capture. Another cause for the low birthrate was an increase in abortion and infanticide, prevalent among California Indians but more frequent inside the missions. Doubtlessly this was associated with divorce, which was easy and common outside of a mission but strictly prohibited within it by church doctrine. It is believed that abortion and infanticide in the missions were often protests against unhappy marriages. Still, the main cause for the population decline was not the low birthrate but the high death rate.

There is no simple explanation for the high death rate; all features of mission life played a part. For instance, diet. Once accustomed to a high protein diet of fresh fish, wild game, roots and acorn, the mission Indians ate barley mush for breakfast, a gruel of barley, peas and beans for lunch, and barley mush for dinner. This diet has led some to conclude that many Indians simply starved to death, which the priests would have never recorded in the records. Surely some did starve to death. But probably more died from European diseases, smallpox, measles, and diphtheria, which are also connected to an inadequate diet and to the unhealthy environment of mission life. The California Indians experienced plagues before the Europeans arrived but had an effective way of dealing with a startling number of deaths. Although they could not name the affliction or its cause, when a plague hit they would burn their village to the ground, march down the road for 10 miles or so, and start all over again, which partially explains why they thrived in the new world for 9,000 years. This practice stopped with missionization, as did other sanitary habits. Mission Dolores was only one of several missions that dumped its sewage in the same stream it used for drinking water.

Missionization also required forced labor, which figured into the high death rate. However, it is unfair to say that the Indians were "worked to death." The work load was mild and work was done on a piecemeal basis; Mission Santa Barbara is typical. Men were required to make 360 adobe bricks a day, and women had daily quotas for weaving cloth and grinding corn. These quotas were easily met by mid-morning, leaving the rest of the day open for leisure-time activities and religious instruction. To the credit of the Franciscans, they created a labor system that reflected Indian culture: to work at a task until it was completed and then rest.

The problem for California's natives was the *idea* of labor itself—it was alien to them. Their culture called for the group to do whatever had to be done on any given day. If salmon were running, they took fish night and day until the run stopped. If it was time for the acorn harvest, that's what the group did. And if enough salmon and acorns were stored for the foreseeable future, the group did nothing, nothing, that is, that we would call "work." The important point here is: to the Indian there was little difference between spearing a salmon and doing nothing. Life was life; nature and the seasons determined what one did. Consequently, the Indians did not divide time the way we do, divide the day into 8 hours of work, 8 hours of rest, and 8 hours of play with a "happy hour" and a "social adjustment" period to ease the transition. They understood life in the same way that a bird building a nest understands life; it does not stop building the nest at 5:00 P.M., and when the nest is done it moves on to other things. In this way, the *idea of work* was alien to the Indian. He could never understand why he had to make 360 adobe bricks every day. He could understand this no better than the sparrow who is forced to build a nest every day.

The inevitable result of forced labor was rebellion, followed by punishment and sometimes death. According to mission records kept by Franciscan priests, when an Indian refused to work or was deemed "lazy," food was withheld from him and his family. In other cases Indians were bound to the stock and whipped for slouching on the job. That such punishment was ineffective is not surprising; it was frequent and lasted throughout the mission period. Forced labor caused some to scale the mission walls. For many who remained behind, the idea of labor, in a roundabout way, led to malnutrition, disease, and death.

Punishment in the missions was severe and the natives understood it about as well as they understood *labor*. For a slight infraction, such as missing mass or morning prayer, an Indian took 15 lashes. For refusing to work or running away, he took 50 lashes. For fighting (including rebellion), 100 lashes plus two weeks in the guard house in irons. And at Mission San Jose the punishment for conducting a "non-Christian" religious ceremony was 25 lashes a day for nine consecutive days. Soldiers did the whipping while the Franciscans forced other Indians to watch, which further humiliated and shamed the wrongdoer whose culture used ostracism, not a whip, to maintain social control. Whipping was frequent throughout the mission period and often the same Indian was repeatedly beaten for the same offence, such as "wastefulness." The ideas underlying piety, punctuality, mass, prayer, and sexual abstinence made as much sense to a California Indian as his daily quota of bricks.

The amount of sexual abuse in the missions will never be known, and there's no proof that the Franciscans took sexual liberties while they saved souls. But sex did not stop with missionization and it played a role in the high death rate. For soldiers stationed in the farthest outpost of the Spanish empire, California was a lonely place. It did not take the king's men too long to realize there were not enough Franciscans in a mission to watch all the Indian women. Consequently, syphilis and gonorrhea, unknown in California prior to the Spanish arrival, spread rapidly and became a fact of mission life. Syphilis was the second leading

cause of death at Mission Dolores and ranked high in most other missions. Towards the end of the mission period, the Franciscans were reluctant to send soldiers after runaways if women were involved for fear of what would happen to them on their way back to the mission. Abortion and infanticide were often protests against sexual exploitation and acts designed to conceal sin and avoid the whip.

However, none of this should be taken as the bottom line on mission life. In the debate over Serra's canonization, in descriptions of the mission system, the histories of early California, and in Serra's ponderous *summarium*, the most crucial question about the missions is ignored. Ultimately the story of the missions is not about quaint architecture, not about a labor system, not about Franciscan motives, and not about the beneficence of Serra. It is a story about *Indians*. They are the subject. They are what the missions were all about. So the most important question is: what did the Indians think about mission life? It's the same question asked about slavery; did the slave like it? It's the only question that really counts.

Ironically, the answer is found in the mission records. When an Indian ran away, was caught and returned, mission law required that Franciscans ask the fugitive why he fled, then enter the reason in the log. Common sense suggests that this "Indian testimony" about mission life is truthful. The fugitive had everything to lose and nothing to gain by saying he hated the mission. Those who recorded the answers had everything to lose and nothing to gain by making the entries they did. The most common reason given for running away was starvation, followed closely by punishment, and other remarks shed light on daily life in a mission. But there comes a time when all parties interested in the subject should sit down, shut up, and listen. At least, let the Indians speak for themselves.

I ran away because I was hungry.
I had been flogged three times for running away.
I was put in jail for getting drunk.
When I ran away the first time and returned voluntarily I was given 25 lashes.
I was frightened at seeing how my friends were always being flogged.
I wept over the death of my wife and children and was ordered whipped five times by Father Antonio Danti.
My wife and son died.
Because I was put in the stocks while sick.
They beat me when I wept over my brother's death.
My mother, two brothers, and three nephews all died of hunger.
They made me work all day without giving my family anything to eat.
When I left to find food and returned the Father refused to give me a ration, saying go to the hills and eat hay.
My son was sick, they would give him no food, and he died of hunger.
I went out to hunt food and was whipped and I went out to fish and was whipped.
Because I wanted to go home.

When Pope Paul stood in the graveyard of Mission Carmel and declared Father Serra "beatified," few observers noticed the Indians shouting through the wrought iron gate "No! No! No!" The chant barely echoed across the graves of the dead Costanoans to the resting place of a saint. But the group kept yelling and waving placards reading "Indians Say No," "Serra Is The Devil," and "Missions Killed My People." Bill Wahapepah, a Kickapoo-Sauk-Fox and spokesman for the protesters of 1987 summarized the issue of the day: "To make a man a saint after he helped in the genocide of Native Americans in this part of the country is a contradiction of the words the religion preaches."

Genocide is a strong word. It brings to mind Hitler's death camps and the near extermination of European Jews. It can only be applied to Native Americans in the sense that contact with Europeans lead to death and the near annihilation of a culture. As children we are all taught to count by singing the catchy song "Ten little, nine little, eight little Indians . . . one little Indian boy." The tune is useful for reminding us about Indians if we change the lyrics to "Ten million, nine million, eight million little Indians"—for the Native American population in North America in 1492 was about 10,000,000 and in 1910 it was 270,000. In California it was 350,000 in 1769, 100,000, in 1834, 35,000 in 1860, and 16,000 in 1910.

When he reflected on the fate of Native Americans, the philosopher Henry Thoreau got a grimace on his face and made an observation. Perhaps he was thinking of a California Indian about to enter Mission Carmel: "If I knew someone was coming to do me good, I would run for my life."

WORKSHEET I: The Two Worlds of Native Americans

1. Juan Bautista de Anza's contribution to Spanish California settlement is _____

   _____

   _____

2. Anza helped to found the future city of _____

3. Jack Forbes view of the California Indian in the Spanish California is that the

   Spanish _____

   _____

   _____

4. What peculiar traits did Father Serra possess on the frontier? _____

   _____

5. What does Theodora Kroeber's view of Ishi tell us about Native American culture

   that destroys the Digger Indian stereotype? _____

   _____

   _____

   _____

6. What is unique about Jeff Jones' points of observation? List 3 of his points and

   explain their importance. 1. _____ 2. _____

   3. _____

7. Define the Digger Indian stereotype. 1. _____ 2. _____

   3. _____

8. Why does Jerry Stanley believe that Father Serra was detrimental to the California Indian?

   _____

   _____

   _____

   _____

   _____

9. The Ohlone Indians are important as an example of _____

   _____

   _____

10. The number of Native Californians, according to the reader, when the Spanish explorers arrived was _____

11. List three reasons for the Decline of California's Native American population:

    1. _____

    2. _____

    3. _____

12. A temescal is _____

13. Why was Father Serra critical of the Reglamento of 1779? _____

    _____

14. By 1800 there was pro and con argument over Father Lasuen's leadership. Briefly explain these arguments and suggest why Father Serra dominates the debate.

    _____

    _____

    _____

15. Briefly describe the Franciscan missionaries contribution to Spanish-California civilization.

_____

_____

_____

_____

16. Father Serra's impact upon Native-American can be shown by

    1. _____

    2. _____

    3. _____

17. What is meant by the term "The Two Worlds of Native Americans?" Briefly

    describe Ishi and Jeff Jones in terms of the two worlds _____

    _____

    _____

    _____

    _____

    _____

18. Describe the Ohlone Indian story of creation.

    _____

19. After Ishi learned to write his name, he _____

20. How many years did the Native-American spend on the missions _____

    Why is this significant? _____

    _____

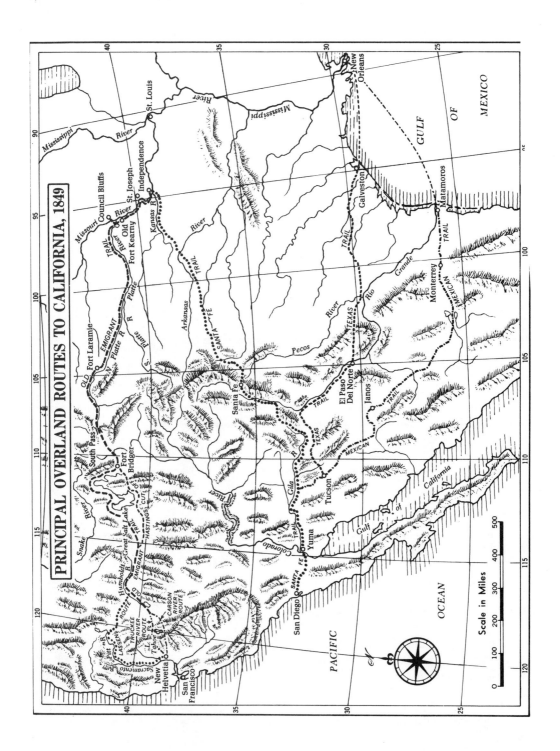

PRINCIPAL OVERLAND ROUTES TO CALIFORNIA, 1849

Mexican-California and the Rise of Foreign Intruders: Foreign Intrigue or Economic Change?

READINGS: HARVEY SCHWARTZ, *"FORT ROSS: HISTORIC RUSSIAN FORT IN CALIFORNIA"* LEONARD PITT, *"HALCYON DAYS: MEXICAN-CALIFORNIA, 1821–1845"*

Mexican California was a brief, but significant, interlude in California history. When Mexico won her independence California was not important in Mexico's future plans. Like the Spanish, the Mexicans viewed California as a remote province with little to add to the new found nation. As the Wars of Latin American Independence raged in the early 19th century, the feeling was that the Californian was somehow not a real Mexican. Combined with this notion was the Mexican tendency to send poorly qualified governors to California. From the earliest days of independence, then, Californians were not happy to be a part of Mexico.

The news of Mexico's political independence reached California in April, 1822. Immediately, Governor Pablo Vicente Sola organized a junta or caucus of military officers, Franciscans and rancheros to swear loyalty to the new Mexican government. This gesture was more or less a pragmatic political move and not an indication of deep seated loyalties toward Mexico. The most important concern of Californians was their economic future and continued political independence. To reflect California's political freedom, Governor Sola flew the Spanish flag for another three months as he urged the Mexican government to prepare a plan for California's future.

On July 14, 1822, the Spanish flag was lowered from the Monterey Presidio and replaced with the green, white and red banner of the Mexican Republic. As news spread throughout California about Mexican revolutionary success, there was speculation about the future.

It didn't take long for discontent to emerge. The Spanish land grant system was an obsolete one which had granted only 25 grants. Many extra legal land grants were settled as local authorities winked at these illegal settlements.

A colonization law enacted in 1824 allowed for five years of tax free land settlement. The result was that fifty working ranches sprung up by 1830. Any Mexican of acceptable loyalty or any foreigner who became a naturalized citizen and converted to Catholicism was awarded a land grant. This provision resulted in 800 plus new land grants.

Ranchos were loosely settled and a chain of hills, a clump of cactus or the center of a river often determined a ranchos boundary. This vagueness clashed with American land law, but in Mexican California the small number of ranchos made boundaries an insignificant question.

Change was rapid in Mexican-California. Social, economic and political institutions evolved into a new direction. The native-born, Spanish speaking Californio controlled the large ranchos, pressed for Home Rule and encouraged foreign settlers.

When Captain John R. Cooper arrived in California in 1823 with the American ship Rover under his command, he fell in love with Monterey. He settled in California and soon two other Americans, Daniel Hill and Thomas Robbins, made their homes in Santa Barbara. These early American residents were import-export traders who were baptized in the Catholic church and married the daughters of prominent ranchers. When William A. Richardson arrived in Yerba Buena on the British whaling ship, the Orion, he converted to Catholicism, married the daughter of the commandant of the port and became a leading business figure. When Yerba Buena became San Francisco, Richardson emerged as a leading businessman.

Throughout early Mexican California there were many foreign traders who questioned Mexican authority. Resentment toward the government in Mexico City increased yearly and by the early 1830s there was an attitude of rebellion amongst local citizens.

Mexico found it difficult to control California, because of the fierce political independence of local citizens. The locals wanted to rule themselves. In 1822 the first Mexican-California Governor was a native-born son, Luis Arguello. He was appointed largely to appease local citizens, and calm the independent attitudes of the Californios. From Mexico's viewpoint Arguello was not really a governor, because California did not become a Territory of Mexico until the Constitution of 1825 went into effect. By that time Governor Arguello had been replaced by Governor Jose Echeandia.

Home Rule arguments plagued Mexican officials during the 1820s and 1830s. Using the local legislature, the diputacion, as a focal point the Home Rule advocates demanded local controls. A decade of political turmoil plagued

Mexican California until 1836 when Arguello was elected Governor by the Diputacion, Marino Vallejo was elected comandante general, and, for once, Mexico readily agreed to the change. The reason for Mexico accepting Home Rule was due to Vallejo's stature.

Since the 1820s when Mariano Vallejo was a well known rancher still in his teens, he argued that Home Rule was necessary because the Mexican government didn't understand California. Vallejo criticized the unstable nature of Mexican government. He wrote Mexican officials and lectured local governors on the need for economic independence for local rancheros.

A series of Mexican Revolutions and Constitutional changes angered Californians. These periodic revolutions and the resulting governmental instability prompted Californians to take a dim view of Mexico. Californians failed to develop a sense of Mexican nationalism. As a result, the political and economic power of the native-born, Spanish-speaking Californios increased dramatically. They owned the key urban businesses, operated successful ranchos and were a strong political force. In addition, their open-minded attitudes and fair manner led foreign businessmen and settlers to flock into Mexican California.

There was a general acceptance of English and American merchants. Many of the newly arrived immigrants had business talents and available investment funds. When the British trader, William Hartnell, profited from the hide and tallow trade, his success attracted other merchants.

In 1822 when William Hartnell arrived in California from Lima, Peru to represent the British firm John Begg and Company, he realized that there was gold in the mission system. It was the consumer market that initially intrigued Hartnell. Soon he was importing Scotch whiskey, items from Peru and taking out a large cargo ship of hides to balance his trading activities.

The missions offered to sell all the hides that Hartnell could ship out of California for $1.00 each. The Franciscans also agreed to sell suet, lard, tallow, wheat, wine, pickled beef and furs. This offer convinced Hartnell to sign a three year contract with the missions to purchase all of their hides and tallow as well as other selected goods. Hartnell's fame as a trader made him a leading citizen. He married a local girl, built the sumptuous Hartnell Ranch in Salinas and in a few years Governor Alvarado appointed Hartnell the mission tax collector. Hartnell built the first important schools in California and was the leading foreign citizen in Mexican California.

Another ambitious immigrant, William Gale, working for a Boston firm, Bryant and Sturgis, also negotiated lucrative contracts for hides and tallow with the missions. The Californios were incensed with the Franciscan friars. Their vows of poverty and loyalty to the mission system had a hollow ring after these lucrative contracts were signed.

Californios vowed to secularize the missions. The decline of the Franciscan's economic influence can be traced to foreign economic successes. By the time secularization was nearing completion in the late 1830s, the Franciscan Friars' cattle trade occupied more than 10 million acres of land and produced almost 400,000 head of cattle, and the same number of sheep. There were more than ten thousand horses roaming the fields. The force of foreign economic investment, coupled with the natural tendency of the Californios to nurture their own economic future, led to the end of the mission system.

Californio policy welcomed the foreign visitor and investor. As a result of local attitudes, American, English and Russian traders planned California economic enterprises. Most traders didn't get beyond the planning stage. But a number of individual settlers immigrated to change the nature of California society. The foreign penetration of California during the Mexican period created a new society. Foreign goods, department stores, trading ventures, ranches and import-export businessmen created a sense of adventure and excitement. Not to mention a new set of financial ideals. Before Mexico's independence, Spain's colonial government kept California closed to foreign settlement. Traders, trappers and visitors continued to enter California but few remained. This changed in the 1820s and 1830s as foreign settlers and observers demonstrated that Mexico didn't have a firm hold upon California.

Mexico's lack of controls prompted foreign corporations to send their representatives to California to found new businesses. During the last days of Spanish-California, the Russian-American Company developed an interest in California. In 1806 Count Nikolai Rezanov visited San Francisco hoping to purchase supplies for the Russian-American Fur Company in Sitka, Alaska. Trade with foreigners was restricted, but Rezanov's engagement to Concepcion Arguello, the daughter of the San Francisco comandante, made it easy for him to bypass the authorities. After Rezanov purchased his supplies, he proposed a Russian settlement in Northern California. This led to the settlement of Fort Ross.

The Russians looked to California because of the decline of the Alaska sea otter. The California waters were rich with otter skins and for a decade the Russians had coveted a California settlement. After negotiating unsuccessfully with the Spanish, the Russian-American Company took advantage of the Mexican revolution to construct Fort Ross. In 1810 Ivan Kuskov mapped out the Bodega Bay area and returned two years later to establish the colony. When construction began on Fort Ross in March, 1812, the twenty-five Russians and eighty Aleut laborers had no idea they were making history. Fort Ross was the first foreign settlement in California. It was established in the Bodega Bay area north of San Francisco. This location discouraged Spanish and Mexican troops from interfering with the Russian settlement.

As visitors sailed by Fort Ross they were struck by the picturesque wooden structures built on a bluff near the sea. Bodega Bay was an excellent port, allowing the Russians to extend their trading influence. They used more than 200 Indian workers to construct a modern fort, and Kuskov established trade ties with a wide variety of Californians. Neither supplies nor workers were a problem for the Russians.

Despite careful organization and vigor, Fort Ross was doomed to failure. The weather ruined crops, an experiment in shipbuilding led to a number of vessels sinking and Fort Ross could not adequately supply the Alaskan trading posts. Mariano Vallejo was also a problem, because he challenged the right of the Russian-American Company to trade in Mexican California.

In the early 1830s Vallejo was sent to Fort Ross to report on its economic success and military strength. The Mexican Governor, Jose Figueroa, instructed Vallejo to look for a site to build a presidio. Clearly, Mexican-California authorities were concerned about the Russian settlement. When the Russian commander, Pedro Kostromitinoff, greeted Vallejo he was struck by the young Californio's youth. At twenty five years of age, Vallejo's cherubic face belied his wisdom. As Vallejo and Kostromitinoff exchanged compliments, the Californio took mental notes. He was surprised at the well developed water mills, the herds of sheep and cattle, the wheat crops and the carefully cultivated orchards at Fort Ross.

It was the wooden walls at the fort which intrigued Vallejo. He realized that they could withstand Indian arrows. But an artillery assault, Vallejo reasoned, would render the walls obsolete. While Fort Ross had an impressive appearance there was minimal security. It had an economic but not a military presence.

Another surprise for Vallejo was how well the Russians understood the Indian. Not only did the Chief of the Tiutuye Indians guard Bodega Bay, but he demonstrated a fondness for the Russians. Vallejo had experienced trouble with the Indians, and he spent an inordinate amount of time talking with the Russians about the Indian problem. After lengthy discussions with the Russians, Vallejo remarked that they had insights into the Indian mind. Few people were able to penetrate the Indians psyche but the Russians understood the Native-American.

Not only did the construction of Fort Ross mark the beginning of foreign intrusion in California, but it created continual confrontation between Vallejo and the Russians. By 1840 Fort Ross was no longer a profitable Russian enterprise. So the Russians decided to look for other trading outlets. They were able to negotiate with the Hudson Bay Company to purchase provisions for their Alaskan posts from Oregon. Once this was completed the Russian-American Company announced its intention to sell Fort Ross.

Vallejo was interested in purchasing it. Sensing that the Russians had no economic leverage, Vallejo offered $9000 for the livestock. This incensed the Russian-American Company and in 1841 they sold Fort Ross to John Sutter for $30,000. Sutter took advantage of the hostile feelings between Vallejo and the Russians and purchased the property with a small down payment. Sutter never made another payment and Fort Ross ended California's pastoral era.

From 1812 to 1841 Fort Ross was a marginally successful Russian settlement. The failure of this short-lived experiment influenced the future of Mexican-California since it left the coast open to American settlers.

The significance of Russia's venture into the American West is analyzed by Professor Harvey Schwartz. His article places the activity of the Russian-American Company in the broader context of imperialistic activity among the major world powers. Professor Schwartz also examines the economic and technological successes at Fort Ross and assesses the fort's subsequent impact upon local agricultural growth. Despite Fort Ross's successes and accomplishments it was not a profitable venture, and when it was sold to John Sutter in 1841 many Californians doubted that foreign economic success was possible.

The sale of Fort Ross is frequently cited by historians as the end to California's pastoral period. This is a period of history in which strong foreign powers could coexist without the threat of war or revolution. The sale of Fort Ross led to a period of aggressive political and military posturing which culminated in the Mexican War. In 1846, when the Mexican War broke out, there was no longer the quiet, peaceful countryside that had characterized California during Fort Ross's heyday. Suddenly the calm was shattered by American troops, foreign settlers and a host of new ideas. Mexican-California's very existence was threatened by this change.

Before the invasion of Americans was brought about by the onset of Manifest Destiny, Californians lived in a virtual oasis of peace and tranquility. The Mexican Constitution created a liberal political climate by granting the Indian equality. By outlawing slavery and preparing the Indian to enter the mainstream of California society, Mexico established the cardinal tenets of political reform. In fact, many nations applauded Mexico's attempt to allow Indians to vote, hold public office and own property. In terms of constitutional guarantees, Native-Americans were granted virtually the same privileges as a Mexican or Californio.

This liberal attitude made it difficult for the Franciscan Mission system to survive. The missions depended upon Indian labor to cultivate the land. The attempt to place the Indian in the mainstream of California society was an indication that private business interests would take over the mission economy. In the 1830s secularization became the most important political issue in Mexican-California. This was an indication that a pluralistic society had triumphed. This is a society where political and economic forces determine the future of the people. Religion was deemphasized and became secondary to capitalistic and political concerns. The selling of mission land and livestock to California businessmen altered the structure of California society. The dominance of Spanish-speaking capitalists ended the historic influence of Catholicism.

Secularization also broke down another Mexican-California stereotype. For years early Anglo historians, notably Hubert Howe Bancroft and Josiah Royce, pictured the Californios as an indolent people. Nothing was further from the truth. Local Californios like Mariano Vallejo, Juan Bautista Alvarado and Luis Arguello believed that Catholicism impeded private business interests. In fact, Garcia Diego, the Bishop of California, complained that church services were little more than a meeting place for women, children and a few Indian converts. The revolution in Mexican-California life clearly reflected the secularization controversy.

When rebellious Indians seized control of the missions at Santa Barbara, Santa Ines and La Purisma Concepcion in 1824, there was a great deal of property damage. The violence and loss of life exploded the myth that California mission Indians were happy. Another example of Indian unrest surfaced when Lt. Mariano Vallejo commanded the Native Cavalry against hostile Miwok Indians in the San Joaquin Valley. In half a century there had been no reason to take up arms against the Indians. During the mid-1840s, bands of California Indians continued to block Mexican settlement in the San Joaquin Valley and to raid local ranchos. It was this action which brought an end to the mission systems influence and led to secularized Franciscan wealth among the Californios.

The turmoil resulting from the secularization debate is brilliantly analyzed in Leonard Pitt's, **The Decline of the Californios: A Social History of the Spanish-Speaking Californians, 1846–1890.** Professor Pitt of California State University, Northridge, argues that there existed a stronger business impulse than California historians have suspected. He believes that an entrepreneurial spirit was a cardinal tenet in Mexican-California. In addition Pitt's pathbreaking study examines the sophisticated attitudes regarding new settlers which prompted Californios to welcome foreign intruders.

The readings in this section suggest that California was a multi-cultural, cosmopolitan civilization long before American conquest. As Professor Schwartz demonstrates, the Russian and Mexican frontier outposts co-existed peacefully. This set the stage for the growth of capitalism and the development of the entrepreneurial spirit. Professor Pitt's study points to Mexican-California as a period of exciting growth.

Fort Ross: Historic Russian Fort in California

by Harvey Schwartz

The following selection is a complete history of the Russian settlement in northern California. The short-lived history of Fort Ross provides an excellent means of analyzing foreign intruders in Spanish and Mexican-California. Harvey Schwartz of the City College of San Francisco presents a very detailed sketch of a Russian colonization scheme. The significance of Fort Ross is that it encouraged foreign settlers to immigrate into California. The resulting foreign business impulse brought important changes into Alta California life.

Fort Ross: Russian Outpost in California (Photo Courtesy of Irving Schwartz)

Harvey Schwartz, "Fort Ross, California: Imperial Russian Outpost on America's Western Frontier, 1812–1841." Reprinted from *Journal of The West*, Vol. XVIII, No. 2, April 1979, pp. 35–48, with permission. Copyright 1979 by the Journal Of The West, Inc.

Fort Ross was the only substantial, permanent outpost of the Russian Empire ever established in California. It marked the southernmost point of Russian expansion in North America and culmination of two and a half centuries of Russian movement eastward from Europe. Although Englishmen and Spaniards had explored and claimed the Northern California coast during the sixteenth century, when the Russians built Fort Ross in 1812 they founded California's first significant European settlement north of San Francisco. Together with their otter-hunting Aleut servants, the Russians lived close to the area's first inhabitants, the Kashia Pomo Indians. They used Ross as a fur-trading, agricultural, trade, and ship-building base for twenty-nine years before selling their property to John Augustus Sutter in 1841.

I. From Moscow to California

Russian expansion into North America in the eighteenth and early nineteenth centuries was the farthest phase of a protracted movement eastward begun by Moscow in the mid-sixteenth century. Between the 1580's and 1630's Russian pioneers seeking furs crossed Siberia and reached the Pacific Ocean near Okhotsk. By 1706 the Russians had taken the Kamchatka Peninsula northeast of Japan. Shortly before Tsar Peter the Great's death in 1725, the Russian ruler sent the Danish explorer Vitus Bering to determine whether America and Asia were connected by land. During 1728 Bering explored the strait named for him. On a second voyage in 1741, Bering discovered the Aleutian Islands and the Alaskan

mainland. Although the famous navigator died during the expedition, the trip's survivors returned home with valuable sea otter furs. Because the sea otter population was declining in Russian waters, this treasure in pelts stimulated Russia's movement eastward. Accordingly, the first permanent Russian settlement in North America was established on Alaska's Kodiak Island, where Gregory Shelikhov founded a hunting base in 1784. By 1790 Shelikhov was considering extending Russia's claims as far south as California.

Although Shelikhov died in 1795, his enterprise gave rise to the Russian-American Company, chartered by Tsar Paul I in 1799 and awarded a monopoly over Russian activity in America. Alexander Baranov, the company's first Chief Manager, ably directed the affairs of Russian America until 1818. From Sitka, established as the region's capital in 1804 and known to the Russians as New Archangel, Baranov presided over the expansion of Russian interests in Alaska, California, and even, for a short time, Hawaii. The Russian-American Company, which in fact represented the authority of the Russian government in the New World, was even granted its own flag by Tsar Alexander I in 1806.

When the Alaskan sea otter population declined because of over-hunting, the Russians looked to California's otter-rich waters. In 1803 Baranov contracted with a New England sea captain, Joseph O'Cain, to divide the proceeds of the first joint Russian-American hunting expedition to California. Baranov furnished the Aleut hunters, and the Yankee provided the transportation with his vessel, the *O'Cain*. The *O'Cain's* spearmen netted eleven hundred furs, turning half over to the Russians in early 1804. During the next decade, Americans and Russians often joined in hunting ventures, generally splitting the catch of sea otters evenly. In these expeditions, the Yankees provided the supplies essential to a Russian enterprise so far afield. At the same time, the Russians were crucial to the Americans, for the Russian-American Company controlled the Aleuts, the region's only skillful sea-otter hunters. Without the Russians providing the Aleuts, the Americans could not have hunted sea-otters successfully.

Because of the tremendous difficulty in transporting supplies from Siberia and cultivating supplementary crops in Alaska, the Russians began looking to California for agricultural products as well as furs. In 1805, when Nicholas Rezanov arrived at Sitka on a Russian-American Company inspection tour, he found the colony short of food and afflicted by scurvy. With famine threatening Sitka in 1806, Rezanov sailed to San Francisco aboard the schooner *Juno* to seek emergency provisions. Diplomatically maneuvering around Spanish regulations against trade with foreigners, Rezanov concluded an agreement for grain and, in one of the most famous romances of California history, became engaged to Concepción Argüello, the daughter of the Spanish commander. Rezanov not only provided relief for Sitka, but also recommended that Russia established an agricultural supply point and hunting base on the Northern California coast, which the English explorer Sir Francis Drake had called "New Albion." After falling from a horse while crossing Siberia en route to St. Petersburg, the Russian inspector died in 1807 before his scheme could be realized.

Determined to implement Rezanov's ideas, Baranov sent his assistant, Ivan A. Kuskov, on a series of exploring and hunting trips to Northern California during 1808–1811. Kuskov, who eventually became the first commander at Fort Ross, was initially interested in Bodega Bay—he called it Port Rumyantsev—where the first Russian American Company structure was built in 1809. Finally, however, Kuskov picked the present site of the fort for the Russians' principal settlement because of its superior soil, timber, pasture land, water supply, and defensibility, and its greater distance from the Spanish authorities in San Francisco. Accompanied by twenty-five Russians and eighty Aleuts, Kuskov began construction of the fort in March 1812 on a bluff 110 feet above the ocean beach. The redwood stronghold, called *Slavyansk,* or "Ross," by Kuskov ("Ross" is an old form of the word *Rossiia*, meaning Russia), was dedicated at the end of the summer but was not completed for many more months. By 1817 the stockade wall accommodated a pair of two-story blockhouses, several cannons, a commander's house, some barracks and storage facilities, an office, a well, a bell tower, and a flag pole. Outside the main fort, a windmill, a shipyard, a bathhouse, a smithy, a cemetery, some gardens, and some animal shelters completed the complex. Forming the nucleus of Russian California, "Colony Ross," as the Russians called it, came to extend approximately eight miles inland between Cape Mendocino and Cape Drake, and included Port Rumyantsev and several farms. During the summer months, the Russians also stationed a hunting party on the Farallon Islands some thirty miles beyond the Golden Gate.

Lithograph of Fort Ross, 1828 (Courtesy of Bancroft Library)

II. The People of Colony Ross

Kuskov selected the site of an old Southwestern (Kashia) Pomo Indian village called *Meteni*, or *Madshui-nui*, as the most suitable strategic location for Fort Ross. The Kashia Pomo, masterful basket-makers, occupied the coast and hills from the mouth of the Gualala River to a point below the mouth of the Russian River. With the arrival of Kuskov, the Pomo near the fort, who called themselves *Chwachamaju*, resettled beyond the stockade area, probably in conical structures made of vertical poles covered with slabs of redwood bark. In 1817 the Russian claim to Fort Ross was formalized by an exchange of gifts and the signing of a deed of cession by several Indian leaders. The Russians not only provided trade items and employment but also, the Indians felt, constituted a buffer against the advance of Spanish colonization. Surprisingly cordial much of the time, Russian-Pomo relations were ocassionally troubled. Because Russian discipline was sometimes stern and remuneration for work sometimes meager, by the early 1830's it was difficult for the Russians to secure Indian laborers. Visiting the fort in 1833, Ferdinand Wrangell, the Governor of Russian-America, reported that during his stay the overseers at Colony Ross had rounded up reluctant Indians, tied their hands, driven them to the Russian settlement, and forced them to work the grain harvest. Nonetheless, Russian-Pomo relations were sufficiently harmonious that Russians often stayed overnight among the Indians. Commander Kuskov's wife, Katherine, learned the Pomo language, acted as an interpreter, and taught Russian to the Indian children. As time passed, the Kashia Pomo incorporated dozens of Russian words into the vocabulary of their own language.

The Russian hunting supervisors were called *promyshlenniki*, which, roughly translated, means frontiersmen or fur trappers; the term is traceable to an old Novgorod word for freelance exploiters of natural resources. Fort Ross's *promyshlenniki* depended upon their Kodiak Eskimo and Koniag Indian hunters—usually identified simply as "Aleuts" in contemporary documents—who had been brought to California from Kodiak Island in Alaska. The Aleuts lived in their own redwood plank houses outside of the fort's stockade walls. Among the world's greatest small-boat hunters, these people pursued sea otter, seal, and sea lion in their *baidarkas*, or two-man skin-covered kayaks, of which forty were brought from Alaska in 1812. Tireless and sea-hardened, the Aleuts would wait motionless in the kayaks for ten to twelve hours. They would approach a surfaced otter silently and swiftly and would impale it with a pronged, detachable bone-tipped spear. A wounded otter would dive under water for about twenty minutes, its course marked by a bladder-balloon attached to the spear tip by a cord. When the struggling otter surfaced again for air, it would be dispatched. Such sea-otter hunting was at first profitable to the Russians. During his exploring voyages along the California coast, Kuskov took 1,453 pelts in 1808 and 1,238 in 1811. But between 1812 and 1815 the otter kill declined to only 714 adults and 163 young. In 1820 only 16 prime pelts were taken. By the mid-1820's sea otter hunting had ceased being a profitable venture at Fort Ross. Thereafter, the Aleuts were often used in lumbering and herding.

The population of Russian-California varied over time, but rarely included over one hundred Russians or five hundred people in all. After twenty years of Russian occupation, only fifty Russians, seventy-two adult Pomos, eighty-three Aleuts, and eighty-eight "Creoles" (persons of mixed Russian and Aleut or Pomo blood) resided at the fort. At Port Rumyantsev, the largest population center outside the fort vicinity, about twenty Russians and fifty Aleuts were stationed during the early days. Very few Russian women and children resided at Colony Ross. In 1833 only about four adult Russian-born females and five Russian children lived at the fort. The largest group of adult females consisted of Pomo women, several of whom were married to Russians and Aleuts. The division of labor at Ross was quite clear. While the Aleut men served chiefly as hunters, especially in the early years, the Russians and Creoles acted mainly as guards, overseers, artisans, and cooks. The Pomos—both men and women—performed most of the colony's agricultural labor. With expanded cultivation, the number of Pomos in the fort's vicinity increased, the Russians employing one hundred Pomo agricultural workers in 1825, one hundred fifty in 1833, and two hundred in 1835. The constant shortage of labor at the sparsely-populated frontier colony was often aggravated by desertion and disease. The Russian-American Company imported some Russians described in the documents as "riff-raff" and criminals.

Desertion among these employees was always a threat. Disease could hamper operations badly, as it did in 1828, when twenty-nine Creoles and Aleuts died of measles. Five years later an epidemic incapacitated most of the fort's personnel and killed many Pomos.

III. Economic Activities at Fort Ross

Agriculture became a leading activity at Colony Ross with the decline of otter hunting. From the beginning of their settlement in California, the Russians hoped grain production at Ross would supply Russian-Alaska with needed food. Unfortunately for the Russians, the amount of grain sent north was neither consistent nor sufficient. With few experienced farmers—the Russian system of serfdom kept most of the nation's peasants tied to the land at home—the colony failed to rotate crops or to fertilize fields. The arable land along this rugged coastal region was not particularly abundant or fertile, and the ocean fog frequently caused stem rust, which could ruin an entire crop. For a long time Ross did not even have an efficient method for threshing. During their first few seasons in California, the Russians had to depend upon the Spanish for grain and seed. Even in later years the residents of Colony Ross were often compelled to trade manufactured goods to the Spanish and Mexicans for supplemental grain to ship to the Russian-American Company's Alaskan outposts. Still, agriculture did expand significantly in the 1820's and early 1830's, yielding good wheat and barley crops in 1828 and 1832. During the latter year Fort Ross was able to send one-quarter of its bumper wheat yield to Sitka. Although from 1826 through 1833 Ross exported 4,000 bushels of grain to Alaska, this still fulfilled only one-twelfth of the Russian-American Company's needs; and in 1835, 1836, and 1837 Russian California experienced serious crop failures. The commanders of Fort Ross never succeeded in making the post a bread basket for the Russian-American Company.

Russian agriculture at Colony Ross was hardly limited to wheat and barley production. Among the supplemental farming activities undertaken by the Russians, stock raising was probably the most important. As early as 1813 the Spanish brought twenty cattle and three horses to Fort Ross. Over the next three decades the cattle, horse, mule, and sheep population at Ross increased substantially. Although a serious epidemic during 1823–1826 killed many animals, stock numbers doubled after 1833 with the opening of new Russian ranchos inland from the fort. The residents of Colony Ross produced beef, butter, tallow, hides, mutton, and sheep's wool, and even sent moderate shipments of salted beef to Alaska in the late 1830's. An 1841 inventory listed seventeen hundred cattle, nine hundred forty horses and mules, and nine hundred sheep in the Russian settlement on the eve of its closing. Pigs, goats, chickens, turkeys, ducks, and geese were also raised at Fort Ross. But because of limited pasture land and over-slaughtering, Russian stock raising at Ross remained only marginally successful. The Russians always had far fewer animals than the Spanish and Mexican Californians. In 1838 the Mexican General Mariano Guadalupe Vallejo, for example, had ten thousand cattle and approximately five thousand horses on his Petaluma rancho alone.

Vegetable gardening and fruit growing, though smaller in scale, succeeded rather better than grain production and stock raising at Colony Ross. While there were substantial vegetable shipments to Alaska in good years, most of the Russians' produce was grown in private plots for local consumption. Many vegetables survived the year around and could be double cropped, some species reproducing in great abundance and yielding remarkably large specimens. Commander Kuskov's extensive gardens included potatoes, carrots, onions, garlic, radishes, beets, turnips, lettuce, cabbage, peas, beans, muskmelons, watermelons, grapes, pumpkins, and horseradishes. Employing a great variety of harrows, plows, carts, and other equipment—as the 1841 inventory discloses—the Russians also cultivated corn, oats, and tobacco. To supplement the vegetables, the Russians planted a number of fruit trees near the fort, many of which remained productive into the twentieth century. The first specimen, a peach tree imported from San Francisco in 1814, bore fruit after six years. In 1818 new peach trees were introduced from Monterey, and two years later one hundred apple, pear, cherry, peach, and bergamot seedlings were added. These trees produced fruit by 1828. Grapes were being harvested six years after vines from Lima, Peru, were set in 1817. By 1833 Fort Ross had four hundred trees and seven hundred vine stalks, and, shortly before the Russian departure, the Chernykh Rancho located nearby had two thousand vines. The Russian inventory of 1841 listed two hundred seven apple trees, twenty-nine peach trees, ten pear trees, ten quince trees, and eight cherry trees as growing in the fort's orchard. In good years Russian California produced a surplus of fruit.

Shipbuilding assumed central importance at Ross with the decline of otter hunting. The first seaworthy vessels launched in California were constructed by the Russians at Fort Ross Cove. Alexander Baranov, the Russian-American Company's Chief Manager, dispatched shipwright Vasily Grudinin from Alaska to oversee construction. Four two-masted ships were completed during 1818–1824: the 160-ton brig-schooner *Rumyantsev*, the 200-ton brig *Buldakov*, the 160-ton brig *Volga*, and the 200-ton brig *Kyakhta*. For a short time these vessels ranged from San Pedro in Southern California to Okhotsk in Siberia. Unfortunately, because the ships were made largely of improperly seasoned tanbark oak, which was poorly suited to ocean-going vessels in any case, rot made all four ships unfit for sea duty within six years of construction. This disaster caused the Russians to discontinue building large vessels after 1824. Thereafter, the Fort Ross commanders encouraged agriculture. The Russians also made skiffs, longboats, rowboats, and barges, several of which were traded or sold to the Mexicans at the Bay Area missions in the middle 1820's. Manufacturing for trade with the Spanish and Mexican Californians—as well as for local use and for export to Alaska—carried far beyond ship and boat construction to include a wide range of activities, such as barrel, tar, brick, leather, boot, wool, flour, furniture, candle, soap, and possibly pot making.

IV. Commercial and Diplomatic Relations

Concern about possible Russian expansion was among several considerations moving the Spanish to found the first

California missions at San Diego and Monterey in 1769–1770 and the Mexicans to establish the last California missions at San Rafael and Sonoma in 1817 and 1823. Spanish and Mexican officials frequently questioned the Russians' right to maintain a base along the Sonoma coast. Although Russia's diplomats never achieved official recognition of Colony Ross from Madrid or Mexico City, however, the Russians maintained agreeable commercial relations with their Spanish and Mexican neighbors because trade benefited everyone on the Northern California frontier. Even in the early years of Russian settlement in California, when Spanish regulations deemed commerce with foreigners illegal, California's Russians and Spaniards carried on a lively contraband trade. In 1816 Spain lifted its ban on colonial trade with foreigners, although local authorities limited the amount of Spanish-Russian commerce officially allowed in California ports. Trade with the Spanish became so important to the Russians that in 1820 they seriously considered abandoning Fort Ross in exchange for a formal commercial agreement guaranteeing a steady supply of provisions for Alaska, but Spain rejected all Russian overtures for such a pact. Finally in 1821, when Mexico became independent of Spain, Alta California opened its ports to unrestricted foreign trade. At first pleased with this development, the Russians soon faced higher tariffs as well as stiff competition from increasing numbers of American and British trading vessels visiting Mexican California's ports. Also, after the secularization of the California missions in 1833, far less Mexican wheat and beef was available for purchase. Besides trading with the Californios, the Russians

concluded a renewable hunting contract with the Mexican authorities in 1823 which enabled them to seek otters as far south as San Diego and to trade pelts for Mexican grain. After the Mexican governor of California terminated the contract in 1831, however, the Russians could legally hunt only as employees of Mexican entrepreneurs. Although very important to the Russians, commercial relations with the Spanish and Mexicans never completely fulfilled Russian hopes in California.

The Tsar's officials, moreover, never achieved international recognition of Russian California from any other major power. In 1819 Russian hopes for worldwide sanction of Colony Ross were badly damaged by the Adams-Onis treaty, by which Spain and the United States formally acknowledged Spanish possession of all land below the Oregon country border. Although the Russians in Alaska periodically traded for provisions with the British and Americans and sometimes entered into joint business ventures with the latter, the Anglo-American powers saw no reason to recognize Colony Ross, especially after 1819, because Russian aims also competed with British and America economic and strategic interests in the Pacific. In September 1821, Tsar Alexander I issued an imperial ukase unilaterally expanding the Russian-American Company's exclusive rights in the northwest into the Oregon country, then jointly claimed by the United States and Britain. American President James Monroe, however, seized upon this appearance of a Russian expansionist threat to rally support for his hemispheric noncolonization principle, embodied in his famous doctrine of 1823. By 1824, no closer than before to achieving international recognition of its California claim, Russia abandoned its expansionist pretentions in North America by agreeing to a Russo-American Convention withdrawing Russia's claims to the Oregon country. The Russians signed a similar treaty with the British in 1825. These agreements denied the Russians future land access between Alaska and Russian California, and left the legal status of Fort Ross unresolved. A final opportunity for international sanction arose in the mid-1830's when the Mexican government invited Ferdinand P. Wrangell, Chief Manager of the Russian colonies in America, to mediate in establishing diplomatic relations between Mexico and Russia. Wrangell hoped to convince the Mexicans to cede a small amount of arable land east of Colony Ross to the Russian-American Company, because, with Mexican grain and beef becoming scarce following secularization of the California missions, he favored increased Russian cultivation. Traveling to Mexico, Wrangell found the officials there prepared to confirm Russian claims to Ross, but ultimately nothing came of his efforts because the conservative Tsar Nicholas I refused to recognize the Mexican Republic, which he identified with revolution. The last serious Russian effort to achieve international recognition for Fort Ross was thus defeated by the Russian Tsar himself.

V. Russian Explorers and Scientists

An impressive number of Russian explorers and scientists visited Northern California during the early nineteenth century. Ivan Kuskov, the first Russian to explore inland from the Sonoma Coast, journeyed fifty miles up the Russian River in 1811 and gave the river its Russian name, *Slavyanka*. Russians also entered Humboldt Bay and may have travelled up the Sacramento River and overland to Clear Lake. Ferdinand Wrangell surveyed the Santa Rosa plain in 1833 when contemplating the expansion of Russian agriculture. Eight years later a Russian expedition to the same region named and mapped several local tributaries of the Russian River. Russian scientists, too, did much field work in Northern California. They were the first Europeans to conduct serious studies in Sonoma Coast botany, zoology, entomology, and ethnology. The naturalist Georg H. von Langsdorff accompanied Rezanov to California in 1806, gathering plant and animal specimens which were added to museum collections in St. Petersburg. In 1816, while on his first voyage around the world, Otto von Kotzebue brought the naturalist Adelbert von Chamisso and the entomologist and zoologist Johann Friedrich Eschscholtz to California. During a short stay in San Francisco, Chamisso collected the now-famous California poppy, naming it *Eschscholtzia California* for his friend and for the new land. Eschscholtz made extensive insect collections at Fort Ross in 1824 while accompanying Kotzebue on a second world tour. Although Wrangell was interested in wildlife, geography, and meteorology, his most important work was probably done in the field of ethnology. In 1833 he conducted the first extensive anthropological study of Indians in the Santa Rosa area. Father Ioann Veniaminov, a missionary who spent many years studying Alaskan Indians, visited Fort Ross in 1836. Finally, while traveling in Northern California during 1840–1841, Ilya Gavrilovich Voznesenskii, who was a zoologist, botanist, geologist, and ethnologist, produced some of the most informative drawings ever done of the inhabitants of Colony Ross. In 1841, a Russian climbing party, including Voznesenskii and Yegor Chernykh, who was a Colony Ross agronomist and rancher, made the first recorded ascent of Mount St. Helen. The climbers left a metal plate at the north summit as proof of their accomplishment. The numerous achievements of Russian explorers and scientists in frontier California deserve our recognition.

VI. Fort Ross Commanders, Agricultural Expansion, and the Sale of Fort Ross.

The five commanders at Fort Ross during the twenty-nine years of Russian occupation in California had in common one important activity—the encouragement of farming. Although the fort's first commander, Ivan Kuskov, assumed hunting to be the main function of Colony Ross and lacked experience as a farmer, he began agriculture and stock raising at the fort. Kuskov's successor, Karl Schmidt, who became commandant at Ross in 1821, attempted to stimulate agricultural expansion by distributing free seed among the Aleut hunters as well as the Russians and Creoles at the settlement. Although Schmidt, a navigator by training, invested much time in the ambitious shipbuilding program of the early 1820's, Paul Shelikhov made significant contributions to the agricultural development of the colony, such as ordering the planting of the last uncultivated arable land near the fort. Peter Kostromitinov, following Shelikhov as commander at the

end of the decade, encourages agriculture even more than his predecessors. Kostromitinov's administration established several new farms (ranchos) in the interior, planted grain along the Russian River in 1831, and may have directed cultivation in the Freestone area eight miles east of Bodega Bay. In 1833 the commander developed another inland farm called Khlebnikov Rancho by the Russians and Three Friends Rancho by the Californios. Kostromitinov also founded Kostromitinov Rancho, or Halfway House, which stood midway between Fort Ross and Bodega Bay. Another farm, labeled New Rancho for a short time, but best recalled as the Chernykh or Jorge Rancho, was put under cultivation shortly after Alexander Gavrilovich Rotchev, the last Fort Ross commandant, assumed command in the mid-1830's. Encouraged by each Fort Ross commandant since 1812, agriculture had become the primary function of the colony by the end of the Russian era in California.

Despite the agricultural activity near Fort Ross, it was clear by the late 1830's that the colony was a financial liability to the Russian-American Company. Fur hunting had declined with the near extinction of the sea otter, shipbuilding had failed outright, stock raising had remained a marginal enterprise, and farming had disappointed Russian expectations. The company found itself operating the colony at a deficit not compensated for by Ross's benefits as a trading outpost. The collapse of Wrangell's diplomatic efforts ended any possibility that agricultural expansion might rejuvenate the colony. To limit Russian growth, the Mexican government induced its citizens to populate the Sonoma region by awarding land grants, and Mexican and naturalized Yankee settlers just a few miles inland from Fort Ross were encircling the Russians. When the Hudson's Bay Company agreed to provision the Russian-American Company's Alaskan bases, the last reason for retaining Colony Ross disappeared. The Russian-American Company opted to withdraw from California, and Tsar Nicholas I formally sanctioned the decision on April 15, 1839. Alexander Rotchev, the last commander of Fort Ross, was made responsible for the negotiations leading to the sale of the company's property in California. This arrangement was ironic, for Rotchev and his wife Helena Gagarin, having come to love Fort Ross, had made it a model of urbane living during the years of their residence. Rotchev had built a new commander's house which included a piano, an impressive library, and imported French wines; and Helena, a princess, according to tradition, who was renowned for her social graces, had cultivated a fine rose garden. After the first potential buyer of the fort, the Hudson's Bay Company, failed to purchase in 1840, the Russian-American Company instructed Rotchev to approach the Mexicans. Early the next year, Peter Kostromitinov, a former Fort Ross commander then serving as the Russian-American Company's San Francisco agent, assisted Rotchev by negotiating for the sale of the property to the Mexican commandant at Sonoma, Mariano Guadalupe Vallejo. Confident that the Mexican government would acquire the colony at no cost once the Russians left, Vallejo merely offered $9,000 to buy the livestock. Meanwhile, Kostromitinov

and Rotchev found a more interested customer in the Swiss-American pioneer, John Augustus Sutter, who agreed to purchase Russian California's buildings, equipment, weapons, and livestock for $30,000 in produce and coin. The formal papers were signed December 13, 1841; two weeks later Rotchev and most of the inhabitants of Colony Ross set sail for Alaska. Although Rotchev himself returned to California briefly during the Gold Rush, the evacuation of Fort Ross ended the twenty-nine year "Russian period" in California history. Besides a schooner and other property at Bodega Bay, Sutter acquired in the stockaded fort itself two blockhouses, the old and new commander's houses, officials' and employees' quarters, storage facilities, a small kitchen, a well, and the famous Fort Ross chapel built in the mid-1820's. Outside the stockade, his inventory included workshops, sheds, kitchens, barns, bathhouses, wooden grain threshing floors, windmills, orchards, gardens, and even a cemetary with wooden grave markers. Sutter used these acquisitions principally for salvage. He had his employee John Bidwell dismantle much of the Ross property and transport it to Sutter's Fort at New Helvetia, or Sacramento. The passing of Fort Ross into Sutter's hands symbolized the end of California's pastoral era, when Russian and Mexican frontier outposts could coexist peacefully, and anticipated the coming of its entrepreneurial period, when aggressive Northern European and Yankee pioneers would compete for gold and profits.

Halcyon Days: Mexican-California, 1826—1845
by Leonard Pitt

The most sophisticated analysis of Mexican-California is Leonard Pitt's, The Decline of the Californios. This pathbreaking study, published in 1966, inaugurated a new look at the Spanish-speaking, native-born leaders, the Californios. Rejecting old myths and stereotypes Professor Pitt demonstrated how Spain's strong heritage was molded by the Californios. The rejection of Mexican political ideas and the rise of local Californio politicians were influences which helped shape California's character. Equally important is Pitt's analysis of the secularization crisis and the changes it brought to California. Halcyon days is a time of a new social order.

California Rancheros Roping a Steer

Leonard Pitt, THE DECLINE OF THE CALIFORNIOS, (Berkeley 1966). Reprinted by permission of the author and the University of California Press.

Californians caught an early glimpse of the modern era on November 20, 1818, when the Argentine pirate and patriot, Hippolyte de Bouchard, seized Monterey to imbue it with the "spirit of liberty." His hopes were soon dashed, however, when the men of Monterey neither rallied to his noble banner nor fought him, but instead preferred to stay at home with their panicking womenfolk and children. "Liberator" Bouchard, understandably discouraged, sacked the town and sailed away at the first opportunity. Ten years more would elapse before California would feel ready for "liberation" and for the ideas that shattered Spanish power and inaugurated social revolution throughout Latin America.

The school of thought that celebrates the Spanish era as California's golden age marks its decline with Bouchard's raid, or, more properly, with the arrival of Mexican Governor José María Echeandía in 1826. This school argues that the saintly piety of the mission fathers and the heroism of the *conquistadores* gave way to the cruelty, materialism, and bathos of the Mexican *politicos*. Liberalismo became the villain, an ideology whose effect George Tays likened to that of a "malignant malarial epidemic." Another school regards the Mexican era as the "true Arcadia," the culmination of the promise inherent in the Spanish beginnings. In considering the decline of Hispanic California it is, however, more relevant to assess the Californians' own response to Mexicanization and gauge its future implications, rather than to bemoan or celebrate it. The problem, in other words, is to delineate the leading tendencies of the era 1826 to 1846 and to learn how they conditioned the Californians for their final ordeal, the confrontation with *Americanos*.

In 1826, California's Spanish heritage was still in strong evidence. Only one generation separated California from the pioneer stage, a fact still obvious in the crudity and sparseness of settlement. Stretched along a 500-mile coastline, the "rationals," the *gente de razón*, numbered about 8,000 and in Monterey, the capital, 300. From the beginning, California had been little more than an outpost of empire, a remote frontier. Since the province lay at the farthest reaches of New Spain, itself a Spanish colony, California's colonial status was twice removed. This geographic and political isolation bred provincialism. An essentially medieval and clerical society, California had twenty-one Franciscan missions which subordinated all and sundry to their will. Neither the military officers at the *presidios*, nor the civilians in the *pueblos* and *ranchos*, could rival the power of the padres in their heyday.

The Spanish heritage, however, compared with the Mexican, creaked with decrepitude. Thus, liberalismo kept filtering into the province despite a wall of conservatism. Mariano Vallejo, ten years old during Bouchard's raid, gradually caught the drift of world history and acknowledged of those "liberators" that "patriotism was their incentive and liberty their god." The idealism of youth made a rebel of Vallejo, but he was forced to bide his time because his elders remained "all very much attached" to king and pope and "prayed at the break of dawn, at noon, at sunset, and at bedtime." His young nephew, Juan Bautista Alvarado, the their cousin, José Castro, also became rebels. These three young "conspirators" formed a secret junta for the study of politics and history and had absorbed a good dose of *radicalismo* by 1826, when Governor Joseí María Echeandía arrived and became the chief resident apostle of the new ideology. In 1831, young Mariano boarded a Mexican vessel and took home a small library of banned books. As ill luck would have it, his sweetheart reported the "sin" to a priest, who promptly caught the youths redhanded with a forbidden work (*Telemachus*) and commanded them to yield the books, go to confession, and do penance. Much to the horror of their relatives, especially their mothers and sisters, the trio refused and were unofficially "ex-communicated."

This circle of Monterey youths was experiencing nothing more than the awakening typical of the Creoles of Mexico and, indeed, of all Latin America. Because they lived on the farthest perimeters of revolution, they caught only partial glimpses and heard merely fugitive rumors of the main movements many months, and even years, later. Nevertheless, the message came through: They began to yearn vaguely for education, the reduction of clerical power, freedom of expression, liberation of bondsmen, the end of colonial status, and self-government. However belatedly, the Enlightenment was overturning the old order. Castro, Vallejo, and Alvarado soon had accomplices in every community—Carlos and José Antonio Carrillo of Santa Barbara; Juan Bandini, a Peruvian resident of San Diego; the brothers Pio and Andrés Pico at Los Angeles; Santiago Argu-ëllo; and Pablo de Portilla—until eventually most of the younger generation and some of their elders professed the liberal heresy proudly.

The first mutation caused by the spread of liberalismo was in the religious realm. The temporal authority of the clerics continued to annoy the younger men as they matured. As a grown man, Don Mariano flatly refused to pay a tithe to finance the "impracticable" schemes of the first bishop of California, Bishop Garcia Diíego, although he never rejected Catholicism itself and single-handedly patronized the village chapel at Sonoma. Outright resistance among the communicants everywhere except in Santa Barbara left the Bishop virtually penniless and paralyzed. At the same time, the new generation deliberately rejected Spanish forms of piety. Domestic devotions fell off among the male part of the population until, by the end of the Mexican régime, Sunday Mass had become an affair for women, children, and neophyte Indians; men participated in the livelier religious fiestas, but as nominal Catholics only. Doubtless, the decline of Catholicism represented an unfortunate disintegration of a unitary way of life. Yet, liberalism was a satisfactory surrogate for religion, and religious change probably prepared the Californians for a future life in a pluralistic society.

Politically, California remained wrapped in its cocoon until 1831. It then began to stir out, goaded by Yankees and Mexicans made restive by a willful Mexican governor, Manuel Victoria, whose credo was "love of order, respect for authority and constant consecration to duty." Although vague at first and always beclouded by petty interests, rebel aspirations hardened during a score of rebellions in the next fifteen years. Among the more important episodes was the unsuccessful assault of the Sonoran *vaqueros* of Los Niëtos (near Los Angeles) against

Governor Pio Pico: The Last Mexican-California Official

Governor José Figueroa in 1834; the attack on Governor Mariano Chico in 1835, which ousted him; and, most important, the uprising of the "federalists" Alvarado and Castro against the "centralist" governor, Nicolás Gutiérrez, in 1836, which secured the province virtual self-government. Thereafter, the Californians had many fallings out among themselves until José Castro was about to battle Pio Pico in 1846, when the sudden intrusion of Captain John C. Frémont's "topographical engineers" ended that squall. By then, however, the Californians had realized their most important aspirations: autonomy within the Mexican Republic, separation of the military and civilian branches of government, and secularization of the missions.

Republicanism created new offices and expanded old ones, and thus gave the local gentry a practical knowledge of self-government. The numerous ceremonial positions aside, many offices carried an authority that nurtured in the incumbents a degree of sophistication. In a short time hundreds of Californians served as governors, delegates to the Mexican Congress and the provincial junta, prefects, alcaldes, *juezes del campo* (judges of the plain), and representatives in the town councils and thus passed through a political or an administrative apprenticeship. Most observers questioned whether many *Californios* ever graduated to the rank of "journeyman"; Mexican Governor Chico asserted that all but a few Californians were intimidated by energy and . . . bluster." Yet, even as apprentices they were not as bumbling as the Mexicans and Yankees made them out to be; Chico discovered this when they turned on him and sent him packing from the province.

As preparation for service in gringo government, however, the old politics proved only partly useful. Its stock-in-trade was intrigue, not debate; rebellion, not compromise; élite leadership, not mass support; and, of course, the flaming *pronunciamiento*. When everything else failed, men reached for their guns. Such tactics conformed badly with the Anglo-Saxon scheme of things.

Because the Californians mixed serious ideological goals with naïive methods, their politics assumed a tragicomic air. Like the tribes of the Stone Age ever preparing for war but rarely fighting, the Californios cultivated a state of perpetual excitement which culminated in anticlimatic decrees or minor skirmishes; three casualties in one of these fights would represent a major tragedy. Some of the rebels themselves complained of speeches that rang too gloriously, of politicos who were too soft-hearted, of "great struggles" that were more like comic-opera episodes. Governor Carlos Carrillo, the first native-born governor, knew that his own family laughingly compared him to Sancho Panza.

By Anglo-Saxon standards, California government came to be judged invidiously. Weighed properly by Latin-American standards, however, in the perspective of the movement for independence in the Spanish Empire, it fares much better.

Viewed that way, correctly, California demonstrates an impressive unanimity on fundamental principles. After about 1835, scarcely a single active royalist remained in the realm, nor a major civilian opponent of secularization of the missions. The "religious question," which then wracked all of Latin America, yielded to acclamation in California. That province demonstrated, further, a talent for leadership. Local leaders had to manufacture civil government from the whole cloth, with little formal preparation, and had to work in a province of vast distances without steady finances, military support, and genuine respect from the mother country. Yet, they accomplished their main goals. Best of all, they shed less blood and destroyed less property in the process than any comparable group of Latin Americans.

The new era produced yet another innovation: an ambivalence toward Mexico and things Mexican. Though freely mimicking Mexico's new ideology, the Californios struggling for autonomy learned to despise the bearers of that ideology—governors, soldiers, and colonists from *la otra banda* (the other shore). Since, among the upstanding citizens of Mexico, "to speak of California was like mentioning the end of the world," the government had to empty the jails of Sinaloa and Sonora to encourage colonization and military occupation of the northern part of the province. As a sort of Siberian work camp, California acquired hosts of petty thieves and political prisoners—18 in 1825, 200 in 1829, 130 in 1830, and so on. Those convicts usually arrived in a state of wretchedness exceeded only by that of the Indians. Bands of these so-called *cholos* (scoundrels) would brawl drunkenly on the public streets and commit theft and other assorted misdeeds—even homicide—while the political prisoners among them organized rebellions. This state of affairs greatly distressed the more genteel settlers.

Second-generation Californians, although often themselves the children of cholos, nevertheless greeted the newcomers dismally, in many cases making no distinction between the outright felons and the dedicated colonists. In 1834, the Hijar-Padrés Colony, a group of respectable Mexican artisans, teachers, and tradesmen, had to flee northern California, while the *nativos* hounded them with cries of "Death to Mexico!" and "Kill the Mexicans!"

Resisting the "degraded" influences of Mexico made men conscious of their California birth. In response to the new identity, the local nomenclature changed, until the native-born ceased calling themselves *Españoles* or *Mexicanos* and began to insist on the name *Californios*.

The province was, however, vast, and the Californios felt the strongest ties to an immediate locale. This led to another innovation in the Mexican period, a north-south regional consciousness; it, too, proved divisive. Regionalism polarized around Monterey, Los Angeles, and Santa Barbara, although the latter town, often caught in a cross fire remained indifferent and confused. After the capital had been moved from Monterey to Los Angeles in 1835, each passing year intensified the rivalry until, in 1845, *abajeños* (southerners) and *arribeños* (northerners) were ready for open warfare. No matter what Alvarado or Castro wanted for Monterey, Pio Pico and others spitefully demanded the opposite for Los Angeles; when northerners spoke of stronger ties with Mexico, southerners

espoused greater independence, and vice versa. The best that could come of this rivalry was a division of power and a truce. In 1846, Monterey's Castro seized control of the military headquarters and customhouse and gave the *Angeleño* Pico the governorship. North-south rivalries were further complicated by family feuds and personal ambitions, which later led to failures of communication and a lack of unity among the nativos—an inability to reach across space to make common cause against the superior gringo enemy. The final gift of political apprenticeship, then, was confusion and bickering.

Unquestionably, the chief reform of the Mexican era was secularization of the missions. Beginning in earnest after 1831, reaching full flood by 1839, and completed by 1845, secularization cut the last cord still linking California to its Spanish "mother." It upset class relations, altered ideology, and shifted the ownership of enormous wealth. It totally destroyed a fiefdom that in its heyday had included twenty-one mission establishments, 15,000 Indian wards, great herds of livestock, millions of acres of land, and proceeds from a lucrative foreign trade. That revolutionary social and economic transformation was California's most important event before the discovery of gold; indeed, nothing in the experience of the Californios compares with it, except possibly the dissolution of the ranchos in the 1880's.

That secularization came bloodlessly is a credit to both the padres and the civil officials. Authorized by the Mexican Constitution of 1824, it was set in motion late in Echeandia's régime by his decree of 1831 but made little headway until 1836. Even liberals conceded that the California Indians "do not possess the qualifications" for freedom and needed protection "against themselves," a thought probably shared by the governor when he made a tentative promise of citizenship to the Indians and rather gingerly asked the friars to limit their floggings to fifteen lashes weekly and to allow married couples immediate freedom. Another governor sought to ease the friars out of their mission establishments and onto the frontier for new labors among the heathens, but he was unsuccessful. The most onerous burdens the government managed to impose on the missionaries were a mild civil tax and ideological sniping, both of which the Franciscans could handle with ease.

The Franciscans held nearly absolute sway over their communicants and threatened to resign en masse, should the government take more strenuous measures. A missionary strike would have brought a crippling work stoppage throughout the province. Fortunately, this threat never came to pass, since the friars settled for token resistance by refusing to swear allegiance to the Mexican constitution and by sermonizing against the republicans. They castigated the "radicals" who went among the Indians "preaching and dogmatizing that there was no hell." Father Narciso Durán, head of the mission system, easily parried every thrust of the civil officials who were, in his words, "but yesterday savages" and are skilled at no greater art than horsemanship, yet presume to "teach the way to civilize men." The fact that the Franciscans tried to prevent the *emancipados* from becoming slaves or savages and yet bowed graciously to the inevitability of secularization partly accounts for the absence of the bloodletting provoked elsewhere in Mexico by religious strife.

When the Californians took over the helm of provincial government in 1836, matters moved more swiftly. Doubtless, high ideals impelled them; but, whether a ranchero professed liberalismo and signed his letters "For God and Liberty!" or had no political persuasion at all, he knew that secularization might bring him wealth—he stood to gain whatever the padres and the Indians lost. The program thus proceeded apace in Alvarado's governorship, from 1836 to 1842. He sold or leased the mission lands and assets to private individuals for the supposed benefit of the creditors, of the government (which would collect a tax in the transaction), of the Indians (who would obtain land grants), and of the missionaries (who would be guaranteed subsistence).

The new owners and lessees began a rapid slaughter of mission livestock. By 1839, an investigation by Alvarado showed that two-thirds of the cattle had been butchered, three-quarters of the sheep, and half of the horses, for which the Franciscans and neophytes had received practically none of their rightful compensation. The governor, a better rebel than administrator, was guilty of favoritism and laxness, although not of lining his own pockets. To maintain the treasury, he issued drafts on mission property to government creditors, without recognizing the dwindling rate of mission inventories. His later attempt to reverse this policy and to salvage some property for the former mission inhabitants failed with the premature end of his term of office. By 1845, the original herds of 150,000 had dwindled to 50,000.

In the eyes of the gente de razón, Indian liberation had succeeded famously, but for the Indians themselves it was a painful experience. The neophytes were torn tragically between a secure, authoritarian existence and a free but anarchic one. Those who had spent their lives in the shadow of the Cross often rejected the proffered liberty, not out of fear of the padres' wrath but of the uncertainties of the outer world. Although examples of neophyte self-leadership were rare, Pacifico, an untypically forward young Indian of Mission San Buenaventura, demanded in 1828 that the 150 neophytes receive immediate release and land allotments. At best, however, the emancipados gained an illusory freedom. By 1829, the number of mission Indians had fallen from 15,000 to 4,500; by 1847 virtually all the remaining ones had gone free and either melted into the lower class of the pueblos, took up residence on the ranchos, went back to their *rancheriías* (villages), or disappeared behind the pale. There, from 1836 to 1839, the "civilized" Indians stirred up their "wild" brethren so much that, in San Diego, for example, entire ranchos had to be abandoned. Even by the 1850's, the neophytes remained a demoralized class, alternately a prey to disease, liquor, violence, submission, and exploitation.

Mexican Governor Manuel Micheltorena, in 1843, gave the Franciscans a respite by calling a moratorium on secularization, an act that was of little use to the friars for lack of morale and of material support. California Governor Pico, who succeeded Micheltorena, returned to Alvarado's policy and, in fact, extended it by liquidating the missions altogether. For this some writers have maligned him, yet he evidently acted in good faith—perhaps even wisdom—since the remaining institutions were too small, too encumbered with debts, and too expensive for efficient operation. Through a controlled liquidation, Pico hoped to guarantee to the Indians some small measure of communal property, to the state a small tax, and to the friars subsistence. The final sale and lease of mission property came in May, 1845.

The dethronement of the padres elevated the rancheros and introduced a new social order based on their authority. More than eight hundred of them shared in the carving up of 8 million prime acres. So swift was the division that, between 1841 and 1844, thirty new ranchos appeared in the Los Angeles district alone. Land in parcels up to 11 leagues could be had practically for the asking by those with the right connections or with a record of civil or military service. Some families obtained several great adjoining parcels and thus prevailed over 300,000 acres or more. By 1846, according to a list compiled by Thomas Oliver Larkin, forty-six men of substance, influence, or political power ruled California. They were largely self-made men, the *arriviste* corps of the recent past who had inherited little wealth from their fathers and mostly were landowners.

WORKSHEET 2: Mexican California and the Rise of Foreign Intruders

1. Why did Californians feel that Mexico didn't understand them? _____

   _____

   _____

   _____

   _____

2. What was Governor Pablo Vicente Sola's response to Mexican independence?

   _____

   _____

3. What role did land grants play in Mexican California? _____

   _____

4. Why was Mariano Vallejo important to local attitudes on economics and politics? _

   _____

   _____

   _____

5. William Hartnell was an example of _____

   _____

   _____

6. What economic and technological changes did Fort Ross bring to California? _____

_____

_____

_____

_____

7. The first native born Mexican-California Governor was _____

8. In what way did Fort Ross challenge local political power? _____

_____

_____

9. Why was Vallejo surprised about Indian labor at Fort Ross? _____

_____

10. What is meant by the term Halcyon Days? _____

_____

11. Define Home Rule _____

12. Telemachus is a _____

13. What role does Leonard Pitt see liberalism playing in Mexican California? _____

_____

_____

_____

14. Secularization is defined as _____

_____

_____

15. The first schools in California were established by _____ and they were important

because _____

16. Joseph O'Cain was _____

17. Did the Tsar's officials receive international recognition of Russian California
from any major power?
a. Yes   b. No (Circle One)

18. Alexander Rotchev was _____

The American Conquest: Manifest Destiny or Conspiratorial Imperialism?

READINGS: LETTER FROM SECRETARY OF STATE JAMES BUCHANAN, *SECRET AGENT THOMAS OLIVER LARKIN* ALLAN NEVINS, *"JOHN C. FREMONT: GREAT PATHFINDER OR AVERAGE PATHMARKER?"* RICHARD DILLON, *"MARIANO VALLEJO: CALIFORNIO LEADER"*

The background to the American conquest of California is a complex and controversial topic. A historiographical debate rages which suggests that Manifest Destiny was only one of many influences upon California's annexation. Manifest Destiny is a theory that implies it was the God given right of the United States to expand from the Atlantic to the Pacific Ocean and to annex all western territory between Canada and Mexico. Popular writers used this phrase in the 1840s to excite American nationalism. Politicians found it a useful device to build electoral support. The average citizen embraced Manifest Destiny as a rationale for conquest.

In 1835 President Andrew Jackson expressed the first official interest in the Mexican possession when he dispatched a friend, Anthony Butler, to negotiate the purchase of Alta California. Not only was Butler a devious negotiator, but he displayed open racial hostility toward the Mexican government. Butler offered Mexico a half a million dollars for the area from San Francisco north, but his inability to convince the Mexican government of his willingness to negotiate a fair deal killed the purchase of northern California.

In 1837 Martin Van Buren became President and he was not in favor of California annexation. But the national mania surrounding the California mystique failed to ebb and interest remained high in this obscure Mexican possession. In the United States Senate, Thomas Hart Benton of Missouri urged Americans to explore the West. Soon official parties sent out by the U.S.

War Department and unofficial bands of American intruders roamed Mexican-California. They challenged Mexican authority and power at every turn. From 1838 to 1842 Lt. Charles Wilkes was a constant observer of the California coast. He hoped to land in California, but he never received permission to occupy any part of the Mexican possession. Wilkes had the imperialist mentality but he was unable to carry out his desires.

A good example of the United States' imperialist mentality occurred in October, 1842, when Commodore Thomas O. P. Jones sailed into Monterey on the false assumption that war had broken out between the United States and Britain. Jones reasoned that by seizing Monterey he was holding a military area strategic to American interests. After sailing into Monterey, Commodore Jones declared it an American possession. When Jones realized that peace prevailed, he good-naturedly explained his mistake to local residents. After raising the Mexican flag again, Commodore Jones attended a fiesta in a vain attempt to apologize to local Californios. Jose Castro suggested that Americans had maintained a strong interest in California for some time but simply couldn't quit meddling in local affairs. Castro failed to realize that the main reason Jones seized Monterey was due to War Department orders to occupy California in the event of hostilities.

The United States was nervous about foreign influences in California. Since the mid-1830s the War Department had maintained a lengthy intelligence file on California. There was a strong feeling among key government personnel for annexation. The general thrust of Manifest Destiny convinced Americans that California was at least a spiritual possession. Since large numbers of settlers had migrated from the Middle West and South to Sutter's Fort, American diplomats believed that they had to acquire California.

In 1842, as the United States and Great Britain negotiated the Webster-Ashburton Treaty to define the American-Canadian border, there was also a plan by President John Tyler to purchase Mexican territory. The United States offered to help Mexico pay off her debts to British and American businesses in return for Texas and a portion of California. This complicated deal broke down when Secretary of State Daniel Webster failed to convince American expansionists that the United States should give up claims to land north of the Columbia River. The territory north of the Columbia River was occupied by the British and it was rich in farm and timber lands. In an aggressive and bellicose stance, Americans demanded the annexation of California.

Some historians argue that a conspiracy by the War Department and American Presidents to annex California had been in existence for some time. While the evidence to support this contention is slim, there are some facts which suggest its validity. The lengthy and intriguing American interest in California reached a fever point in the mid-1840s.

The election of President James K. Polk in 1844 is cited as the chief argument in support of the Manifest Destiny thesis. When he campaigned for the presidency, Polk talked long and hard about annexing Texas and California. Polk, a close friend and protege of former President Andrew Jackson, was concerned about British influences, and he campaigned on the notion that aggressive imperialism would hamper foreign influences. Polk advocated the annexation of Texas and the occupation of the Oregon territory. Although Polk hoped to annex California, it was not a high priority. When Polk sent John Slidell to offer Mexico $40 million dollars for Upper California and New Mexico, he continued the American plan to seize the Mexican territory.

It was the aggressive policy of the U.S. War Department which helped annex California. The most controversial figure during annexation was John C. Fremont. As a lieutenant in the elite Army Corps of Topographical Engineers, Fremont was one of the first official explorers to travel into the American West. The publicity from his three exploration ventures made Fremont a national hero. His journals became nationwide best sellers and encouraged the migration of permanent settlers. In his second expedition, Fremont discovered Lake Tahoe and spent a month at Sutter's Fort. The suspicion that Fremont was an advanced agent of American Imperialism and not a scientific observer, as the War Department maintained, caused many Californios to complain about the devious nature of American annexation.

It was Jose Castro, the Californio military leader, who pointed out that Fremont's Army Corps of Topographical Engineers was supposed to be a party of scientific observers. How could they be scientists, Castro chided, with some many uneducated American soldiers? The earliest Army Corps exploration ventures sent twenty scientists into the American West. But Fremont's Third Expedition into California included 60 Kentucky long rifles. They had neither the scientific training nor the military temperament of the Army Corps. Castro charged that Fremont had explored the San Joaquin Valley for the U.S. War Department. Most Californios scoffed at Fremont's explanation that he was leading a scientific party to collect samples of natural wildlife, to map the west, and to record weather and terrain conditions. In reality, Castro, argued, Fremont was the first wave of American military intervention.

In the spring of 1846 when Fremont constructed Fort Gavilan near Hawk's Peak, Castro, the Commander of the Native Cavalry, ordered Fremont to leave California. Fremont's Fort Gavilan was a direct challenge to Mexican and Californio authority. Not only did Fremont ignore the repeated demands of local authorities to leave California, but he organized a group of Americans who were armed to repel local controls. Finally, Fremont's boisterous demands and ingratiating remarks prompted Thomas Oliver Larkin, the American consul in Monterey, to order Fremont to march north to Oregon.

While camped near Klamath Lake in southern Oregon, Fremont was visited by Lt. Archibald Gillespie. A secret agent for the United States Marine Corps, Gillespie provided Fremont with information on California's conquest. There were a series of War Department directives that Gillespie and Larkin had in their possession to guide their course. These materials dated from the mid-1830s and demonstrated the War Department's lasting interest in California. Among the tasks that Fremont was requested to complete were reports on military preparedness, loyalty to Mexico and economic growth. All of these areas were vital to American interest as the annexationists hoped to conquer California peacefully. The main objective of Fremont and other American adventurers was to interfere with Mexico's control of California.

An interesting example of American governmental interference in Mexican affairs occurred in 1845 when President James K. Polk appointed the wealthy American merchant, Thomas Oliver Larkin, as a secret agent. It was Larkin's job to gather military intelligence, report on the attitudes of key Californios, notably Mariano Vallejo and Jose Castro, and, finally, to deduce the level of loyalty to Mexico.

When Thomas Oliver Larkin was appointed an American agent, President James K. Polk's Secretary of State, James Buchanan, wrote a letter to Larkin thanking him for his time and effort. In this letter, Buchanan stressed the importance of Larkin's "spy activity" and suggested that the future of the United States depended upon Larkin's efforts. This overstatement was typical of the times. The zeal and fervor associated with Manifest Destiny blinded most Americans to Mexican rights. After Secretary Buchanan finished his October 17, 1845, letter to Larkin, he placed it in a brown-leather satchel and instructed Archibald Gillespie to carry it aboard a ship that he was sailing around the Cape of Good Hope to California. Once Buchanan's letter was delivered to Larkin the mysterious process of annexation unfolded in California. What Secretary Buchanan's letter demonstrated was that the War Department had been interested in annexing California for a decade.

Another catalyst to annexation was the formation of the American dominated Bear Flag Republic. This strange experiment began in the early morning hours of June 14, 1846, when a group of Americans seized Mariano Vallejo's ranch in Sonoma and proclaimed the Bear Flag Republic. The twenty Americans had no plan and poor organization. After Vallejo was seized he offered his conquerors copious amounts of wine. William Ide, a Mormon, was the only Bear Flagger who escaped intoxication. Therefore, he was selected to lead the new American styled Republic. This action reflected the tensions between Californio residents and American settlers. The Bear Flag revolution provided an excellent excuse for annexing California. This was all the encouragement American officials needed to take the final step in conquering the Golden State.

One important legacy of the Bear Flag revolution was an early sign of ethnic conflict. When Don Mariano Vallejo was seized as a hostage, it was due to his wealth and prestige. Vallejo's mammoth ranch spread from Sonoma, north of San Francisco, into what is now Contra Costa County. In the 1830s Vallejo's wealth had increased dramatically with the secularization of the missions, and he represented the economic success of the local Spanish-speaking Californians. Despite his wealth and political prominence, Vallejo was a strong supporter of American annexation. This contradiction suggests how complex Mariano Vallejo was as a historical figure. He believed that American institutions, particularly governmental and economic ones, would benefit Mexican-California. So he tried to persuade the Bear Flaggers that he was an ally. Vallejo was also friendly with Thomas Oliver Larkin, John Sutter and many other early American settlers. When arrested by the Bear Flaggers, Vallejo was commander of Mexico's military forces in the San Francisco Bay Area.

In July, 1846, Commodore John Drake Sloat sailed into Monterey bay to claim California as an American possession. Once U.S. troops occupied Northern California, a number of military men began to distinguish themselves. The most important was John C. Fremont. Yet, there were many nagging questions about Fremont. Was he one of the instigators of the Bear Flag revolution? Had he fomented racial unrest? The tales of Fremont lingering near the Battle of Olompali and spreading racist tales to the Bear Flaggers has caused his historical reputation to suffer. Many Californios, like Vallejo, charged that the Great Pathfinder was a racially motivated trouble-maker.

The great tragedy of American annexation was that California could have been purchased or acquired through friendly diplomatic negotiations. There were many indications that Vallejo and other Californios were eager for American annexation. Despite the overwhelming circumstantial evidence that Fremont was a troublemaker, many historians see him as a "gallant, daring and useful" figure in California. One such historian is Allan Nevins. In a pioneer book published in 1928, Nevins justified the Great Pathfinder's belligerent attitudes on California conquest. Although Nevins points out Fremont's overzealous actions, nonetheless, he believed that Fremont did have leadership qualities. Years later Nevins remarked that his positive view of the Great Pathfinder changed dramatically. This was one indication that Fremont continued to be a controversial historiographical figure. In fact, in subsequent editions of Nevins book, the subtitle was changed to the Great Pathmarker. As Nevins suggested, Fremont discovered nothing that was new but he was able to compile most of what was known about California and the West.

If Secretary's Buchanan's letter to Larkin and Professor Nevins' assessment of Fremont are correct, there is need to analyze the role of Mariano

Vallejo. As the leading Californio, Vallejo was a seminal figure in California from the 1820s until his death in 1890. Young Vallejo watched the Spanish settle Monterey, and when he died at 82 he had witnessed the building of the transcontinental railroad and the triumph of American civilization. Richard Dillon's, **Humbugs and Heroes,** published in 1970, contains an excellent sketch of the venerable Californio. By tracing Vallejo's career from the 1820s to the late 1840s, Dillon concluded that Don Mariano was an exceptional Californian whose contributions were never fully appreciated.

Secret Agent Thomas Oliver Larkin

In 1845 President James K. Polk instructed Secretary of State James Buchanan to appoint Thomas Oliver Larkin an American agent in Mexican-California. Larkin, a well-known merchant, was the United States Consul at Monterey and frequently passed on secret military information to the War Department. There is little doubt that members of the War Department desired to annex California. The following letter from Buchanan to Larkin is a revealing glimpse in American Imperialism in the mid-nineteenth centure.

Department of State

Washington Oct 17th 1845

Thomas O. Larkin Esqre
Consul of the United States at Monterey, California

SIR

I feel much indebted to you for the information which you have communicated to the Department from time to time in relation to California. The future destiny of that Country is a subject of anxious solicitude for the Government and the People of the United States. The interests of our Commerce and our Whale fisheries on the Pacific Ocean, demand that you should exert the greatest vigilance in discovering and defeating any attempts which may be made by Foreign Governments to acquire a control over that Country. In the contest between Mexico and California we can take no part, unless the former should commence hostilities against the United States; but should California assert and maintain her independence, we shall render her all the kind offices in our power as a Sister Republic. This Government has no ambitious aspirations to gratify and no desire to extend our Federal system over more Territory than we already possess, unless by the free and spontaneous wish of the Independent people of the adjoining Territories. The exercise of compulsion or improper influence to accomplish such a result, would be repugnant both to the policy and principles of this Government. But whilst these are the sentiments of the President, he could not view with indifference the transfer of California to Great Britain or any other European Power. The system of colonization by foreign Monarchies on the North American continent must and will be resisted by the United States. It could result in nothing but evil to the Colonists under their dominion who desire to secure for themselves the blessings of liberty by means of Republican Institutions; whilst it would be highly prejudicial to the best interests of the United States. Nor would it in the end benefit such foreign Monarchies. On the contrary, even Great Britain by the acquisition of California would sow the seeds of future War and disaster for herself; because there is no political truth more certain than that this fine Province could not long be held in vassalage by any European power. The emigration to it of people from the United States would soon render this impossible.

Larkin Papers, III, 705, Doc. 337. Published by permission of The Bancroft Library.

I am induced to make these remarks in consequence of the information communicated to this Department in your Despatch of the 10th of July last. From this it appears that Mr. Rea, the Agent of the British Hudson Bay Company furnished the Californians with arms and money in October and November last, to enable them to expel the Mexicans from the Country: and you state that this policy has been reversed and now no doubt exists there, but that the Mexican troops about to invade the province have been sent for this purpose at the instigation of the British Government: and that "it is rumored that two English Houses in Mexico have become bound to the new General to accept his draft for funds to pay his troops for eighteen months." Connected with these circumstances, the appearance of a British Vice Consul and a French Consul in California, at the present crisis, without any apparent Commercial business, is well calculated to produce the impression, that their respective Governments entertain designs on that Country which must necessarily be hostile to its interests. On all proper occasions, you should not fail prudently to warn the Government and people of California of the danger of such an interference to their peace and prosperity—to inspire them with a jealousy of European dominion and to arouse in their bosoms that love of liberty and independence so natural to the American Continent. Whilst I repeat that this Government does not, under existing circumstances, intend to interfere between Mexico and California, they would vigorously interpose to prevent the latter from becoming a British or French Colony. In this they might surely expect the aid of the Californians themselves.

Whilst the President will make no effort and use no influence to induce California to become one of the free and independent States of this Union, yet if the People should desire to unite their destiny with ours, they would be received as brethren, whenever this can be done, without affording Mexico just cause for complaint. Their true policy, for the present, in regard to this question, is to let events take their course, unless an attempt should be made to transfer them, without their consent, either to Great Britain or France. This they ought to resist by all the means in their power as ruinous to their best interests and destructive of their freedom and independence.

I am rejoiced to learn that "our Countrymen continue to receive every assurance of safety and protection from the present Government" of California, and that they manifest so much confidence in you as Consul of the United States. You may assure them of the cordial sympathy and friendship of the President, and that their conduct is appreciated by him as it deserves.

In addition to your Consular functions, the President has thought proper to appoint you a Confidential Agent in California: and you may consider the present Despatch as your authority for acting in this character. The confidence which he reposes in your patriotism and discretion is evinced by conferring upon you this delicate and important trust. You will take care not to awaken the jealousy of the French and English Agents there by assuming any other than your Consular character. Lieutenant Archibald H. Gillespie of the Marine Corps will immediately proceed to Monterey and will probably reach you before this Despatch. He is a Gentleman in whom the President reposes entire confidence. He has seen these instructions and will cooperate as a confidential agent with you, in carrying them into execution.

You will not fail by every safe opportunity to keep the Department advised of the progress of events in California, and the disposition of the authorities and people toward the United States and other Governments. We should, also, be pleased to learn what is the aggregate population of that Province, and the force it can bring into the field: what is the proportion of Mexican, American, British and French Citizens, and the feelings of each class toward the United States; the names and character of the principal persons in the Executive, Legislative and Judicial Departments of the Government, and of other distinguished and influential Citizens; Its financial system and resources, the amount and nature of its commerce with Foreign Nations, its productions which might with advantage be imported into the United States, and the productions of the United States which might with advantage be received in exchange.

It would, also, be interesting to the Department to learn on what part of California the principal American settlements exist, the rate at which the number of Settlers have been and still are increasing, from what portions of the Union they come and by what routes they arrive in the country.

These specifications are not intended to limit your inquiries. On the contrary it is expected that you will collect and communicate to the Department all the information respecting California which may be useful or important to the United States.

Your compensation will be at the rate of Six dollars per day from the time of the arrival of this Despatch or of Lieutenant Gillespie at Monterey. You will also be allowed your necessary travelling and other expenses incurred in accomplishing the objects of your appointment; but you will be careful to keep an accurate account of these expenditures and procure vouchers for them in all cases where this is practicable without interfering with the successful performance of your duties. For these expenses and your per diem allowance, you are authorised to draw from time to time on the Department. I am, Sir, Respectfully Your Obedient Servant

James Buchanan

John C. Frémont:
Great Pathfinder or Average Pathmarker?
by Allan Nevins

The controversial John C. Frémont has proven to be as enigmatic to historians as he was to contemporary observers. The Harvard philosopher, Josiah Royce, was one of the earliest to write about Frémont's misadventures. Born in Grass Valley and educated at the University of California, Berkeley, Royce was an unusually analytic critic. In 1886, Royce's early history of California made Frémont into a veritable villian. This set the tone for the general historiography of California conquest. It was not until 1928 when Allan Nevins of Columbia University published his multi-volume study that Fremont's tarnished image was resurrected. It is ironic that Nevins changed his own attitudes about Frémont during the course of his future research. In the 1956 revision of the Frémont biography, Nevins made it clear that he no longer considered Frémont a great pathfinder. In fact, the book's sub-title was changed to the "Great Pathmarker." What is interesting about the following selection is that Nevins justifies Frémont's bellicose activity in California in 1846.

. . . Here we are confronted by one of the most baffling problems of Frémont's career. What were the instructions brought by [Lt. Archibald H.] Gillespie which caused Frémont to cut short his explorations, turn south, invade California, and begin in earnest the war which he had threatened a few weeks earlier? He knew that mere re-entrance upon California soil, from which he had been expelled with a warning to keep off, would be construed as a hostile act. Did he have genuine warrant for his course? Or did he, with his usual precipitancy, leap to conclusions and base a bold and stubborn policy upon inadequate authority?

Gillespie, a headlong, high-spirited young officer, had left Washington in November, 1845, and reached Monterey on April 17, 1846, on the ship *Cyane* by way of Hawaii. He brought Frémont a copy of an official dispatch from Buchanan at the head of the State Department, a packet of family missives from Senator Benton and Jessie, and some verbal explanations, as well as much news picked up en route. The family letters, of course, had no official weight. Frémont knew that the Senator's long experience, his position as chairman of the Senate Military Committee, and his great political prestige, made him powerful with the Administration. He knew that Benton would stand by him loyally in anything he did. But, as an army officer, Frémont also knew that nothing the Senator wrote could be used as warrant for any military step, and that to launch his force of sixty upon a warlike

John C. Frémont

course he required some direct official authority, unless he were ready to take the risk of disavowal and punishment. The only really official document brought by Gillespie was Buchanan's dispatch. What policy did it warrant Frémont in pursuing?

The answer appears simple. The dispatch was directed, not to Frémont, but to the consul, Larkin, though Gillespie had been ordered to take it to Frémont. It contained nothing whatever that the explorer could construe as a suggestion that he employ armed force against the Californians. It instructed Larkin to carry on a peaceable intrigue for the secession of California from Mexico by the voluntary act of its inhabitants. He was requested to be discreet, cautious, and sleepless. He was to approach the California authorities, assure them of American good will in their disputes with Mexico, and encourage them to break loose with a promise of our "kind offices as a sister republic." Once they became a separate nation, such as Texas had been, they might look forward to annexation. "If the people should desire to unite their destiny with ours," wrote Buchanan, "they would be received as brethren."

One other injunction was laid upon Larkin with special emphasis. He was told that Washington had reason to fear British or French aggression in California: Larkin himself, in fact, had warned the Government of this. He must counteract foreign machinations by friendly appeals: "On all proper occasions you should not fail prudently to warn the government and people of California of the danger of such an interference to their peace and happiness; to inspire them with a jealousy of European dominion; and to arouse in their bosoms that

love of liberty and independence so natural to the American continent." Larkin, that is, was to do his best to detach California from Mexico for the United States, but he was to do so with the aid and good will of the Californians. Obviously, Frémont had here no authority for hostile action. . . .

So much for the official documents; but there remain the private letters and Gillespie's verbal information, upon which Frémont, as he stated later, unquestionably based his actions. Gillespie brought a budget of exciting news. He told Frémont that Sloat had heard of his encounter with Castro through the brig *Hannah*, and had promptly sent the sloop *Portsmouth* to San Francisco to protect the Americans, where it still lay. He told him that Mexico and the United States had now drifted to the very brink, if not beyond the brink, of war; and that Taylor had advanced to the Rio Grande, where fighting was expected at any time. He brought news that the Mexican authorities at Mazatlan, at last accounts, had expected Sloat to blockade the port at once, and had fled to Rosario with the archives. Finally, Gillespie showed Frémont a letter which Larkin had sent him, under date of April 23, to San Francisco, just as he was starting north to find the explorer. "Capt. Montgomery [of the sloop *Portsmouth*] is of the opinion," wrote the consul, "that Commodore Sloat may by the next mail (6 or 8 days) have a declaration on the part of the United States against Mexico, in which case we shall see him in a few days to take the country." He added that the Californians were much disturbed by the *Portsmouth's* arrival. "I have (as my opinion) said to Generals Castro, Carrillo, and Vallejo, that our flag may fly here in thirty days.

The first says, for his own plans, war is preferable to peace."

As a matter of fact, on the very days that Gillespie and Neal reached Frémont, May 8 and 9, 1846, the first sharp battles of the Mexican War occurred. Frémont felt almost certain that fighting was already under way. In the light of Gillespie's news of the imminence of war, the injunctions regarding peace and conciliation in the dispatch to Larkin seemed unreal and out of date. The explorer says as much in his *Memoirs*. "This idea was no longer practicable as actual war was inevitable and immediate," he writes; "moreover, it was in conflict with our own instructions. We dropped this idea from our minds, but falling on others less informed, it came near losing us California." He later adds that "the rapid progress of affairs had already rendered" conciliation impossible, and made it necessary to "carry out the ultimate purpose of the government."

But Gillespie also bore family letters, and verbal instructions from Secretary Bancroft. Upon the nature of the family letters, we have explicit statements from both Frémont and Jessie, and both agree that they warned Frémont to be ready to take a militant stand. Mrs. Frémont asserts that they might be said to be in a family cipher, for they were full of prearranged references to talks and agreements known only at home. Frémont states this more emphatically. Benton's letter, he says, "while apparently of friendship and family detail, contained passages and suggestions which, read by the light of many conversations and discussions with himself and others at Washington, clearly indicated to me that I was required by the government to find out any foreign schemes in relation to

California, and so far as it might be in my power, to counteract them." In a conversation long afterward with Josiah Royce, Frémont said that the letters were particularly clear upon the desirability "of taking and holding possession of California in the event of any occurrence that would justify it, leaving it to my discretion to decide upon such an occurrence." He was warned of the British designs and told that Polk desired that he "should not let the English get possession of California, but should use any means in his power, or any occasion that offered, to prevent such a thing."

No doubt Frémont's recollection of the affair might be regarded as confused or colored; but it is in great measure corroborated by a letter, inaccurate in a few particulars but illuminating, which Secretary Bancroft wrote him in old age, when Royce's book had made the subject controversial. Bancroft speaks of verbal instructions:

You as an officer of the army were made thoroughly acquainted with the state of things in California.

My motive in sending so promptly the order to take possession was not from any fear that England would resist, but from the apprehension that an English man of war in San Francisco harbor would have a certain degree of inconvenience, and that it was much better for us to be masters there before the ship should arrive; and my orders reached there very long before any English vessel was off California. The shameful delay of Sloat made a danger, but still he took possession of San Francisco before a British ship arrived.

Not having my papers here, all I can say is, that after your interview with Gillespie, you were absolved from any orders as an explorer, and became an

officer of the American army, warned by
your government of your new danger
against which you became bound to defend
yourself; and it was made known to you,
on the authority of the Secretary of the
Navy, that a great object of the President
was to obtain possession of California. If I
had been in your place, I should have
considered myself bound to do what I
could to promote the purpose of the
President. You were alone, no Secretary of
War to appeal to, he was thousands of
miles off; and yet it was officially made
known to you that your country was at
war; and it was so made known expressly
to guide your conduct. It was further
made known to you, that the acquisition of
California was become a chief object of the
President. If you had letters to that effect
from the Secretary of War, you had your
warrant. If you were left without orders
from the War Department, certainly you
learned through the Secretary of the Navy
[Bancroft himself] that the President's
plan of war included the taking possession
of California.

   The truth is, that no officer of the
government had anything to do with
California but the Secretary of the Navy,
so long as I was in the Cabinet. It had
been my desire to acquire California by
all honorable means much before that
time. . . .

Of strict legal authority for re-entering
Mexican territory and fomenting an in-
surrection by the American settlers along
the Sacramento, Frémont had none; of
moral authority, he had a great deal. He
knew that the written message to Larkin,
like that to Sloat, had to be guarded and
harmless in tenor, for it might easily fall
into Mexican hands. He would, therefore,
give the greater weight to verbal commu-
nications. The very fact that Gillespie
had been ordered without fail to find and
talk with Frémont was full of signifi-

cance. With the knowledge that immediate war was almost a certainty, which
was he to do: push on north and home-
ward by way of the Oregon Trail, leaving
the scene of action behind him, or return
at once to California? No man of courage
and patriotism could hesitate. It was impossible to stand still; it would have been
a spiritless and craven act to turn his
back on California; the only course was to
retrace his steps. . . .

   His sudden reappearance within forbidden bounds created a commotion
among the American residents, and inevitably the malcontents and adventurers
who longed for a conflict with Mexico
responded most warmly to the excitement. Many came riding into Frémont's
camp. During 1845, a large number of
new emigrants had arrived, so that there
were now fully 800 Americans, nearly all
of them able-bodied men, in the province.
Some were legal landowners who had
gone through the necessary process of
becoming citizens; the great majority,
however, were simply squatters, or men
who picked up a living by combining work
as ranch hands with hunting and trap-
ping. To understand Frémont's relations
with them, it should be understood that
they conformed to the rough frontier
type. While a number showed sterling
character and high ability, the gamut
among the reckless sailors, ignorant, rugged frontier farmers, and buckskin-clad
trappers ran to a low level. With the
Anglo-Saxon's instinctive feeling of superiority, most of them looked down upon
the gay, indolent, inefficient Californians,
who loved gambling, guitars, and fandan-
gos, and who made so little use of the rich
country. They felt that California ought
to be in the hands of their own virile,
energetic race, and that it was only a

question of time and opportunity till they should take it over.

These men brought Frémont a wild variety of rumors—that war between the United States and Mexico had begun; that it was about to begin; that Castro and his merciless greaser crew were planning to fall upon all foreign settlers and scatter them to the winds; that Castro and others were plotting to separate California from Mexico, but were unwilling to place it under American protection; that the British were scheming to annex California forthwith. Samuel Hensley, one of the leading American settlers, and Neal, with whom Frémont had talked at length, agreed that the American residents would either have to leave the country soon, or fight for the homes they had made. Frémont lent an especially attentive ear to stories of aggression against the Americans and of plans of the California authorities to injure and restrict them. His own clash with the Government a few weeks earlier had prepared him to believe anything of Mexican treachery and bullying. . . .

[O]n April 30, 1846, while Frémont was still proceeding northward into Oregon, Castro had issued a proclamation warning the Americans again that they had no right whatever to hold land unless they became Mexican citizens. In this paper he instructed all the judges that they could not legally permit any sale or other transfer of realty to foreigners; while he gave brusque notice to Yankee squatters that not only would they forfeit any purchase they had made, but they would "be subject, unless they retire voluntarily from the country, to be expelled from it whenever the government may find it convenient." Castro, an ambitious,

bombastic man, who liked to strut a bit, even made warlike preparations, and talked of bringing armed forces against the settlers. Reports of this, perhaps exaggerated, quickly reached the Sacramento.

There was really a vast deal of covert ill feeling and distrust between the majority of the American settlers and the general body of Californians. Josiah Royce, in his volume on California, writes as if Frémont's precipitation of the so-called Bear Flag War were the origin of the sullen hostility between the two peoples which followed the annexation of the province. Actually, the tension between the races was already painful. Not merely did the Americans tend to regard the natives as lazy, childlike, untruthful, and cowardly. The Californians, for their part, tended to look upon the immigrants as rough, overbearing, and grasping—as brutal fellows whose one aim was gain. In general, mutual understanding was impossible. Protestant against Catholic, Anglo-Saxon against Latin, strenuous pioneers against idlers—they were sundered by instinctive antipathies. The part which Americans had played in various California revolts had excited animosity and fear. Moreover, the Californians had sufficient racial pride to resent the American annexation of Texas, and had doubtless learned from Mexican writers that the Spanish-speaking people there had fared ill. A few liberal and informed Californians favored American control, but the predominant view was antagonistic.

Frémont was impressed by the reports of Castro's threatening attitude and of the danger of Indian attacks. It seemed altogether likely to him that the Mexican officials would try to incite the savages to an uprising. Some settlers who came into his camp declared that the half-civilized Indians working on the ranches were leaving their tasks and taking to the mountains, an indication of imminent hostilities. Sutter sent Frémont a courier with a message which the Captain interpreted as meaning that an Indian onslaught was in preparation. Inasmuch as California had never had a military force able to cope with the tribes, outlying farms had frequently been sacked, and it was only recently that Sutter himself had felt safe. The province between Lassen's ranch and the Mexican line contained perhaps 20,000 aborigines, of whom half had a smattering of civilization; but current reports exaggerated their numbers to 40,000 or more. They were lazy, unthrifty, and thievish; physically, they were greatly inferior to the best tribes of the plains, as, for instance, the Sioux; but when aroused and collected in numbers, they were a real menace. Frémont shared the frontiersman's usual prejudice against savages, whom he regarded as uniformly treacherous, base, and cruel. Once he had seen a party of emigrants after a band of Indians had wreaked its worst upon them—the men mutilated and flayed alive, the women impaled upon sharp stakes—and he had never forgotten it. He still felt a keen resentment over the death of his faithful Basil Lajeunesse. Telling the settlers that he would take precautions to protect them and their families, he kept a close surveillance over such Indians as he could, and made ready for active operations. . . .

Many of the settlers had reached the conclusion that, no matter what Frémont did, the time had come for them to act. William Hargrave, who had settled in the Napa Valley two years earlier, tells us that his American neighbors there considered the outlook "very gloomy"; that they feared the Mexicans would try to eject them; and that "we foreigners were ready to fight for our new homes." We have a similar account by William F. Swasey, who was for a time Sutter's bookkeeper at the Fort. The settlers had heard, he states, that a large number of the native Californians had met at Monterey to discuss a plan for declaring the territory free and placing it under the protection of a foreign flag, and that a majority were in favor of a British protectorate. The arrival of the British warship *Collingwood* made English annexation seem, to some observers at least, a distinct danger. A spontaneous American revolt was on the point of breaking out when Frémont so fortuitously returned. According to Hargrave, he was one of a party of nine or ten men who came to Frémont's camp to seek assistance. "Kelsey acted as spokesman," he says, "and I do not recollect the language used, but my impression was at the time that Frémont, though very cautious and evidently averse to precipitate action, was willing enough to resume active operations, but he preferred to see for himself in how far the settlers of Napa and Sonoma Valley were ready to shake off the Mexican yoke. At any rate, he peremptorily refused to take any responsibility for sudden action on our part and endeavored to delay or frustrate our efforts. Whether Frémont expressed himself differently when he spoke to Kelsey alone, later in the day, I cannot say."

Frémont was playing a waiting game. He knew that the settlers were determined to act, he gave them at least partial encouragement, and he bided his time. The great object was to gain California for the United States, and this seemed to him the shrewdest course. "We made no secret of our intentions," Hargrave says of the settlers, "to keep up the agitation till the opportunity arrived for a bold stroke. On our return to the Napa Valley we found that the revolutionary movement had gained more ground, and steps were taken at once to organize a force sufficient for our first enterprise—the capture of Sonoma." He adds that a majority of the men on the north side of San Francisco Bay did not feel friendly toward Frémont at the beginning of the Bear Flag War, but became cordial later. The recollections of John Fowler of Napa County strongly corroborate Hargrave's account. He declares that the fear of the Mexicans was such that many settlers had been preparing to leave California for the States or for Oregon. Others wished to fight, and "I was in favor of acting at once, independent of Col. Frémont and without consulting him." Swasey says simply that "the Americans and foreigners generally were called together in Sacramento, Napa, and Sonoma Valleys for the purpose of resistance." It would seem that Swasey, who was very close to Larkin at this time, thought he knew what were the confidential instructions of the Federal Government which Gillespie had brought to Frémont. "Their substance was," he states, "that the Colonel should be governed by circumstances, and, if a movement appeared among the Americans to bring about an annexation to the United States, or to defeat the designs of another government (the object of the *Collingwood* being well understood), he should identify himself there-

with, keeping near to California to be prepared for such emergency." This testimony is worth little as regards the supposed instructions; it is worth a good deal as to what was in Frémont's mind.

He did not need to rouse the settlers to fall upon the defenseless Californians whom Royce pities so much; the Americans had already been aroused by a fear, for which they had only too good grounds, of hostile action by the California authorities. He was glad to see their armed rising. It meant the swift end of Mexican authority, for he had no doubt that the settlers could defeat Castro. It meant the forestalling of any action which the British might contemplate. The settlers' action would be decisive as regarded the future American sovereignty in California, and yet the American Government would not be involved. If they were hard pressed, he might join them, leaving Washington free to disavow his step if it wished. If he heard of the commencement of war with Mexico, he would certainly join them. There can be little doubt that Frémont, speaking confidentially, promised the settlers that if worse came to worst he would come to their aid— though as a blind he still spoke of leaving shortly for the States. While he maintained great reticence as to the instructions he had received through Gillespie, everyone supposed that whatever he did was with the authority of the United States.

Frémont's waiting game was, if you will, the game of an opportunist; but it was precisely his duty to be an opportunist. Royce later criticized him for being bloody-minded and precipitate; the American settlers at the time criticized him for being hesitant and careful. "We left him," says Hargrave, "most of us somewhat disgusted with the result of our interview." His course exposed him to misunderstanding, but any course he could possibly have taken would have done that. Under these circumstances, the first blow was struck.

It happened that Castro had sent a Lieutenant Arce to the north shore of San Francisco Bay to collect some scattered horses bearing the government brand. The officer collected about one hundred and fifty animals, and was taking them southward by way of Sutter's Fort and the San Joaquin Valley. Necessarily, the whole countryside knew of the movement: Arce, in the bright Mexican uniform of blue, red, and silver effects, supervising a dozen men, with their flashy serapes, high Mexican saddles, and lassoes, as they herded the mounts at a trot toward the fords of the Sacramento, the cavalcade raising a thick cloud of dust under the June sky. They reached Sutter's Fort, stayed overnight as Sutter's guests, and went on south the next day to the Cosumnes River, sixteen or eighteen miles distant, where they camped for the night. Here they were surprised by a party of a dozen settlers, under Ezekiel Merritt, who disarmed them, took away their horses, and insultingly told them to carry the news to Castro. Merritt was a tall, rawboned frontiersman, fearless, simple, and fond of risks, who was a natural chieftain for the rougher immigrants. He regarded Frémont with enormous respect, and later Frémont called him his field lieutenant.

. . . [The capture of Arce's horses helped raise in northern California the signal of war.] No one in this remote Mexican province yet knew that almost a month earlier (May 12, 1846) Congress had declared war; that in the battles of Palo Alto and Resaca de la Palma, Taylor had driven the Mexicans across the Rio Grande. The acts of Frémont and Merritt produced a feeling of consternation among the peace-loving Americans and friendly Californians. When Sutter heard that Arce had been attacked by a group of settlers, he expressed astonishment and indignation. Other Americans were immensely pleased. At last, they felt, California was to be brought quickly and decisively under the American flag. Many of high character welcomed the new turn of affairs. Long afterward an observer asked an estimable pioneer who had four sons under Frémont if he felt any compunction in attacking the Californians. "He said he had Scripture example for it. The Israelites took the promised land of the East by arms, and the Americans must take the promised land of the West in the same way."

Frémont now saw that he had aroused forces that could not easily be suppressed; that he had set in motion men of headlong temper, and made it certain that the Mexican authorities would strike back. The result was his decision, still keeping in the background, to instigate an attack upon the small military post of Sonoma, fifteen miles north of San Francisco Bay. Here were cannon, small arms, munitions, and horses, which Frémont needed; here lived General Vallejo, once commandant general of the province—a firm friend of American annexation—who might be used to influence the public. A quick stroke, with the raising of the American flag, would once for all end the danger that England, in collusion with Mexico, would occupy California. Frémont states that he sent Merritt, his field lieutenant, into the town "instructed to surprise" it. It is clear that he had planned all the steps beforehand, and anticipated little or no resistance.

The feat was quickly accomplished. Sonoma was an old mission establishment, now a dull and ruinous-looking place, infested by countless fleas. The chief buildings—the quartel, the residences of Vallejo, his brother, and his brother-in-law, Jacob Leese, and a few others—looked upon a large plaza, disfigured after the careless California fashion by the skulls and skeletons of slaughtered beeves. At dead of night, some thirty-three or thirty-four armed settlers rode into the unsuspecting hamlet, or as they grandiloquently called it, fortress, routed the astonished Californians out of bed, and took possession of the military equipment. These included eight fieldpieces, two hundred stands of arms, and almost a hundred weight of powder. Vallejo, protesting, was taken with the rest to Sutter's Fort, where Merritt and Frémont had planned to jail them. . . .

Events now moved rapidly. Some of the settlers who had taken Sonoma had ideas of their own as to how a revolt should be conducted. At such figures as William B. Ide, a shrewd, fussy, dogmatic Jack-of-all-trades, who had wandered west from Vermont, successively a farmer, schoolteacher, carpenter, and rancher, or as Dr. Semple, an unbelievably long and lanky Kentuckian, who was quick on the trigger and loved an illiterate kind of rhetoric, it is easy to sneer. Josiah Royce has sneered at these typical frontier figures in the best Boston-Brahmin manner. They were not drawing-room ornaments. They did not have the horror which a philosophical

pacifist like Dr. Royce felt for the rude acts of warfare which have usually accompanied the American conquest of new territory. But they did organize carefully their little uprising, thus touched off by Frémont, give it an orderly form, and attempt in the best Jeffersonian manner to justify it.

Sonoma was held by the settlers as a combination of fort and headquarters, and the little garrison there rapidly increased from fifteen or eighteen to forty men. On the very first day, June 14, 1846, the captors redeemed themselves from the charge of being a loose mob of marauders by declaring the "Republic of California." This scheme of an independent republic had been revolved by Americans for years. One recruit, William L. Todd, a nephew of Mrs. Abraham Lincoln, took a piece of whitish brown cloth a yard and a half in length, and with either some paint or some pokeberry juice (the accounts are conflicting) placed upon it a large star in the upper right-hand corner, and facing this at the top the figure of a grizzly bear. Native Californians gazing contemptuously at this design were heard later to call it "the shoat." Across the middle of the flag were painted the words "California Republic." When it was hoisted on the empty Mexican staff, the Bear Flag Party and the Bear Flag War had found an imperishable name. This flag was a symbol to which the settlers attached the utmost importance. It meant order. Only one unruly fellow dared to suggest that Sonoma be sacked, and "an unanimous indignant frown made him shrink from the presence of honest men." It meant liberty; Dr. Semple was voluble in preaching the abstract principles of republicanism. It meant American rule forever replacing Mexican rule, as Ide formally asserted [in his proclamation of June 18, 1846]. . . .

The raising of the Bear Flag, the circulation of Ide's proclamation of the "Republic," and the news of the occupation of Sonoma aroused the immediate anger of the Mexican officials. Castro replied with two proclamations on June 17. He had no forces beyond San Francisco Bay, but he promptly collected what troops he could farther south, and dispatched them under an officer named De la Torre to the relief of Sonoma. Their approach became known on June 23; the Bear Flag forces sent couriers to ask Frémont's help, and marched out under Lieutenant Ford to repulse the Californians. The result was a brisk engagement about a dozen miles from San Rafael, in which the Bear Flag men killed two Californians, wounded several more, and put the whole body to helter-skelter flight. While this happened, Frémont was casting off all disguise and taking the field. He was glad to have the call to arms. He had made up his mind that the crisis had come, and that it was "unsafe to leave events to mature under unfriendly, or mistaken, direction."

Frémont and his rescue party reached Sonoma on June 25, 1846, and with an augmented force of 160 men in all he at once took up the pursuit of De la Torre's retreating troops. The Captain had not acted without serious thought. He believed that his open entry into the struggle would prevent the Bear Flag settlers from being ultimately crushed by the stronger forces of Castro, and would deter any British agents from proclaiming a protectorate of California. If war had begun between the United States and Mexico, all would be well. On the other hand,

if peace were maintained and it became necessary to disavow Frémont, little harm would have been done. The Captain took steps to make disavowal easy by drafting his resignation and laying it aside in an envelope to be sent to Senator Benton, who could transmit it to the War Department at his discretion.

It was only by great luck combined with an adroit ruse that De la Torre's crippled force escaped south of San Francisco Bay to a point of safety. The Californians had better horses than the Americans. De la Torre, having thus gained the head start, put a false message into the hands of an Indian, announcing an imminent attack upon Sonoma by Castro himself, and when the Indian was captured, Frémont hastily turned back from his pursuit to protect the threatened town; and De la Torre was then fortunate enough to find a large boat at Sausalito on the north shore of the Bay, and to make his way across. The anger and chagrin of the Americans at failing to crush their antagonists were extreme. They had as yet lost no men in open battle, but when Lieutenant Ford was marching to repulse De la Torre near San Rafael on the Bay, the settlers had come upon the bodies of two American immigrants, Tom Cowan, or Cowie, and a man named Fowler, murdered by the roadside. It was plain that they had been tortured to death, and their disemboweled and mutilated corpses presented a shocking spectacle. Cowan had been well-known and greatly liked, and the episode aroused a stern desire for revenge. A little later, when the Americans were in possession of San Rafael, some Californians landed from a boat, were intercepted by Kit Carson, who was on patrol duty, and when they offered resistance, were shot down. This appears to have been a cold-blooded murder. In excuse, it has been said that they were messengers bearing official Mexican orders, and that they tried to escape; and a long controversy has raged over the question whether the killing of the two—some say three—was defensible. There is little doubt that it was not. . . .

Had Frémont foreseen how harshly a group of later historians would criticize his daring series of acts in turning back from his explorations, fomenting the Bear Flag uprising, and finally assuming its open leadership, he would have been dismayed and incredulous. Without partiality for Frémont, it is impossible to believe that this criticism, in the extreme terms in which Royce and Hittell state it, is justified. Frémont is accused of acting without specific authority, and of course that charge is true. He was six months' travel by a dangerous and difficult route from Washington; through Gillespie he had received news which made him feel it was his duty to assume a certain independent responsibility. He did just what a long line of officers of the English-speaking race have always done in emergencies. The British Empire owes half its territory to subalterns, generals, ship captains, and merchants who have acted without authority and been applauded later. Andrew Jackson had no authority in 1818 to invade the Spanish territory of Florida and seize Pensacola, but he did it. Commodore T. A. C. Jones had had no authority in 1842 for the occupation of Monterey, but he occupied it. An officer who will not go beyond out-of-date and insufficient orders in an emergency, who will not use his own discretion, is not worth his salt. Admiral Sloat was just such an officer, and the Administration in Washington regarded Sloat's timidity

and vacillation on the Pacific Coast as a national misfortune, and made that fact clear to him.

Frémont has been accused, again, of taking action which, orders or no orders, was not justified by the facts of the California situation, or his knowledge of the general wishes of the Federal Government. But it is useless to deny that he had left Washington with verbal instructions from the Administration; besides his own word, we have that of Senator Benton, Mrs. Frémont, and Secretary Bancroft for the fact, and they all had a high regard for the truth. It is useless to deny that the fear of an Indian attack was general; Sutter himself feared it. It cannot be denied, finally, that Castro was acting in a way which filled the American settlers with apprehension for their property and personal safety—his own orders and proclamations prove that—or that Frémont had good reason for fearing a sudden British proclamation of some form of protectorate. Royce is especially caustic in his treatment of the panic of the Bear Flag leaders regarding Castro. But of this one of our ablest historians writes:

First, many of the settlers had ample reasons to feel alarmed: the illegality of their presence; Castro's sudden and cruel seizure of Americans in 1840; his attack upon Frémont in violation (the Americans believed) of a promise; official notices, issued about May 1, to the effect that a majority of the Americans were liable to be expelled at the convenience of the authorities; Castro's warlike preparations; his talk of moving against the immigrants with armed forces; and reports, more or less authentic, and reliable, from various persons regarding what he said or intended. Secondly, the contemporary testimony of Frémont, Gillespie, and other Americans—some of it given under oath—that alarm was actually felt is too strong to be rejected. Much has been made [by Royce] of Bidwell, a clerk of Sutter's, who tells us that alarm was not felt. But (1) his statement was made thirty years after the events; (2) he admits that he was not on good terms with Frémont, and his statement aims to show that Frémont invented the story of alarm as an excuse for his conduct; (3) his statement is in other respects clearly inaccurate; (4) it assumes that he knew the sentiment of all the persons on the Sacramento, yet proves that an important fact may have been known to but few; (5) it shows that at the critical time he was absent in the mountains; (6) it says, "Californians were always talking of expelling Americans," and therefore were talking of it in April, 1846; (7) his book mentions that in 1845 an attack upon New Helvetia was so confidently expected that he rode night and day to warn Sutter. . . .

Almost equally violent is Royce's attack upon the "legend" that the British had designs upon California; but the British archives show that these designs were well matured. The apprehension that England would forestall us was dwelt upon in the Senate early in 1846; it filled Secretary Bancroft's mind. "The expansive course of Great Britain," says the historian just quoted, "remarks dropped by English writers, repeated warnings dropped from our diplomatic and consular agents at Mexico, and the consensus of opinion in California, Mexico, France, and the United States were quite enough to warrant suspicions of England." Sloat, Stockton, and Larkin all feared Rear Admiral Sir George Seymour's intentions. British policy since 1815 has usually been extremely considerate of American

susceptibilities, and it was so in this instance. But the English naval contingent on the Pacific coast would have been glad to secure a diplomatic foothold if it could be done without antagonizing the Americans. This was perceived with growing clarity in Washington. Frémont's activities along the coast, and his return at a critical juncture from the north, accentuated the feeling of the British officers that the United States was determined to obtain California, and that it would be impossible to act without coming into sharp collision with American aims and agents.

Above all, Frémont has been assailed as a mischief maker who split innocent blood, aroused a resentment among the native Californians which quadrupled the difficulties of the subsequent American occupation, and laid the foundations for a lasting animosity between these Californians and the Americans. Actually, the Bear Flag uprising did not cost a dozen lives all told. A more nearly bloodless conquest or revolution it would be hard to find. In weighing Josiah Royce's denunciation of it, we must recall that Royce was a thoroughgoing pacifist to whom any fighting of any character was abhorrent. An armed clash, in view of the outbreak of the Mexican War, was inevitable, and northern California could not have been secured with a shorter casualty list. As for the ill-feeling aroused by the Bear Flag uprising, much of it appears quickly to have evaporated. The Americans, after Frémont took full control, bore themselves for the most part in an exemplary manner. There were no outrages, no depredations, and few aberrations from the rule of strict obedience and orderliness; Alexander Godey tells us, truthfully, that Frémont's operations "were eminently characterized by a regard for the rights and interests of the inhabitants of the country through which his forces marched, which secured to him the kindest feelings of regard and respect of the entire California population." It is true that there was a sudden angry flare-up of the Californians against the Americans after Sloat raised his flag, and much semiguerilla warfare. But where did it occur? Not in northern California, where Frémont had acted, but in southern California. As for the legacy of ill feeling which the events of 1846 left, that was largely inevitable. Any historian who supposes that two races so alien in blood, religion, habits, temper, and aims as the Americans and the Mexican-Californians could have lived together without sharp friction is very naïve.

Frémont was not the liberator of California. It would in all probability have fallen safely and surely into American hands had he gone unambitiously north to the Oregon Trail in the spring of 1846. But he did play a gallant, daring, and useful rôle in expediting the American conquest, making it easy for the Navy to act, preventing the possible occurrence of complications with Great Britain, and enabling California to be almost wholly pacified before the first overland forces under General Kearny arrived.

Mariano Vallejo: Californio Leader
by Richard Dillon

Mariano Vallejo was one of California's most important leaders during the Mexican-California era. From his sprawling Sonoma rancho, the venerable Californio was a political and economic power broker who helped to develop workable institutions. Vallejo was also a commissioner appointed by the Mexican government to supervise the secularization of mission lands. When he died at his Sonoma home in 1890 at the age of 82, Vallejo was the most respected of all early California leaders. Richard Dillon's portrait of Vallejo in Humbugs and Heroes *offers some excellent insights into the last days of Mexican-California and the early period of American annexation.*

Hardly "typical" of the settlers of Spanish and Mexican California was Don Mariano Guadalupe Vallejo. Like John Sutter he stood head and shoulders above most of the leaders of Arcadian California and, while he was never governor, he became one of the most powerful individuals in the entire province. And still the Yankee take-over of California was as disastrous for him as for Sutter or Vallejo's less impressive ranchero friends. What made Vallejo's case so distressing was that he had welcomed the Americans (and earned the name of "traitor" in some quarters, as a result) because he believed their rule would mean peace and order and growth instead of the directionless drifting of the Mexican.

Vallejo and Sutter, rivals at first, became firm friends in mutual misfortune during the Bear Flag Revolt, Mexican War, and Gold Rush. Both were efficiently looted of their lands and other property by gringo squatters and shysters. Withal, Vallejo remained the most effective link between the two regimes and he accepted his disaster with more grace than the embittered Sutter. He lived out a useful life at his Sonoma estate, Lachryma Montis (Tears of the Mountain, so called for the hillside springs which watered his vines), a 280-acre remnant of his onetime feudal domain of tens of thousands of acres. Vallejo saw the urgent need of reconciliation between the two peoples; "Let the wound heal," he urged.

During his heyday, Vallejo's kindness and hospitality rivaled that of John Sutter, himself, and Reverend Walter Colton, U.S. Navy chaplain and Alcalde of Monterey, may have been thinking of him when he contrasted the native Californians with his fellow Americans: "The shrewdness and sharpness of the Yankee . . . and the liberality of the Californian . . . Give me the Californian!"

Whether Vallejo was, or was not, the most distinguished *Californio*, the "Noblest Roman of them all," as historian Rockwell D. Hunt used to insist, there is no challenging his importance to California in pre-Gold Rush days. He was born

Richard Dillon, HUMBUGS AND HEROES, (Garden City, Doubleday, 1970). Reprinted by permission of the author.

Mariano Vallejo (Courtesy of the Bancroft Library)

on July 7, 1808, in Monterey and profited more than most of his peers from the limited and haphazard education available from Alta California's few tutors. The young man was something of a protege of Governor Pablo Solá, who appreciated the benefits of education, and Vallejo's talents were also recognized by Governor Luis Arguello, who appointed the young man his private secretary. Later, Vallejo imported the best library in California, although the clergy was outraged since many of the books were taboo because of the *Index Librorum Prohibitorum*. Mariano entered military service as a cadet at the age of fifteen, and by the time he was twenty-three he was in command of the San Francisco garrison and elected to the provincial legislature (illegally, since he was a soldier). In 1834, he was elected an alternate delegate to the Mexican Congress, but was never called to Mexico City.

But Vallejo saw himself as a soldier, not a politician. He rose from ensign to colonel and even to *commandante general* of all California. He led punitive expeditions against hostile Indians and in 1829 won a considerable reputation when he whipped the rebel forces of renegade mission Indian Estanislao (or Stanislaus). However, his achievement was tarnished by his callousness in allowing his Indian allies to murder some of his prisoners. He supported the home-rule rebellion of 1832 by the Californians against the governor, Manuel Victoria, imposed upon them by Mexico City, and took part in the

Isaac Graham affair, in which a number of Americans (suspected of being fillibusters) were exiled. Later, however, Vallejo tried to remain more aloof from the chaotic rebellions and counterrebellions which dominated politics during the Mexican regime. He preferred to play a lone hand rather than galloping off at the drop of a sombrero to reinforce Juan B. Alvarado or José Castro in one of their power plays. Similarly, he was able to stay out of the sticky Micheltorena War of 1844, in which the governor was thrown out and Sutter was defeated and humiliated. (Vallejo had to go to the extreme of disbanding his military company—pretending that he could no longer afford to support it—but it worked.)

When Governor José Figueroa began to worry in 1833 about the presence of the Russians at Fort Ross and Bodega, he sent his most trusted officer, Vallejo, to reconnoiter the outpost of Russian Alaska and to make recommendations. The two men decided that a military post was necessary north of San Francisco Bay, as much to contain warlike Indians and potential Yankee filibusters as Russians, who seemed peaceable enough to Vallejo. Vallejo was not only named commander of the new post at Sonoma, he was given the title of Military Commandant and Director of Colonization of the Northern Frontier. In this new position, his power compared to that of Sutter and José Castro, *commandante general of* California. By stabilizing Mexico's northwesternmost frontier Vallejo played his greatest role in California history. He whipped hostile Indians, won over others with just treatment, and made a powerful ally in Chief Sem Yeto (Mighty Army) of the Suisunes. He, several times, put a stop to the enslaving of Indian children by Mexicans and Indians alike, even by Chief Solano himself, none other than Sem Yeto after he became a Christian.

When the missions were secularized in 1833, Vallejo was named administrator of the Sonoma Mission, San Francisco de Solano. He was so efficient that he was accused of feathering his nest at the expense of the Indians and the ex-missions. But he took better care of the Indians than almost any other administrator; he increased the livestock while the herds of the other missions dwindled away. Small wonder the governor paid little heed to the complaints against Vallejo, most of them made by two discredited priests, so demoralized that they should have been defrocked long before. Later, Vallejo would protect the mission lands and herds (and the Indians) from the plans of the Hijar-Padres Company to "colonize" the missions with newcomers from Mexico and elsewhere.

One reason why Vallejo cared little to meddle in governmental politics was that Governor Juan B. Alvarado, his nephew, was jealous of him and saw him as a rival. So he devoted himself to building up Sonoma and, in time, he became a sort of *cacique*, or chief, although his allegiance to Monterey was never in doubt, as was Sutter's. His domain, with his brother Salvador's, now stretched from Sonoma to Petaluma to Napa and all the way to Carquinez Strait. The Government paid no attention to his suggestions, reforms which might have delayed the American conquest. He repeatedly urged that the presidial companies not be allowed to waste away: "the only hope of salvation of the country, which needs positive and efficacious remedies before it is submerged in ruins." Unheeded, he built up his own extraofficial presidio at Sonoma, although he was forced to outfit and pay his troops from his own pocket most of the time. (In twenty-four years of military service to Mexico, Vallejo himself was apparently never paid so much as a plugged peso in salary.) At times, as when the governor wished to use his men in some ill-advised adventure, Vallejo could fall back on the fiction that they really constituted his private bodyguard. At another time he answered Alvarado's request for some of his men by saying, "My troops will always be ready to support the law, but not to abuse it."

The ambitious and ruthless John C. Frémont mistreated Vallejo just as he did Sutter, and, through the farce of the Bear Flag Revolt, captured and jailed Vallejo at New Helvetia. When Sutter protested the gross injustice of the act, Frémont threatened to hang the Swiss from his own oak tree. It took Commodore Robert Stockton himself to secure the release of Vallejo and his aides, on parole, from the little dictator, Frémont.

Belatedly, Vallejo was rewarded for his loyalty to the new government by being elected to the constitutional convention of 1849 in Monterey. There, he was largely responsible for naming the various counties of the state. He was also elected to the first State Senate, but his efforts to place the capitol in the town of Vallejo failed. After a brief itineracy, the capitol came to rest in Sacramento. When he heard of Marshall's discovery at Coloma, Vallejo wished his friend and erstwhile enemy the best: "As the water flows through Sutter's millrace, may the gold flow into Sutter's purse." Vallejo did virtually no gold mining himself. He devoted himself to his Sonoma estate, becoming a great vineyardist and vintner like his neighbor, Agoston Haraszthy, whose two sons married daughters of Vallejo. Don Mariano also helped Bancroft write his history of California. On January 18, 1890, Vallejo died, and with him passed the last important tie with the Mexican period of California's history.

WORKSHEET 3: The American Conquest: Manifest Destiny or Cospiratorial Imperialism?

1. Manifest Destiny is defined as _____

_____

2. How did President Andrew Jackson show interest in Mexican California? _____

_____

3. What role did Anthony Butler play in the early attempt to purchase Mexican California?

_____

_____

4. What was President Martin Van Buren's attitude on annexing Mexican

California? _____

_____

5. Commodore Thomas O.P. Jones is important because _____

_____

_____

6. How strong is the evidence that there was a U.S. War Department conspiracy to

annex Mexican California? _____

_____

7. President James K. Polk's attitude on Mexican California annexation was that ___

_____

8. President Polk was concerned about the influences of which European nation in

Mexican California? _____

9. Jose Castro called Fremont's Third Expedition _____

10. The Hawk's Peak incident saw Castro _____

11. How clouded or distorted were Fremont's recollections of his role in California?

_____

_____

_____

12. How did Fremont provoke war like attitudes? Did he need to do this? _____

_____

_____

_____

13. What role did the Bear Flag revolution play in American annexation? _____

_____

_____

_____

14. Briefly analyze the importance of Mariano Vallejo to Mexican California?

_____

_____

_____

15. Thomas Oliver Larkin was important because _____

_____

_____

16. Who was jealous of Vallejo? _____

The California Gold Rush, Economic Blessing or Disaster?

READINGS: W. TURRENTINE JACKSON, *"THE NEW MELONES RESERVOIR PROJECT AREA: THE GOLD RUSH YEARS"* RICHARD H. PETERSON, *"THE FOREIGN MINERS' TAX OF 1850: EXPLOITATION OR EXPULSION?"*

On January 24, 1848, James W. Marshall accidentally discovered gold in the Sierra Nevada foothills. While he was constructing a sawmill for John A. Sutter on the south fork of the American River, Marshall noticed some glittering particles in the water. In a small lumber camp called Coloma, Marshall scooped up the magical gold specks. Realizing that his discovery validated tales stretching back to the Spanish explorers, Marshall quickly journeyed to Sutter's Fort.

When Marshall arrived at Sutter's Fort with a small sack of gold, there was an atmosphere of secrecy and intrigue. John Sutter looked skeptically at the gold. He went to a book shelf and picked up an encyclopedia looking for information on how to test the precious metal. Sutter bit it. His lip bled. Sutter then subjected the yellow rocks to some crude laboratory tests and verified that gold had been discovered.

Gold! Sutter couldn't believe his good fortune. He began planning how he could monopolize California's mineral wealth. Sutter envisioned a California Republic in which he would be the exalted ruler, the King of California, and the Emperor of the Golden State.

After negotiating a treaty with the Coloma Indians for $150 worth of goods, Sutter petitioned General Richard B. Mason, the Military governor, for exclusive right to mine California gold. While Sutter prepared his documents to control mining wealth, he negotiated with a group of Mormon workers to remain in his employment after they had finished building a sawmill on the American River. They refused. Soon a mining colony, known as Mormon Bar, was producing gold from one of California's richest veins.

Shunned by the Mormons and ignored by Governor Mason, Sutter entered a partnership with Isaac Humphrey, a Georgia miner. The plan was for Humphrey to teach simple placer mining techniques to Sutter's Indian workers. This experiment failed, but it created further interest in Sutter's gold find. While no substantial wealth was discovered, there was a great public curiosity in Sutter's activity. Suddenly Sutter's behavior was monitored, and his movements became a matter of local concern.

One reason for the interest in Sutter was his eccentric behavior. When Sutter learned of the gold discovery, he swore Marshall to secrecy. Sutter then drank copious amounts of alcohol and staggered out into the streets surrounding Sutter's Fort screaming "Gold, Gold, Gold."

If Sutter could not be trusted, perhaps there were other reasons to reexamine the gold fables. The old tales of Indian wealth were not forgotten. Many people remembered the Spanish and Mexican gold legends. It was not long before gold lured miners, adventurers and the curious into the mother lode, setting the stage for a social, political and economic revolution in California. The popularity of the Gold Rush wouldn't spread throughout the nation until 1849. Since California was a remote settlement and Sutter exaggerated everything connected with his small colony, the gold find was a suspicious one.

Few people realized that California mining wealth was discovered only nine days before the signing of the Treaty of Guadalupe Hidalgo. Mexico's weak political and military position made it impossible to challenge California annexation. Generally, Mexico was not interested in retaining California because of the problems with the native-born, Spanish-speaking Californios. When Mexico learned that gold had been discovered, key government officials laughed off the tale. Since 1822 California had cost the Mexican government large sums of money and they looked upon the gold story as a last ditch attempt by Californios to maintain Mexican interest.

Most Americans didn't take the gold rush seriously. The slow dispersion of news and the lack of general interest ended when Sam Brannan became involved in gold mania. From his small general store at Sutter's Fort, Brannan watched with curiosity as gold tales monopolized conversation. Since he had arrived in California in 1846 as an Elder of the Mormon Church, Brannan had established an enviable reputation as a businessman and a respected church leader. After gold was discovered, Brannan stockpiled goods in his warehouse to supply his general stores.

A larger than life figure with a knack for self-publicity, Brannan brought a bottle of gold dust into San Francisco. On May 12, 1848, cries of "Gold! Gold! Gold!" filled the streets. Brannan's wagon was filled with large pickle jars brimming to the top with gold painted sand and a few nuggets on top to satisfy the skeptical observer. In less than a month Brannan was selling almost $5000 worth of goods a day. In time Brannan opened new mercantile stores, sold city lots, invested in a railroad, bought a shipping company and developed San Francisco waterfront lots. The entrepreneurial spirit in California was born with the Gold Rush and Sam Brannan was one of its earliest successes.

As word of Brannan's wealth spread, Brigham Young, the leader of the Mormon Church, sent a messenger to collect the $40,000 that Brannan owed the church. When the money wasn't available, Brannan was excommunicated from the Mormon faith. Undaunted Brannan continued to influence California history. He formed the Society of California Pioneers and endowed fire brigades and other civic organizations with funds. He opened a bank, began a mail service and by the early 1860s purchased most of the Napa Valley. Brannan's estate in Calistoga was an early monument to his wealth.

During the 1860s Brannan's investments turned sour, and he began to lose money. An argument with a squatter left Brannan paralyzed by a bullet fired in a heated argument. He also lost money in Hawaiian land speculation, Nevada silver mining and a Mexican economic and political venture. Brannan's wife sued for divorce, and she was awarded half of his estate. Undaunted, Brannan moved to San Diego where he sold real estate and raised figs on an Escondido rancho. When he died in 1889, Brannan had been living with his landlady, Magdalena Moraga, but he was a broken man bereft of his fortune.

While Brannan was a celebrity millionaire, most Californians only survived the Gold Rush. In June, 1848, when gold samples were distributed in Monterey, Walter Colton, the local alcalde, reported that everyone in town left for the Sierra Nevada foothills. "My messenger sent to the mines, has returned with specimens of the gold," Colton wrote, "and many were soon busy in hasty preparations for the mines." As Colton pointed out there were few miners who found any degree of wealth. This was largely because the Gold Rush was a social romp. The vast majority of miners remained impoverished. Energy, enthusiasm and legend were the byproducts of the Gold Rush.

In 1850 Walter Colton's book, **Three Years in California**, documented the unbridled enthusiasm created by the Gold Rush. In Colton's view Californians were not skilled enough to properly mine the lucrative gold veins. The Gold Rush era, Colton maintained, led many Californians to leave everything behind and flee to the Sierra Nevada. Governor Richard B. Mason complained that he had to prepare his own breakfast because the army cook had gone in search of gold. "A general of the United States Army, the commander of a man-of-war, and the Alcalde of Monterey, in a smoking kitchen grinding coffee, toasting a herring, and peeling onions," Colton wrote in awe. As Colton's book pointed out virtually everyone left Monterey and San Francisco. Mining fever hit California. It produced a drunken social atmosphere, one that created strong interest in the Golden State among Americans.

No one realized the enormity of the gold find. In 1848 fewer than 6,000 miners produced ten million dollars worth of gold. The following year 40,000 California miners extracted thirty million dollars worth of precious metals. By 1852 one hundred thousand miners turned out eighty million dollars in mining wealth. Generally, there was far more disappointment than reward, but the myth persisted that anyone could get rich. The search for the ultimate El Dorado occupied the thoughts of every miner. The fortune hunters labored over glasses of barely drinkable alcoholic beverages and talked about gold. That vein which would produce instant wealth was just around the corner for most miners. This myth kept miners in California.

It is very difficult to analyze the historical significance of the Gold Rush. Many historians believe that it was a curse, because gold brought wealth and statehood long before California was ready. There were also business problems during the Gold Rush. One of the characteristics of early gold seekers was to form joint-stock companies and partnerships. These speculative economic ventures opened up investment opportunity for businessmen and created a spirit of frontier capitalism.

In turn this capitalistic impulse manifested itself in the small towns that American settlers founded. As towns like Hell's Delight, Gouge Eye, Poker Flat, Devil's Retreat, Murderer's Bar, Poverty Hill and Gomorrah sprung up, there was a hard-drinking and fast-living atmosphere dominating California civilization. There were also permanent developments. The Gold Rush towns flourished as small business brought a sophisticated consumer mentality to these pioneer communities. When John and Daniel Murphy founded gold at Vallecito, they became wealthy by maintaining cordial relations with the Indians. John Murphy took one and a half million dollars from his diggings.

Murphy's gold find highlighted problems between the French and the Americans. Soon Mexican-American miners were in conflict over claims with the Anglos and lawless night riders plagued Vallecitos. Ethnic conflict was one of the byproducts of the California mining frontier.

In order to understand California during the Gold Rush, it is helpful to analyze a specific mining region. Professor W. Turrentine Jackson of the University of California, Davis, offers a valuable history of gold fever by concentrating upon changes in Calaveras and Tuolumne Counties. In an essay on settlement patterns around the New Melones Reservoir project, Jackson examines the complexity of Gold Rush civilization. Combining thirty years of academic research with the literary skills of a novelist, Jackson weaves tales of men who made the gold country California's most exciting frontier. His conclusions destroy the myths and stereotypes which have prevented full understanding of the Gold Rush.

As Professor Jackson suggests there has been an emphasis upon "the romantic, hectic and bizarre aspects of life in the mining districts and towns." This viewpoint ignores the concern that small town miners had for their community. It also obscures the settlers who remained as permanent residents and who were working to improve the quality of life.

When gold was discovered in August, 1848, in the Tuolumne area, there was an immediate surge of multi-ethnic settlers. Since the mining town of Sonora bore the name of the state in Mexico, there were large numbers of Spanish-speaking miners throughout the motherlode. As a result of this concentration of non-resident laborers, the Foreign Miners' Tax Law of 1850 was passed by the California legislature. This law imposed a licensing fee of $20 a month upon French, Mexican, Chilean, Peruvian and German miners. It wasn't long before the Spanish-speaking complained that the tax wasn't collected equitably. Soon ethnic conflict was prevalent throughout the Sierra Nevada. The strained relations between ethnic groups challenges the popular notion that egalitarianism prevailed in the mines.

By 1850 there were 15,000 Mexicans in the southern mining regions of Calaveras, Mariposa and Tuolumne counties. This concentration of Spanish-speaking miners prompted State Senator Thomas Jefferson Green of Sacramento to urge passage of the Foreign Miners' Tax Law of 1850. Senator Green defended the law as a means of raising much needed state revenue. As a result of the tax law, ten thousand foreign miners left the region.

The uneven manner of collecting the Foreign Miners' Tax Law of 1850 has drawn a great deal of criticism from historians. Professor Richard H. Peterson of San Diego State University poses the question of whether or not the law was exploitive, and he examines the manner in which the tax forced Latin-American miners out of California. Although Senator Thomas Jefferson Green defended the law as a necessary tax measure, the evidence indicates that it led to expulsion of the Spanish-speaking miners.

The Foreign Miners' Tax Law of 1850 inaugurated a double standard in all aspects of California life. Soon the schools were segregated, job opportunities for ethnic minorities decreased and the courts dispensed a tough brand of justice. This led to the formation of ethnic political groups to end this type of harassment by the Courts, the school system and the employer.

In Sonora more than 5,000 miners demonstrated in 1850 against the law. American merchants protested that they were losing good customers due to politics. In the summer of 1851 mob violence between American and French miners near Mokelumne was averted by lengthy discussions. In 1852 tensions eased when Chinese miners became the target of the Foreign Miners' Tax Law of 1850. The taciturn Chinese were singled out because they were an ethnic group with different ways and a new culture. Since the Chinese mined marginal claims on the outskirts of mining towns, there was little disruption to the local community. The tax, which was now only $3 to $5 a month, was collected easily, and the majority of Chinese miners quickly moved to the San Joaquin Valley. The tax on foreign miners was the perfect justification for the prejudice of American miners.

The impact of the Gold Rush upon California society was the key factor in shaping the Golden State's future. Not only were the entrepreneurs attracted to the Sierra Nevada, but the permanent settlers, the foreign adventurers and the politicians who hoped to profit from statehood. The rise of a multi-lingual, multi-ethnic civilization led to increased tensions over land and mining claims. Because of the rich, cosmopolitan Hispanic heritage, many Americans found it difficult to accept the original Spanish and Mexican settlers. The clash of lifestyles and customs eventually produced the modern Californian. During the Gold Rush these differences created a volatile civilization. As Professor Peterson suggests the Foreign Miners' Tax Law of 1850 drove "Mexicans and other Latin-American miners from the diggings by the thousands. . . ."

Gold Mining in California

Historical Survey of the New Melones Reservoir Project Area: The Gold Rush Years

by W. Turrentine Jackson

The revolutionary changes brought to California by the discovery of gold at Coloma in January, 1848, is the subject of the following essay. Professor W. Turrentine Jackson of the University of California, Davis, provides an in-depth view of Calaveras and Tuolumne counties. This interpretive look at the men who made mining country such a vibrant part of the early American period is important in analyzing the problems of post-statehood California. Jackson's study also destroys many of the pioneer myths about the contributions of gold country. He sees gold as the catalyst to permanent settlement and workable political and economic institutions.

Immediately following the discovery of gold at Coloma in January, 1848, one of the largest folk migrations in history occurred. Within two years the placed called "California" was known throughout the civilized world. By the end of 1848 the population had only increased to 20,000 from the 14,000 Euro-Americans in the area at the time of discovery. By the time the "Rush of '49" came to a close the population had swelled to almost 100,000. The Argonauts had come by land and by sea with Americans forming from one-half to two-thirds of the total. Fanning throughout the future state, prospectors concentrated their efforts in three distinct sections: the "northwestern" section along the Trinity, Klamath, and Scott rivers and their tributaries; the "northern" or "central" section including Amador County, El Dorado County where gold was discovered, and all the mining counties to the north—Placer, Nevada,

Yuba, Sierra, Butte, and Plumas; and finally the "southern" mines extending all the way to Mariposa County. The mines of Calaveras and Tuolumne counties were, without doubt, the most important of these southern mines. As Rodman Paul has stated, "The heart of this last section was the mining region in Calaveras, Tuolumne, Mariposa, and upper Stanislaus counties." Several important mining discoveries were made along the banks of the Stanislaus River and within the area included in the New Melones Reservoir Project Area.

The physical feature that served as a landmark to guide miners to the region was a long mountain ridge formed by an ancient lava flow, forty miles long and over a half mile in width, so flat and level that it became known as Table Mountain. This elevation can easily be traced as it intersects the Mother Lode running from the vicinity of Angels Camp, across the

W. Turrentine Jackson, HISTORICAL SURVEY OF THE NEW MELONES RESERVOIR PROJECT AREA, (Sacramento, 1976), pp. 21–30. Reprinted courtesy of the author and the U.S. Army Corps of Engineers, Sacramento District.

Stanislaus River towards Jamestown. In the ravines and nearby streams many gold seekers sought precious metal.

The discovery of gold at Coloma was followed immediately by similar discoveries in the vicinity of *Mokelumne Hill*, in the northern part of Calaveras County. Captain Charles M. Weber had visited the Mokelumne River as early as April or May, 1848, and with a company of eight men worked the stream for two months, each man taking several thousand dollars in gold. Colonel Jonathan D. Stevenson came to the river with approximately a hundred men from his Mexican War "regiment" that had just been mustered out of service. One of the first mining codes was drawn up here. Soon numerous discoveries were made along the Mokelumne River. However, in 1848 Mokelumne Hill was not an important mining town but within a year it gained importance as a central trading center. Rich discoveries were soon found in volcanic mounds on a ridge above the stream at "French Hill," "Nigger Hill," and "Stockton Hill." The diggings were so rich that only sixteen feet square was allowed to each miner. Mokelumne Hill was noted as one of the toughest communities in Calaveras County. Water was in short supply and the town burned on three occasions only to be built again. *Chili Gulch*, two miles to the south, was a center for Chilean miners in 1848–1849 and was a scene of continuous violence.

James H. Carson, of Stevenson's regiment, learned of the gold discoveries in Monterey and headed for the mining region with a group of fellow soldiers. In August, 1848, in association with George Angel, he traveled south from Mokelumne Hill until Angel stopped at the junction of two streams, later known as Dry Creek and Angels Creek, to establish a trading camp and to prospect. By the spring of 1849, the population of *Angels Camp* had reached three hundred and was known as a trading center. When Friedrich Gerstacker, a German from Leipsig, visited Angels Camp in April, 1850, he thought the entire surface of the camp and all the soils along the creek had been worked by the miners. J. D. Borthwick visited the town in 1851 and discovered, "A village composed of well-built houses of wood, and altogether a more respectable place than San Andreas." When the placer operations played out in 1853 the town had a population of forty-five hundred. Rich gold-bearing quartz was discovered shortly thereafter, the population increased, and the permanency of the community was assured.

Carson had continued further south to the present *Carson Hill* region and he and his party dug in the gravels of Carson Creek where, according to his memoirs, they "took out, in ten days, an average of 180 ounces each." He recorded in addition:

We lived on beef and beans—beef dried, fried, roasted, boiled and broiled, morning, noon and night: as much as every man wanted, without money or price; with a change, at times, to elk, venison, and bear steak.

Apparently the success was short-lived, for Carson traveled on south to diggings along the Tuolumne River. In the early spring of 1849, he returned to Carson Hill and to Angels Camp. He noted,

When we reached the top of the mountains overlooking Carson's and Angel's Creek,

*we had to stand and gaze on the scene
before us—the hill-sides were dotted with
tents, and the Creeks filled with human
beings to such a degree that it seemed as if
a day's work of the mass would not leave
a stone unturned in them.*

Carson also penned an account of life in
the mines when he wrote:

*The morals of the miners of '48 should
here be noticed. No person worked on
Sunday at digging for gold—but that day
was spent in prospecting the neighborhood,
by the more sedate portion of the miners;
while others spent it in playing at poker,
with lumps of gold for checks; others,
collected in groups, might be seen under
the shades of neighboring trees, singing
songs, playing at 'old sledge' and drinking
whiskey—in all of which proceedings,
harmony, fun and good will to each other
were prominent features. We had ministers
of the gospel amongst us, but they never
preached. Religion had been forgotten,
even by the ministers. . . .*

Although Jim Carson was inflicted with
wanderlust, he left his name behind at
Carson Hill along the Stanislaus, the
center of what has been considered the
richest camp in the Mother Lode.

At a nearby point on the river, later
known as *Melones*, John W. Robinson and
Stephen Mead, who had also been with
the Carson party, established a trading
post and ferry in the summer of 1849.
Harvey Wood came to Melones in August,
1849, and mined successfully at what was
known as the "Stanislaus" mine, and
eventually purchased the interests of
Robinson and Mead.

Among the mining camps to the north
and east of the Mokelumne Hill-Melones

route were *Murphys* and *Vallecito*. The
Murphy brothers, John and Daniel, also
associates of Angel, found gold at Vallecito, once known as "Murphy's New Diggings." John Murphy maintained exceptionally good relations with the Indians
whom he prevailed upon to mine for him
in exchange for blankets, food, and other
provisions. He reportedly took out a fortune in gold during the 1848 season,
amounting to one and a half million dollars. Murphys, as a town, was not initially as prosperous as Angels Camp. Only
fifty miners were there in August, 1849.
Soon the ground was found to be so rich
that the size of claims was limited. In
April, 1850, Gerstacker arrived in Murphys and reported:

*To prevent abuse, the American diggers
called a meeting in which it was resolved
that no one should have a larger
placer—and only one—sixteen feet long
and eight feet broad, with a space of two
and a half feet around it for throwing dirt.
Such a claim might be registered for a fee
of two dollars with the Alcalde.*

The German also wrote a description of
Murphys in these months:

*There was a large woody plan in the midst
of which a small town arose. A broad
street of large store tents extended along
the middle of the flat. Not only the
necessary provisions and unnecessary
drinks might be had in these shops, but
also real articles of luxury. The main
street was thus solely occupied by the
different stores and shops. A mass of small
blockhouses and tents lay behind them,
scattered as far as the next range of hills.*
*Although consisting only of tents, it
had, during the summer of 1849, been
raised to the rank of a real town, where an*

*alcalde, a sheriff, and a constable were
duly elected. The whole town comprised
about fifty tents, two or three blockhouses,
and a house built of planks; yet, it already
boasted nearly as many "bars" as tents,
besides three American and four French
dining rooms, two doctors' shops, at least
twenty gambling tables.*

Murphys was the scene of constant national conflict between the French and Americans. There was a never-ending search for adequate water, and successful ditch companies were organized to provide the necessary supply. Even so, the town suffered a disastrous fire in 1859. Murphys greatest glory as a mining center came in the late fifties and sixties when more elaborate placer operations and hydraulic mining produced rich returns. Quartz mining developed there much later than at Angels Camp and was never as important.

At nearby Vallecito numerous Mexican-American miners worked. The town gained a reputation for being a place of rendezvous for lawless night riders. The diggings here were deep and could not be worked effectively in winter because of the high water table that accumulated in the mines.

To the south and west from the Mokelumne Hill-Melones trace were the camps at *Copperopolis, Milton*, and *Jenny Lind*. *San Andreas*, near the geographic center of the county today, was first settled by Mexicans and it was not until the spring of 1850 that a few Americans arrived. There was a continuing increase in the number of Mexican miners, and by the fall of 1850 there were fifteen hundred residents in camp. Not until the spring of 1851, comparatively late, did Americans in large numbers arrive, though soon

they were in the majority. Like other nearby towns, San Andreas gained notoriety for crime and violence. In addition, the lack of water proved a major obstacle to placer operations until water companies were organized to deliver the essential supply to the rich gravel deposits. Numerous sizable nuggets were found here. The mines around San Andreas were in full operation in 1853. The following season the old channel of a prehistoric stream was found directly under the town, one hundred to one hundred and fifty feet deep, and production increased in spite of the declining placer operations.

On the road from Carson Hill through Angels Camp and on to San Andreas were a number of lesser camps including Altaville, Dogtown, Upper and Lower Calaveritas and Fourth Crossing.

The first discovery of gold in Tuolumne County was made in August, 1848, at *Wood's Crossing* on Wood's Creek, tributary of the Stanislaus, a site named for the Reverend James Wood. According to Carson's reminiscences, "the few who were there then were realizing two and three hundred dollars per day, with pick and knife alone." Wood's Crossing was about a mile southwest of *Jamestown*. A lawyer from San Francisco is credited with having discovered gold on the latter site, also in August, 1848. In the spring of 1849, Carson returned to the vicinity of Wood's Creek and reported:

*On the long flat we found a vast canvas
city, under the name of Jamestown, which,
similar to a bed of mushrooms, had
sprung up in a night. A hundred flags
were flying from restaurants, taverns, rum
mills, and gambling houses. The gambling
tables had their crowds continually, and
the whole presented a scene similar to that*

of San Francisco. . . . I have there seen Spaniards betting an arroba *of gold at a time, and win and lose it as cooly as if it had been a bag of clay. Gold dust had risen in value from what it was in 1848—as high as ten dollars per ounce was given for gold dust at the monte banks. Wood's Creek was filled up with miners, and I here for the first time after the discovery of gold, learned what a miner's claim was.*

One Judge A. H. Tuttle built a log cabin at the site of Tuttletown this same summer. Previously only tents and Mexican *Ramadas*, or brush houses, had existed at this stopping place for packers and prospectors travelling the route from Angels Camp to Sonora.

Sonora was established by a party of Mexicans, presumably from the state of Sonora, Mexico. Not until the spring of 1849 did the first American settlers arrive. In July an estimated one thousand five hundred foreigners, largely Mexicans and Chileans, poured into the camps of Tuolumne County, and by the fall Sonora had a population of five thousand. *Columbia*, "The Gem of the Southern Mines" has long been considered one of the most typical, most populous, and most significant of the towns on the Mother Lode. The discovery was comparatively late. Dr. Thaddeus Hildreth and his brother George were leaders of a party that made an overnight camp on the site in March, 1850. According to one account, a heavy rain during the night washed away surface dirt revealing to John Walker, a member of the party, gold particles in the nearby gulches. Temporarily known as Hildreth's Diggings, the name was changed to Columbia by the hordes of miners, disappointed in neigh-

boring districts, who rushed to the new find. The center of activity was on Kennebec Hill where six thousand men labored.

Towards the southwest from these major mining communities were many lesser, but once exciting mining camps, including *Jackass Hill*, just west of Tuttletown, that gained notoriety in 1851 and 1852. *Springfield*, southwest of Columbia, was largely dominated by a woman, Donna Josefa Valmaseda, who had been forced to flee her native town of Guaymas because she gave aid to the crews of the United States warships attacking the town during the Mexican War. She employed many of her fellow-countrymen in working the mines near Springfield. *Chinese Camp*, ten miles southwest of Sonora, was so named because of the early concentration of Chinese miners in the area. *Jacksonville*, on the Tuolumne River, established in the summer of 1849, was second only to Sonora in size in 1851.

When the historian attempts to ascertain the distinguishing characteristics of these well-known communities in the southern mines, in Calaveras and Tuolumne counties, both in and near the New Melones Reservoir Project Site, in comparison with the rest of California's mining counties, he immediately notes the exceptional heterogeneous nature of the population. French, Mexicans, Chileans, and Chinese, for example, were found in far greater numbers here. This "foreign" influence was felt both in mining methods, such as the Spanish use of the arrastra or the Chili mill and pans with rounded sides for panning, and the methods of "scratching" in the shallow, surface diggings by the Chinese. There was also an institutional impact, for example, recognition of the position of the alcalde, a unique Spanish institution combining executive, administrative, legislative, and judicial functions, in places like Sonora. Only in time was the alcalde's position replaced by the Justice of the Peace, an officer in the Anglo-American tradition. A negative aspect of this cultural mix was an expression of prejudice. The California legislature passed a Foreign Miner's Tax in 1850 imposing a tax of twenty dollars a month on all foreigners as long as they remained in the mines. Not until 1853 was it reduced to a more reasonable rate of $4. a month. Nowhere was the legislation as vigorously enforced as in Calaveras and Tuolumne counties. Naturally conflict followed from the discrimination expressed in such special taxes. The so-called "French War" broke out at Mokelumne Hill; a few miles to the south at Chili Gulch the Chileans and Americans came to blows: the Mexican community in Sonora was periodically under attack by Anglo-Americans; in Columbia a law was passed providing that Asians could not work the mines for themselves or anybody else and any person selling a claim to an Asian would forfeit his own right to mine in the district for the next six months. Outbreaks of violence always followed the same pattern; minorities would protest and temporarily drive out the Anglo-Americans only to be overcome by the majority who seized control and established additional discriminatory regulations. A Vigilance Committee, so typical of many mining areas, was established in Tuolumne County in June, 1851. As an outgrowth of these developments, organized groups of desperadoes also appeared in the region. Frustrated minority residents were often leaders of those who worked outside the law they considered unjust. Joaquin Murieta is the most notorious example of this type of leader in the Southern Mines.

Historians of the California Gold Rush have emphasized the romantic, hectic and bizarre aspects of life in the mining districts and towns. The narrative has usually included an account of the chance discovery of hidden wealth, the frantic rush to the new bonanza, the inadequacy of communication and transportation, the privation of individuals working in a difficult terrain with inadequate housing in inclement weather, the lack of supplies, the eternal restlessness of the prospectors, the violence which led to vigilance committees and law and order movements, and the vast array of amusements for the predominently male society.

More recently historians have emphasized the transitory nature of these characteristics of the mining kingdom, suggesting that they lasted but a season or two, at the most three. Quickly the population became stabilized in towns that were governmental, transportation, mining, or milling centers. The residents became town dwellers with typical concerns about improving the streets, with maintaining stage, express, mail and freight services, with earning a living as laborers, shopkeepers, or such professional people as teachers, lawyers, and doctors. They were concerned with raising funds, through taxes, for public improvements in the water system, for fire protection, for maintaining the police service, or for construction of a school or hospital. All mining towns had problems relative to community sanitation and health. The local newspaper editor became a key individual in maintaining community pride and optimism. Thus, the life style of individuals in the mining population centers was more like those on the "town frontier" or even the "urban frontier" than those on the "agricultural" or "ranching frontier." Moreover, the problems, anxieties and ambitions of the individual were not greatly different from residents in these same communities in the twentieth century.

Scholars have also suggested that the more significant mining story is to be found in understanding the technology whereby miners actually dug the gold, the science and technology of reclaiming the precious metal, the roles of labor and investment capital. Only with a thorough understanding of such topics can we explain why some discovery sites ended up as ghost towns and others continued as viable communities.

The Foreign Miners' Tax of 1850 and Mexicans in California: Exploitation or Expulsion?

by Richard H. Peterson

The question of discrimination in the California mines is one that historians have debated for many years. In the following article Professor Richard H. Peterson of San Diego State University examines the debate over the implementation of the Foreign Miners' Tax Law of 1850. This controversial tax was randomly collected causing many Californios to cry out against the double-standard of law enforcement. More traditional scholars have suggested the socio-economic decline of Mexican-Americans was directly related to this tax.

The troubled history of the Mexicans on the California mining frontier has been subjected to close scrutiny. They suffered more discrimination and violence from American miners than did other foreigners in the early diggings. A letter from a Mexican War veteran to the *Stockton Times* for April 6, 1850 helps explain the conflict:

> *I was in the Mexican War—I was—and I can tell you was some pumpkins at Chapultepec and Monterey—I know what Mexicans are—I do. They are no men; an army of Mexicans is of no more account than an army of Quiotas (coyotes) and didn't I smash 'em. Mexicans have no business in this country. I don't believe in them. The men were made to be shot at, and the women were made for our purposes.*
> *I'm a white man—I am! A Mexican is pretty near black. I hate all Mexicans.*

In addition to racial and cultural prejudice, economic competition and social disorder in Gold Rush California influenced American Behavior.

Whatever the causes of Mexican-American conflict, enactment of the Foreign Miners' Tax gave the confrontation a new dimension.

> *. . . in the history of . . . (American) contact with the Latin races in the mines, . . . the Foreign Miners' Tax looms up as the one overwhelmingly important event. This did more, probably, than any other thing, to set the foreign population against the American miner. Neither group really ever got over the effect of this law.*

Another student of the tax has called it "one of the most original if benighted laws ever passed in a California legislature." In view of the special significance of the tax, an investigation of its causes seems appropriate. In particular, was it designed to exploit or to expel the Mexican miners? Considerable disagreement can be found on this question.

Richard H. Peterson, "The Foreign Miners' Tax of 1850 And Mexicans In California: Exploitation or Explusion?", *The Pacific Historian*, Vol. 20, No. 3, (Fall, 1976), pp. 265–270. Reprinted with permission of the author.

The California State Constitution guaranteed full property rights to foreigners who were or would become "bona fide" residents. However, U.S. Congressional inaction on California mining tenure and the mounting pressure of anti-foreign and especially anti-Mexican sentiment led to discussion of a foreign miners' tax during the State Legislative session, 1849–1850. Out of the discussion, on April 13, 1850, was born "An Act for the better regulation of the Mines, and the Government of Foreign Miners," imposing a tax of $20 per month in the form of a license upon all non-citizens of the United States working in the California mines. The act, furthermore, authorized license collectors to retain $3 from each $20 payment as compensation for their services and sanctioned the forcible removal of aliens from their mining sites for failure to comply with the tax collectors.

In an important article Leonard Pitt contends that the Foreign Miners' Tax "was not an exclusionist measure as has been assumed, but a system of taxation an indenture. Its object was to exploit alien caste laborers rather than expel them and to aid American mining capitalists by blocking foreign capitalists." State Senator Thomas Jefferson Green, the author of the tax bill and the chairman of the Senate Finance Committee, was, "convinced that foreign servile labor could play the role he had earlier intended for the Negro," and that the tax would allow California to have access to a steady supply of dependent foreign workers. Professor Pitt's "exploitation interpretation" is documented by reference to Green's statement in the Senate Finance Committee report on the objectives of the tax:

Upon the arrival in our waters of shiploads of foreign operatives . . . (an American) can employ their services at a fair rate, and advance money for their license(s), which he holds until the labor is performed according to contract. Under this law the operative so employed will not flee from the performance of his contract, because the privilege of gold digging is in the hands of his employer. The newcomer who arrives penniless upon our shores, at the end of his first contract, can either seek a new employer, or having made money enough to control a license, go to work on his own accord.

Mentioned in only a short paragraph of a four page report, this statement probably was not intended for special emphasis. More important, in early 1850, there were relatively few large-scale, capitalistic mining operations which required the employment of foreign contract labor. River mining produced company organization on the Tuolumne with the hiring of some Mexican workers. However, according to a most knowledgeable student, "the real beginning of lode (quartz) mining in California is to be found not in 1849 and 1850, but rather in the half-dozen years that commenced in 1850–1852 and extended throughout the ensuing period of depression and doubt." Hydraulic mining, another extensive employer of labor, awaited the mid and late 'fifties for technical efficiency and widespread use. In 1850, California's mining economy, for the most part, did not require a foreign miners' tax as a means of making possible the exploitation of alien caste labor by American mining capitalists. Individualistic placer mining still prevailed.

There is convincing evidence that the

Foreign Miners' Tax was designed more to exclude than to exploit such foreigners as the Mexicans. By 1850, the latter had comprised the bulk of the foreign population in the southern mining region. Within California's entire mining population, the Mexicans, as a group, were the most experienced and probably the most successful of the early miners. As a result, they soon became an unique object of American jealousy and resentment. William Kelly, an astute English visitor to the mines, observed:

> . . . *Americans . . . resorted . . . in the first instance, to the Chileans and Mexicans for (mining) instruction and information, which they gave them with cheerful alacrity; but as soon as Jonathan got an inkling of the system, with peculiar bad taste and ungenerous feeling, he organized a crusade against those obliging strangers. . . .*

Printed and distributed in only Spanish and English and rigidly enforced primarily against the Mexicans and Chileans, the tax was an outgrowth of this crusade. As San Francisco's *Alta California* declared on April 22, 1850, ". . . riot and bloodshed instead of being prevented, will ensure from any attempt to enforce it. In many instances it will be merely legalizing the most desperate attacks upon portions of the foreign population. . . ."

The severity of the tax amounted to expulsion from the mines. The exorbitant cost of food, clothing, and mining equipment in California's inflationary economy diminished the earnings of the average prospector, who managed about $80 per month before expenses. In addition, the declining productivity of the placers, river mining inactivity during the rainy season, and long periods of preliminary labor building a flume or a long-tom or diverting a stream from its channel, made it almost impossible to pay the $20 assessment. Regarding the Mexicans, the *Alta California* on July 10, 1850 remarked that "a moderate tax they could afford . . .' but the tax as it stands at present amounts to exclusion. . . ." Speaking of the unlucky or less skillful miner, Etienne Derbec, a French journalist in the diggings, observed that "everyone knows it is impossible to pay such a tax; there are some poor devils who do not earn $20.00 in an entire month."

The willingness of the Mexicans and other Spanish-Americans to pay a more moderate fee suggests the expulsionist objective of the tax. Their feelings are aptly expressed in the following petition to Peter H. Burnett, Governor of California, from foreign representatives of Sonora, which was largely Mexican:

> *Without assuming any tone other than that of the deepest respect for the government under which we live and are protected, we beg humbly to suggest to your excellency that a larger state income could be raised, and that too, without causing the slightest dissatisfaction, by the imposition of four or five dollars per month, instead of the large sum of twenty.*

The exclusionist motive of the tax further is implied by the doubtfulness of the alleged state income objective. Green's Finance Committee ostensibly proposed the tax, in part, as a means of financing the State Treasury:

Your committee believe that, as a matter of finance, while that is secondary in character, it will prove to be the best, and surest, and readiest means of collecting a large amount of public revenue . . . $200,000 per month may be safely calculated upon.

However, the prospective income was inconsistent with the tenets of laissez-faire capitalism prevalent at this time. In the words of William Perkins, a perceptive Canadian visitor to the mines, the severity of the tax "seemed to display a desire either to drive the foreign population entirely out of the country, or to amass an amount of money that could hardly be expended in the legitimate business of government. . . . It is not to be wondered if Uncle Sam should deem this a little too large a bite for our State to indulge in." State government expenditures for the fiscal year ending June 30, 1850—$585,702.83—tend to substantiate Perkins' argument against the magnitude of the projected tax revenue.

If the tax was designed to provide income for the state, why were non-Hispanic aliens, who comprised a substantial segment of the foreign population, largely exempt from payment. Moreover, the State legislators must have realized that the exorbitant rate would be evaded by every possible means, thereby undermining the alleged revenue objective. Further, the economy of California and the nation would have been stimulated to a greater degree by the elimination of the Mexicans' export of gold than by the tax, which, in its first year of operation, enriched the State Treasury by only $33,147.47. Ironically, Green's committee recognized the economic stimulus of gold circulation, thereby suggesting that the tax had an expulsionist purpose:

It is a matter of great national policy, that the vast amount of California gold, or at least a large proportion of it, should first find its way through our own country, and its influence upon the wants of commerce be there felt, before it seeks a market in other nations.

The vehemently anti-foreign tone of Green's report gives additional evidence of the tax's exclusionist intention:

Among others, the convicts of Mexico, Chili, and Botany Bay, are daily turned upon our shores, who seek and possess themselves of the best places for gold digging . . . and carry from our country immense treasure.
The low state of morality which such a population spreads broadcast in the land is to be deeply lamented.
Practiced vice and crime, hardened with the degradation of former punishment, makes these people irredeemably lost to all social equality or national advantage.

Even those who see the tax as a device for exploiting foreign labor recognize Green's almost fanatical hostility toward Mexicans. He had spent some time in a Mexican prison. After escaping he published a "tirade against all things Mexican." He had boasted personally that he could "maintain a better stomach at the killing of a Mexican than at the crushing of a body louse." It is difficult to imagine how he could have put his very personal anti-Mexican hostility aside when writing the tax bill.

Green's remarks constitute only one source of evidence that the Foreign Miners' Tax was designed to expel the Mexicans. In March, 1850, Thomas Butler King, who had been sent to California by President Zachary Taylor to stimulate interest in the constitutional convention, submitted to the U.S. Secretary of State a novel revenue measure for the mines. He proposed the exaction of $16 as the price of a permit or license to dig gold in California for one year. However, in his own words, "I have proposed to exclude foreigners from the privilege of purchasing permits, and from working as discoverers of purchasers in the vein-mines . . . these mines belong to, and . . . should be preserved for, the use and benefit of the American people. . . . During the mining season of 1849, more than fifteen thousand foreigners, mostly Mexican and Chilenos, . . . carr(ied) out of the country . . . gold dust, which belonged by purchase to the people of the United States. If not excluded by law, they will return and recommence the work of plunder." Even Green believed that the outright exclusion of aliens would not be permitted by the U.S. Constitution. Yet, it is plausible that King's report, in part, determined the real objective of the Foreign Miners' Tax, which was enacted a month later. According to Dale L. Morgan and James R. Scobie in their reliable introduction to the *Perkins' Journal*, "the kind of thinking in which King indulged was also being done in the California legislature."

The effect of the tax was to drive Mexican and other Latin-American miners from the diggings by the thousands, especially in response to pressure from armed American miners. However, to argue to this basis that the tax had expulsionist motives is to confuse consequences with causes. Regardless of the results, there seems to be sufficient evidence that the tax was intended at the outset to remove the Mexicans. Despite the alleged "democracy" of the frontier and the mining camp, not all residents were accorded equal opportunity or equal treatment.

WORKSHEET 4: The California Gold Rush:
Economic Blessing or Disaster?

1. What was Sutter's initial reaction to gold discovery? _____

   _____

2. After Sutter realized the magnitude of the gold in Coloma, he _____

   _____

3. Mormon Bar was important because _____

   _____

4. Isaac Humphrey _____

5. How did old tales of Indian wealth influence Gold Rush California? _____

   _____

6. What was the general attitude of Americans toward gold discovery in 1848? _____

   _____

7. What role did entrepreneurs like Sam Brannan play in publicizing and profiting

   from the Gold Rush? _____

   _____

   _____

8. What is important about the Murphy Brothers and their mining camp? _____

   _____

   _____

   _____

9. What was Sam Brannan's business and personal life like after the Gold Rush?

_____

_____

_____

10. Professor W. Turrentine Jackson writes of the Foreign Miners' Tax Law of 1850:
"Nowhere was the legislation as vigorously enforced as in Calaveras and

Tuolumne counties." Why was this the case? _____

_____

_____

11. Why does Professor Richard Peterson argue that the Foreign Miners Tax Law of

1850 led to expulsion? _____

_____

12. Why was John Sutter's role controversial in the discovery of gold? _____

_____

_____

13. How did Thomas Butler King reflect nativist attitudes? _____

_____

A Tale of Two California Political Rivals: David Broderick and William Gwin in the 1850s

READINGS: Howard A. DeWitt, "William Gwin and the Politics of Prejudice"

On June 4, 1849 the steamship the Panama sailed into California. The Panama was a harbinger of change. It brought some of the most important American settlers into the former Mexican province. These new residents became important politicians, key business people and individuals who shaped the direction of American California. They also brought with them two rival political notions. One was a strong support for slavery and the other was an antipathy to the peculiar institution. However, to the casual observer, the Panama appeared more like a vacation boat than an instrument of change.

After a brief stop in San Diego where passengers looked at the remains of the hide and tallow trade and took a tour of the local mission, the Panama sailed to Monterey where the passengers feasted on fine food and drank assorted wines. When the Panama finally sailed into San Francisco Bay the passengers were enthralled by Angel Island. Yet, the first impression of San Francisco was not a pleasant one. The city was little more than seven windblown sandhills with almost no vegetation. The Spanish presidio which guarded the entrance to the bay was in decay and the docks were rickety and in need of repair. One Panama passenger remarked: "Where is the beauty of San Francisco that we have read about?"

Who had described the beauty of San Francisco with such a fictional bent? The answer was a simple one. John C. Fremont's wife Jessie Benton Fremont had helped her husband craft a fictional account of California that became a national best seller. The problem was that Fremont's writings were sold as serious history. The reality was that Fremont's books were more like romance novels than works of serious history. They did excite Americans about California settlement, and the Panama was filled with people who had read Fremont's popular works.

When the Panama sailed into San Francisco the passengers got their first look at the city that had more tents than permanent homes. The large number of abandoned ships in the San Francisco harbor made it look more like a junk yard than a naval repository. Then the Panama passengers found out the ultimate truth about San Francisco. It was dirty, dangerous and unpredictable. When they hired local dock men to unload their luggage, it cost more than the freight charges from New York to San Francisco. The price revolution created by the Gold Rush made San Francisco the costliest city in the world. The criminals added other costs to the journey.

The law and order problem had a dramatic impact upon the Golden State. People jostled one another, cursed and shoved one other on their way to the hotels. Once they entered the less than luxurious lobbies of the local hotels, the Panama passengers found overpriced rooms and unsatisfactory accommodations. There were only one or two women per hundred men but the city was full of "soiled doves," as the prostitutes were known, and there were more bars per person than in any city in the world. San Francisco was a rough and tough frontier settlement with a reputation for heavy drinking, violence and avoiding the rules of civilized society. It was into this atmosphere that the two Democratic party rivals, David Broderick and William Gwin, brought their political ideas.

Corruption was an accepted part of the political process. The secret or Australian ballot would not be written into law until 1891. This allowed politicians to manipulate election results and disregard the people's wishes. When William McKendree Gwin explored California for the first time, he was struck by the human frivolity of the gold rush. No one seemed responsible. Gwin's previous careers in Mississippi politics and in the corridors of the Washington Capitol prompted him to conclude that Californians needed his political wisdom. There was an arrogance to Gwin and a feeling of superiority that reflected the pro-slavery or Chivalry Democratic mentality.

At the core of Gwin's politics there was a maniacal zeal for power and control. Gwin believed that California had an unnatural mixture of the races. He looked in astonishment at what he called "hordes of pig-tailed smelly Chinese." With these attitudes Gwin gave birth to the politics of prejudice. The basic tenets of Gwin's politics would end Democratic politic power by 1859 but his ideas would continue to dominate California politics.

After helping to write the California Constitution of 1849, Gwin served two terms in the United States Senate and led the Chivalry or pro slavery wing of the Democratic party in its fight to bring right wing political ideas into the mainstream of California society. Like many political fanatics, Gwin took a dim view of past California history. He gave little credence to Spanish and Mexican contributions to the Golden State. In fact, he literally ignored the Hispanic tradition.

But Gwin was an equal opportunity bigot. He complained about the Chinese and other foreigners. He was also hostile to Irish Catholics and frequently gave demagogic speeches complaining of their flawed vision. The depth of Gwin's arrogance was demonstrated in political debates when he refused to even listen to another viewpoint. A good example of this took place when Gwin toured gold mining camps urging a vote for statehood. Anyone with a non-statehood viewpoint was ignored and Gwin labeled anti-statehood foes as "ill informed."

As he entered California politics, Gwin was a different breed of Democrat. He was a loyal member of the party but he deeply distrusted the common person. As a result, he was nervous about the mob or the working poor. His early California speeches were demagogic ones designed to excite political passion. He saw conspiracies around him to replace the genteel slave owning aristocracy with a working class democracy.

Gwin's feelings were reinforced by the Hounds. Wearing silly uniforms in an attempt to parody a military order, the Hounds were a private police force who patrolled San Francisco. They were little more than local thugs who extorted money from San Francisco businesses. The Hounds strutted the streets using their power to eat and drink for free at any restaurant. Gwin became one of their strongest critics. Then an incident took place which helped Gwin's rise to power.

One of the Hounds leaders, Samuel Roberts, was a boatman who robbed ships as he unloaded them. He also earned a reputation for abusing women. When he ran off with a young Chilean prostitute, Felice Alvarez, there was a public outcry. To the casual observer it looked as though Roberts kidnaped the young prostitute. She also continued to ply her trade. Then disaster struck.

On July 15, 1849 Felice Alvarez was entertaining two German tourists in her hotel room when Sam Roberts burst in. He took the German, Leopold Bleckschmidt, into the street and attempted to whip the frightened, naked man. When the whip failed to kill the German, Roberts began beating him over the head with the whip's metal handle. As a horrified crowd looked on, the German slumped to the ground. Everyone presumed that he was dead. Someone from the crowd shouted: "This is not manly." Roberts glared at the crowd. Then he shouted: "I will kill the next man who sleeps with Felice Alvarez." At that point Roberts rode off to drink with his fellow Hounds.

Gwin used this incident to suggest that the Hounds were on a rampage and law and order had to be brought to San Francisco. Locals listened and soon

Gwin had a strong base of support in San Francisco. He was the law and order candidate. Gwin frequently commented that he would save the city from the Irish Catholic riff raff. In lapses of monumental bad taste, Gwin skewered women he described as Chilean whores, then talked of dissipated Europeans, the lack of morality in the anti slavery forces and condemned those who would support the rights of immigrants. Gwin also argued that the wrong type of Americans would produce a demented civilization. Not surprisingly, these people were Irish Catholic followers of David Broderick. With these attitudes, Gwin introduced the rights wing political mentality that became a major part of California politics. He was the primary focus of the politics of prejudice.

Gwin's political rival, David Broderick, entered San Francisco Bay on June 13, 1849, when he arrived on the steamship Stella. The son of an Irish stonemason, a gifted craftsman, a seasoned New York politician in the Tammany Hall machine and a skilled businessman, Broderick represented the anti slavery, liberal Democratic political faction.

During his youth, Broderick worked in the New York slums with a volunteer fire company. He noticed how easy it was to manipulate votes by using the fire company as a vote getting source. People would turn out and give the fire companies funds to protect their homes. Candidates for public office would promise to establish a city fire department. The lesson that Broderick learned was that good city services could get you elected to public office. The appointment of Irish Catholics to city jobs was another way to get votes. Broderick used these devices to dominate San Francisco politics.

He was a politician who was not only civil rights oriented but responsible for government aid to the less fortunate. The wards or neighborhoods allowed the Tammany Hall machine to dominate San Francisco politics. This was a brand of New York Tammany Hall politics that Broderick brought into the Golden State. Unlike Gwin, who concentrated his power in the United States Senate, Broderick selected the California Senate as his power base.

Like many of his contemporaries, Broderick purchased a saloon and named it, The Subterranean. This was an allusion to its underground location and Broderick's desire to serve the working class. As The Subterranean owner he got to know the roughest San Francisco workers. He urged the locals to support his workingmen's politics. They did and he was elected to the California Senate. Soon he became the acknowledged leader in the state legislature. Eventually, Broderick became a U.S. States Senator and his political influence was a catalyst to California's growth.

Broderick's world was one of prostitutes, criminals, shady characters and anti Chinese workers. In his moments of screaming out against Gwin, Broderick charged that his rival was not a gentleman. He would tell anyone who would listen that Gwin was a hypocrite. He often said that men like Gwin had their own private houses of prostitution. Many locals citizens wondered about Broderick's mental health when one day he announced that Gwin's prostitutes were prettier than his own. Broderick would also complain that Gwin was a foppish gentleman with a penchant for fine clothes that hid an abnormal mentality. There was a strong hatred in Broderick's politics. One that suggested he had never escaped the slights of the New York Irish Catholic ghetto. It was not long before the voters tired of these personal attacks.

In contrast to Gwin, Broderick was sloppily dressed, found it difficult to speak without swearing and was prone to overstatement and outrageous generalizations. But at the heart of Broderick's Tammany Hall, Irish Catholics politics was a liberal Democratic program. One that prompted him to defend the Irish Catholic worker, and urge the state to fund special programs to provide land for the common person.

David Broderick's rise to political prominence was legendary. Between December 1848 and April 1851 he went from being the foreman of a volunteer San Francisco fire company to the president pro tempore of the California Senate. He would remain the voice of the liberal wing of the Democratic party until his untimely death in 1859. The force of reform politics in the Golden State owes its birth to Broderick.

The Gwin-Broderick political feud defined the politics of the 1850s. The differences between Gwin and Broderick defined the hostility between a number of political factions. Gwin was pro slavery, Broderick was anti slavery and the American or Know Nothing Party worried about immigrants, the Irish Catholic and the Chinese. The result was that California split into liberal and conservative political camps with definable ideological directions. A century a half later many of these political ideas remain an integral part of the California landscape.

The following reading suggests the differences between Gwin and Broderick. Howard A. DeWitt's biographical sketch of Gwin argues that he practiced the politics of prejudice to sway California elections. He was also an ardent defender of a civilization long in decline. Not only was Gwin a pro-slavery Secesh or Chivalry Democrat, but he was a staunch defender of the southern way of life. The fear of the wrong type of white people (Irish Catholics), the demand to limit Chinese labor and the general mob like attitude of Gwin's supporters created sharp divisions in California society. The following reading suggests the nature and direction of Gwin and Broderick's differences. It also delineates how the politics of prejudice became an integral part of the California political landscape.

Senator William Gwin and the Politics of Prejudice

by Howard A. DeWitt

California's politics of prejudice emerged in the 1850s. In this selection, the role of Senator William Gwin is analyzed against the backdrop of the Golden State. As a pro-slavery Democrat, Gwin had an ideological direction which gave birth to the institutiona-lized right wing. During the 1850s, Gwin was not only the leading voice of local conservatism, but he was the catalyst to those who feared the impending changes in California society. These fears were largely fueled by Gwin stressing that immigration and assimilation threatened the social balance. By the eve of the American Civil War, Senator Gwin's politics produced an identifiable prejudice in California politics. As a result, he popularized many political ideas that still are fashionable. The use of demagoguery, the oppressive power of the majority and the idea of limiting the rights of ethnic groups has remained an integral part of California civilization. Senator William Gwin didn't necessarily give birth to these notions but he fostered their popularity and permanence in California. This selection examines how Gwin created the politics of prejudice.

California became a pawn in national politics because of the slavery debate. From the time that the United States seized the Golden State from Mexico on July 7, 1846, there was a debate over California's political future. Would it become a free or slave state? This question intrigued everyone and led to prolonged conflict over the ideological direction of the Golden State. One man who benefited from this turmoil was an obscure Southern politician, William Gwin.

Who was William Gwin? He was Southern born on October 9, 1805 near Fountain Bend in the northern part of Sumner county, northeast of Nashville in Middle Tennessee. From birth Gwin was groomed for politics. Early on he learned to defend the basic tenets of slavery. His education created the notion that the working class needed controls. This translated into the use of nativism in Gwin's politics. While he never joined the nativist-minded American Party, Gwin

did agree with its notion of restricting the wrong type of immigrants. These immigrants were invariably European, Catholic and worked in the city. Where did Gwin develop his political ideas?

It was in Gwin's education that he developed his sense of superiority and political wisdom. Like many young Southern aristocrats, Gwin was provided with tutors and had a superior education. At twenty one, he passed the bar exam. But he was a lawyer with a desire for continued education. So Gwin enrolled at Transylvania College in Lexington, Kentucky and at the age of twenty three received a medical degree. His thesis on "Syphilis" ran twenty three pages and he accepted the medical license with the notion of moving into private practice. But he soon caught the political bug. It was the Age of the Common Man and there was opportunity for political and economic gain in the American West.

It was on the frontier that Gwin's education defined his politics of prejudice. His view of Mexican Californians, Native Americans and African Americans was one that emphasized their alleged biological and societal inferiority. It was a cruel and dehumanizing racism that had its genesis in Gwin's nearly two decade apprenticeship in western politics.

In 1831, young Gwin went to work as the personal secretary for President Andrew Jackson. Although Gwin wasn't hired because of his ability, President Jackson owed a personal debt to Gwin's father, he was an excellent protege. While under President Jackson's tutelage, Gwin learned the essential elements of political patronage. He became a staunch pork barrel Democrat who believed that federal funds or the promise of them could buy political power.

Initially, President Jackson set William Gwin up in Mississippi politics. He was nominated as a U.S. Federal Marshall for Southern Mississippi. This appointee position carried an annual income of $75,000, but this was understood to be little more than a stepping stone to running for the United States Senate. None of President Jackson's plans worked out. Mississippi Senator George Poindexter opposed Gwin's appointment thereby making it difficult for him to succeed. It wasn't until President Jackson replaced Senator Poindexter that Gwin finally was appointed to the federal Marshall position.

Mississippi, on to California and the Formation of Gwin's Political Ideology

This background in Mississippi politics taught Gwin a number of important lessons. He realized the importance of party loyalty. With President Jackson as his mentor, Gwin learned how to employ political power. Using patronage to build a political foundation was the main lesson. Eventually, Gwin used this technique to build his California political machine.

He also sought greater personal wealth. He was an opportunist who used his political knowledge for financial gain. When investments in Indian lands were opened up by President Jackson's land policies, Gwin jumped in and became a wealthy man. As a lawyer, Gwin represented the Chickasaw Indian Nation against the federal government. When he finished their case the chiefs were presented with a bill for $56,021.49 and they were forced to pay Gwin with large chunks of their most valuable land. He literally threw local Native Americans off their land. Privately, Gwin mocked their intelligence and reinforced the pro-slavery Democratic party notion that other ethnic groups were inferior.

As a gentleman with a fine education, a degree of wealth and a belief that the aristocracy should control governmental institutions, he was the perfect embodiment of future California prejudice.

In 1840, William Gwin was elected to the United States House of Representatives from Mississippi and served one term without distinction. When the twenty-seventh Congress convened in Washington D.C. in 1841, Gwin was timid around fellow members of the House of Representatives. He seldom spoke during House debate and his only interest was in providing pork barrel funds for his district.

During this time Gwin's finances began to unravel. His land deals hadn't turned out to be as lucrative as he had imagined. So Gwin turned to politics for salvation. He would find a political position and use this to enhance his dwindling fortune. Once James K. Polk ascended to the presidency in the mid-1840s there was speculation that Gwin would become a cabinet member. But opportunities in national politics failed to materialize. Soon the Democratic party looked to California and the party leadership sent Gwin to the Golden State. The Democrats sent Gwin into California to guide the constitutional convention toward statehood. Along the way he would line his pockets with lucrative investments.

On June 4, 1849, the Panama sailed into San Francisco. As the steamship approached the treacherous inlet to the bay, the gray fog seemed to cast a spell on the ship. The passengers on the Panama were not ordinary ones. In addition to future United States Senator William Gwin, there were other important Californians who entered the political-economic-social arena via the trip. After Gwin migrated to the Golden State, Bayard Taylor arrived in San Francisco. He was an aspiring poet who had little interest in politics, economic gain or fame. He was a famous scholar who had translated Goethe's **Faust** into English. The violence and decadence in the Golden State inspired Taylor to write one of the best early histories. Taylor was typically of the wandering American who migrated west seeking a passionate new civilization and embracing it.

Many early Californians were fanatics. Law and order was on their mind. Davy Scannal was a man obsessed with the role of the Sheriff in California. When he arrived in San Francisco on the Panama, Scannal became a member of the extralegal police force known as the Hounds.

This lawless brigade of thugs was responsible for the San Francisco Vigilante Committee of 1851. Scannal complained that San Francisco businessmen didn't understand that the Hounds were simply honorable citizens driving the riff raff from the city. The tragedy is that Scannal terrorized the city for years in the name of his own brand of law and order. He would roam drunkenly on the downtown streets near Market and Montgomery and threaten San Francisco citizens. Ironically, Broderick eventually selected Scannal as a San Francisco Sheriff. Yankee Sullivan, former heavyweight champion of America, remarked that Scannal was the most dangerous man in the Golden State.

There were others who represented the common person. One was Billy Mulligan, a chronic alcoholic as well as a political enforcer for whoever had the money and liquor. He was like a little bull dog with an ugly, pinched face and a penchant for explosive violence. His standing amongst San Franciscans was legendary, since Mulligan became Charles Cora's jailor when the Italian gambler was arrested. Not surprisingly, Sheriff Davy Scannal was a good friend of Mulligan's and one of his drinking buddies.

Another important Californian, William T. Coleman, arrived on the Panama and was instrumental in vigilante activity in both the 1850s and 1870s. When he entered San Francisco vigilante politics, he had matinee idol good looks and claimed to be a direct descendent of the nation's first president George Washington. Like Scannal and Mulligan, Coleman was a law and order fanatic obsessed with the wrong people migrating to the Golden State. Fortunately, his erratic behavior and heavy drinking prevented him from political success. Like the others, Coleman didn't possess Gwin's political pedigree.

As Gwin arrived in San Francisco, he was officially writing a government report. Unofficially, Gwin was defending slavery while seeking a position of power and prestige. When Gwin arrived in California there was opportunity to establish his political reputation by helping to write a state constitution. He was fond of telling people that he came to California for no other purpose than to influence the document designed to bring statehood.

When the Constitutional Convention of 1849 met in Monterey, Gwin was a prominent member. As the delegates met at Colton Hall, a large stone building used as a schoolhouse during the Mexican War, Gwin soon found that local politicians ignored his quest to become the body President. The Monterey Constitutional Convention selected a pioneer resident of the Golden State, Dr. Robert Semple, to handle the proceedings. This comeuppance may have been Gwin's fault, because he often remarked that his political education was superior to that of his colleagues.

How did Gwin distinguish himself at the Monterey Constitutional Convention of 1849? His rhetoric, arguments and general ideological direction made him the spirit of California's political right wing. Then he purchased a plush wagon and toured the Golden State selling the concept of immediate statehood. As he traveled through the gold fields in 1849, Gwin spun stories of Negro revolts, Catholic political chicanery and foreign intrigue. As a result, he helped give birth to nativism. Gwin realized that his argu-

ments would propel him into national office.

In March, 1849, the United States Congress adjourned after a stormy series of arguments over the future of California. There were a number of contentious debates over the future economic direction of the United States. Many Southerners equated slaves with property and this created debates dividing Californians into liberal and conservative groups.

As a leading Chivalry Democrat, Gwin believed that the future direction of American democracy would be decided in California. Still a young man in his early forties, Gwin had a penchant for reading classic English and European literature. His political image was that of a wealthy, well educated and politically astute Southerner. Although he seldom tipped his political hand, he was a calculating politician.

He also had a vision of American history. It was a dark view. One that saw an excess of democracy. Gwin believed that there was too much political and economic freedom in the Golden State. His personal mission was to introduce a semblance of old style Southern politics. His motivation was to become a controlling force in California politics. His political ambition knew no bounds and he was never encumbered by either ethics or integrity.

Seeking Public Office and Cleansing the State: The California Constitutional Convention of 1849

When Gwin arrived in California on June 4, 1849 he announced his intention to become a United States Senator. At forty four years of age, Gwin was one of California's most experienced politicians. He also understood the nature of local politics. The Democratic party was split into two factions. One was an anti-slavery group led by New York Tammany Hall Democrat, David Broderick, and the other was the Chivalry Democrats who were pro slavers with a states rights' penchant. Because of his political prominence, Gwin was selected as a member of the California constitutional convention of 1849. As the forty-eight representatives met to write a state constitution, which led to statehood, Gwin was a prominent voice. As the constitutional convention progressed, Gwin became the acknowledged architect of California statehood.

It was easy for Gwin to assume a leadership role, because the California constitutional convention of 1849 was the work of political amateurs. The convention was scheduled to begin on September 1, 1849, but the delegates who chartered a ship to sail the one hundred plus miles from San Francisco to Monterey failed to arrive on time. They were lost in the fog during the four day trip and the ship could not find Monterey's harbor. When deliberations did begin the members of the constitutional convention lacked the political experience to deal with the complex questions of statehood. Gwin took over and the other delegates often referred to his "haughty and dictatorial manner."

During the Monterey Constitutional Convention of 1849, Gwin fought with the Californio leader Mariano Vallejo, who represented the Hispanic California interests. The earliest signs of Gwin's racial attitudes were revealed in actions towards Vallejo. When Don Mariano defended his fellow Mexican rancheros and

their place in California history, Gwin suggested that they were backward economically. When it became apparent that Gwin was not interested in Vallejo's opinion, the Californio displayed his good manner by simply ignoring his hostile colleague.

As Vallejo refused to criticize Gwin's excesses during the Monterey constitution convention of 1848, Gwin erroneously interpreted this as ignorance. With European manners and a sense of gentility, Vallejo looked upon Gwin as a self-serving politician with little integrity. Early in the constitutional convention, Vallejo realized that the Spanish speaking influence was on the wane. He viewed the developing arguments over slavery as an extension of the American political debate which would lead to the Civil War in 1861 and make the Golden State rife with racial differences. So Vallejo decided to cast his vote with anti-slavery Democrats.

With Vallejo and the seven other Spanish speaking delegates uniting with the Tammany Hall Democrats, the Monterey Constitutional Convention of 1848 included a clause prohibiting the ownership of slaves as well as forbidding California from being a slave holding section. This made the California Constitution of 1849 one of the more liberal and far-sighted documents in the American West. Surprisingly, Gwin did not react to this proposal. He believed that it worked to his personal advantage. He would campaign for the United States Senate as a proslavery or Chivalry Democrat, but also he would support the free state proposal. Gwin could then use the fear of slavery to sell his politics of prejudice.

Along with California hero John Charles Fremont, Gwin was selected as a

United States Senator. The reason that the California legislature selected Gwin was a simple one. He was well known and well connected in national politics. He also was able to promote strong arguments for immediate statehood.

When the Monterey Constitution Convention of 1849 adjourned, Gwin traveled throughout California in search of political support. His strongest argument was that he was connected to the Democratic party leadership. On January 1, 1850, Senator William Gwin sailed out of the Golden Gate aboard the mail steamer, the Oregon, destined for New York. The stage was set for Senator Gwin to enter national politics and bring the politics of California prejudice into the national political arena.

Senator William Gwin: Statehood and the Birth of the Politics of Prejudice

Once he arrived in Washington D. C., Senator Gwin made obligatory calls on the nation's legislative leaders. The object was to convince these powerful political figures to support California's bid to become the thirty first state and the sixteenth free state. Not only would this swing the balance of power to the north in the slavery debate, but it would thrust the Golden State into the mainstream of national politics. Senator Gwin's agenda was to protect the rights of slave owners while maintaining California as a free state. It was a strange position. He was a defender of slavery who worked with anti-slavery forces to funnel large sums of federal money into California.

Thrust upon the national stage, it was now Senator elect Gwin's turn to charm his Washington D. C. colleagues. He suc-

ceeded admirably. There was no question that California would become the thirty first state and Senator Gwin was an important force in this triumph. When California was admitted to the Union on September 9, 1850, it was in part due to Gwin's zealous lobbying for statehood. The **London Times**, the newspaper which best summed up the remarkable atmosphere surrounding California statehood, editorialized: "Here was a community of some hundreds of thousands of souls, collected from all quarters of the known world . . . all organized under old Saxon institutions, and actually marching under the command of a mayor and aldermen." What amazed everyone was California's physical size. The **Times** observed that California was "a state with a territory as large as Great Britain, a population difficult to number, and destinies which one can foretell."

Once California was admitted to the Union, Senator Gwin became its most powerful national spokesperson. Lurking in the shadows was an opponent who would haunt and daunt Gwin throughout the 1850s. This was Senator David Broderick who represented San Francisco, the Irish Catholic migrants and the liberal Tammany Hall oriented Democrats. As a staunch opponent of slavery, Broderick always was present to counter Gwin's political presence.

Gwin's Politics of Prejudice: Hidden Within Federal Improvements

In Washington D. C., Gwin was a celebrity. Since he was the recognized head of the California delegation, there existed special privileges. Among these privileges was the notion that Gwin would assume the mantle of political leadership.

So Gwin took California's Congressmen to meet the House and Senate leaders. He was banqueted and treated like royalty.

Senator Gwin's first task once statehood became a reality was to bring internal improvements into the Golden State. With a zeal which amazed his Senate colleagues, Gwin pushed bills through Congress establishing a branch mint and a San Francisco customs house. The jobs created from these federal businesses was staggering and allowed Gwin to appoint his political followers to well paying positions. He also was instrumental in obtaining federal funds for a naval shipyard, a dry dock at Mare Island and a marine hospital.

Once these projects were underway, Gwin appointed people to positions as project administrators, helped influence bids for contractors and selected federal law enforcement personnel. As a result, he built a political machine which operated on the politics of prejudice. The use of the pork barrel, appointing key supporters to political office or throwing government contracts their way, was an old and established part of American politics. In California, Gwin used the pork barrel to build his own political power. He demanded that anyone awarded a job or a federal contract kick back from 10% to 20% of their pay to the Democratic party coffers. Not surprisingly, Gwin's political campaigns in the 1850s were well financed.

The Land Law of 1851 was Gwin's main triumph. He systematically depleted the Mexican land grantees of their property with a federal law that set up a three man Board of Land Commissioners, sitting in San Francisco, to adjudicate contested land claims. While both the law and process was defended as a fair way to deal with disputed land claims, the end result was to take away the most productive Spanish and Mexican land. Most Mexican land grants were awarded from 1845 to 1846 under the last Mexican Governor, Pio Pico. Gwin argued that these grants were extralegal because Governor Pico realized that American California was a possibility, and he was granting land to his friends.

The result of the Land Law of 1851 appears fair on the surface because most original land grantees retained their property rights. About 600 of the 800 contested Mexican land grants were approved. But these land claims were all one section or 640 acres. The Mexican land grants not approved were those that dominated the area around the San Francisco bay and greater Los Angeles. More than 200 wealthy land owners watched as the periphery of their land was settled. In a twenty year period the Mexican American aristocracy was reduced to second class citizenship. By using intricate American land law and the legal system, squatters could move in and legally seize Spanish or Mexican lands.

While in Washington D.C., Gwin earned an enviable reputation as a shrewd politician. Now it was time to return to California and use his political expertise to forge a strong pro-slavery coalition.

The Triumphant Return of Senator William Gwin and His Rival David Broderick: 1851—1852

When Senator Gwin returned to California, statehood and prosperity created a new atmosphere. When the state legislature met in San Jose on January 2, 1851 it was christened the "Legislature of a Thousand Drinks." It is not surprising that political integrity and personal honesty were not California political traits. The lack of secret elections, open bribery, obvious political corruption and differences between the pro and anti-slavery Democratic factions created a volatile political atmosphere.

The Gold Rush legacy continued to influence Californians. The average politician looked upon the Golden State as a place to get rich. Consequently, the quality of political leadership was so low that members of the state legislature sold lots to unsuspecting buyers that were under water. Local newspapers called this practice a transaction typical of California politics. Then politicians in San Francisco city government swindled the state out of eleven million dollars worth of waterfront property, and local newspapers remarked that it was expected behavior for one branch of government to steal from the other.

The changes taking placing in California in 1851 were profound ones. The gold rush had not only brought in businessmen with get rich quick schemes but also settlers with a defined political position. This created the anti-slavery Tammany Hall Democrats led by Broderick. They controlled a large part of the electoral process and intensified the debate between pro and anti-slavery forces. For a decade these two political factions involved the Golden State in business and racial turmoil and the resulting conservative-liberal split became a hallmark of California society and politics.

The differences between Gwin and Broderick became apparent in the election of 1852. The California Democratic party held a convention to nominate national convention delegates excluding Broderick and his supporters. Broderick was so enraged that he insulted a former governor of Virginia and was challenged to a duel.

On the day of the duel, Broderick sailed in a small boat from San Francisco to an Oakland mud lot. He was dressed in a fine suit and an expensive gold watch hung from his vest. A friend remarked: "If you are going to die, do it with a fine gold watch attached to your vest." As Broderick turned and prepared to fire at his opponent, his gun jammed. His opponent fired and a patch of blood appeared on Broderick's stomach. He then fired his gun six times at his opponent and missed with each shot. As Broderick fell forward holding his stomach, everyone feared that he was dead. After examining the wound the doctor found that his watch had been shattered by the bullet and his stomach was cut with flying glass. Therefore, Broderick was fine and the incident established his firm reputation as a foe of Gwin's Chivalry Democrats. This duel was a portent of things to come as Broderick would die in 1859 in another shooting incident.

Senator William Gwin's Economic Vision Amidst the Turmoil of California Politics

During his early U.S. Senate career, Gwin had an economic vision which would tie California to the eastern markets. In 1852, Senator Gwin proposed a bill to build a transcontinental railroad. This legislation was doomed with the outbreak of the Civil War because of the controversy over slavery. Northerners hoped to have the railroad built through the free states while Southerners argued for a slave state route. While national politics prevented the bill from passing, Senator Gwin's remarks on the California economy clearly demonstrated his vision for the future. From his earliest days in Mississippi politics, Gwin recognized the importance of implementing the pork barrel for his political purposes. He would use federal funds to buy votes, he would appoint federal marshals to control what he viewed as the lawless Mexican, and he would derail the liberal politics of his rival, State Senator David Broderick. But Gwin also urged golden State businessmen to expand their productivity. It was dangerous, Gwin cautioned, to depend upon government funds.

Some of Gwin's pork barrel schemes backfired. When he campaigned throughout California, Senator Gwin suggested that the U.S. Mint would create unbridled prosperity. Gwin argued that the gold the miners were bringing to San Francisco could be sold at great profit to the U.S. Mint, Gwin argued, and therefore he personally selected Moffat and Company to assay the gold.

This led to a controversy alleging that Gwin was receiving kickbacks. Before the money was sold to the U.S. Mint, it was assayed by Moffat and Company and miners were charged a two and a half per cent fee. Since Moffat and Company was selected to be the middle man, local miners charged collusion. Moffat and Company collected an extra twenty one million dollars in assaying fees, the suspicion that Gwin became wealthier in the process was understandable.

The differences between Gwin and Broderick from 1849 to 1854 stemmed from their view of the future of the Golden State. Not only did Gwin believe that

owning slaves was an absolute property right, but he was suspicious of the immigrant. The Mexican, Gwin argued repeatedly, could not be trusted and California needed to emphasize its American roots. By using the federal patronage to appoint his supporters to key political positions and to divert government funds to his friends, Gwin gained strong control over California society. He envisioned a law and order society to control Hispanic influences.

When the California legislature convened in Benicia on January 2, 1854, the temporary capital became a battle ground between Gwin and Broderick. The San Francisco delegates, headed by State Senator Broderick, decided to oppose Gwin's reelection to the United States Senate. They hoped to delay the election of a United States Senator by a year to give Broderick more time to campaign for the Senate seat.

There were numerous fights in the Benicia hotel bars. Billy Mulligan, a tough bully who was only five feet two inches tall, showed up with a famous bandit, Parker H. French, and they announced that they would personally beat up any Gwin supporters. Mulligan was not only a Broderick supporter but he was a legendary barroom fighter. One day Mulligan walked into a restaurant and found a man twice his size verbally berating Broderick. In a new tuxedo and ready for a night on the town, Mulligan walked over and butted the man with his head until he was unconscious. Mulligan then ordered a bottle of champagne and a steak dinner. He emptied the man's wallet and left its contents, more than a $1000, to cover the bill. Then a fierce bully called Snaggle Tooth Billy Williamson rode into town and announced that he would fight a duel with any man who supported the Chivalry Democrats. Not surprisingly, Snaggle Tooth Billy worked for Senator Broderick. These thugs were typical of the wide open California atmosphere and the general level of political corruption.

Gwin's supporters announced that they would not be intimidated. He searched for and found a politician who could charge Senator Broderick with corruption. This member of the California legislature, Senator Elisha T. Peck, informed his colleagues that he had been offered a $5000 bribe to influence the U.S. Senate election. As Peck recounted his story, it was discovered that a follower of Senator Broderick offered the bribe. Although he refused it, he demanded an investigation. In melodramatic fashion, Peck announced that he was putting himself under the protection of the Gwin Democrats. He feared for his life. Then Billy Mulligan was seen stalking Peck. Fortunately, Mulligan had succumbed to the ravages of alcoholism and was sleeping in alleys. He was no longer a threat to anyone but himself.

The end result was that the election wasn't delayed. This was a defeat for Broderick. Since Senator Gwin was in Washington D.C. working on legislation and unable to defend himself from Broderick's vicious attacks, he received both sympathy and support from many Californians. To counter this attack, Gwin used the pork barrel and pushed a bill to create the Mare Island Naval Shipyard. Then he orchestrated a well publicized bill to rebuild San Francisco's marine hospital. He also led the battle for increased funds to settle land disputes. Gwin continued his onslaught by obtaining money for Indian subsistence, the construction of lighthouses, a coastal survey, a comprehensive survey of public lands and an engineering study to create a transcontinental railroad. The use of federal funds to increase California prosperity was a hallmark of Gwin's politics.

Gwin's Political Career Begins Falling Apart: California Nativism in the Mid 1850s

Just as Gwin appeared politically unbeatable, a swing took place in California politics. The American Party, or Know Nothings as they were known, met in 1854 and decried the unlimited immigration, the excessive power of the Irish Catholic San Franciscan and expressed the fear of a papal plot to seize California. The Know Nothings lectured California voters on the need to retain the old American ways. The result was that the nativist Know Nothing separated enough votes to elect J. Neely Johnson as governor.

The influence of the Known Nothing Party established political bigotry in the mainstream of California politics. The resentment toward Hispanics and selected European immigrants, coupled with a rising fear of Chinese immigration, allowed the American Party to triumph. This was a strange defeat because the Democrats had won every election since 1850.

When the campaign to re-elect Gwin took place in early 1855, State Senator Broderick had enough votes to block his reelection. The resulting hate filled atmosphere cut into Gwin and Broderick's political power. As a result, one of California's U.S. Senate seat remained open for two years with Gwin and Broderick on the outside looking in. By April, 1856, Gwin's political managers received word that Broderick was prepared to settle his differences with the Chivalry Democrats.

The California Democratic party was in shambles and the voters were looking toward the newly organized Republican Party.

The Election of 1856: The Re-Emergence of Gwin and Broderick and the End of Democratic Political Power

Although the Democratic party was in dire straits, as the election of 1856 approached, Gwin believed that he had an excellent chance for reelection. A meeting was arranged between Gwin and Broderick at an auction house on Merchant Street near Montgomery in San Francisco and they struck a deal to cooperate with one another. The idea was that the California legislature would elect both of them to the United States Senate. There was only one problem, one of the candidates would have to accept a shortened four year term.

When the California legislature convened on January 5, 1857, in Sacramento, Gwin and Broderick were the only two serious candidates for the United States Senate seats. In California politics, Gwin was at a disadvantage because Broderick controlled the California legislature. So they elected him to the six year term and Gwin to the four year U. S. Senate position. This uneasy truce did little to alloy the differences within the Democratic party. It also created the feeling that the Democrats were so divided that the party could never reform itself.

On February 13, 1857, Gwin and Broderick arrived in New York. The reception for the native son, David Broderick, was like that of a hero returning from war. The Tammany Hall Democrats turned out with a band, banners and speeches proclaiming him the defender of the common worker. The tribute to Broderick was effusive and he was praised in local newspapers. Not only did the New York reception make Gwin uncomfortable, but it rekindled deep feelings of hatred between the two men.

The Lecompton Compromise, the Election of 1859 and the End of California's Democratic Party

The looming specter of the American Civil War found its way into Golden State politics. Since September 9, 1850, when California became the thirty first state, the argument over slavery created deep divisions. As the Chivalry and Tammany Hall Democrats did battle with one another there was a growing uneasiness over the peculiar institution.

In 1858, the debate over the Lecompton Compromise not only split the nation over the future of slavery but it tore California politics apart. The Lecompton issue was a strange one. It was a debate in Kansas where the pro-slavery faction took over the constitutional convention and attempted to establish slavery in a free state. The future of slavery in Kansas quickly erupted into a national issue and pro-slavery California Senator Gwin was one of its staunchest defenders. Naturally, Senator Broderick opposed the slavery faction.

What made the so-called Lecompton Compromise a strange one was that the pro-slavery faction had no chance of carrying the day. Free Soil party Kansas citizens were in the majority, but it was the argument over slavery that mattered. Through a piece of legislative trickery, the pro-slavery faction pushed through language that protected the rights of

Kansas slave owners. This infuriated the free state advocates and most Kansas citizens boycotted the election. The issue was not so much slavery as it was the right of slave owners to maintain their property.

So Senator Gwin put himself in the forefront of those in the Golden State who defended the peculiar institution. In California, while there were only a small number of slave owners, the Secesh Democrats caused the Lecompton attitude to triumph in the Golden State. While slavery was illegal, a California Supreme Court decision, the Perkins case, recognized the property rights of slave owners. Gwin's staunch support of slavery tore the local Democratic party apart and doomed their future electoral prospects. The politics of prejudice turned the voters toward the newly established Republican party and a host of other third party movements promising reform. In 1861, railroad mogul Leland Stanford became the first Republican governor, thereby dampening the future of Democratic politics.

The end of the California Democratic party resulted from the air of violence and recrimination permeating the state. During the electoral campaign of 1859, the Lecompton Democrats won more offices than Broderick's Tammany Hall Democrats. The turmoil surrounding California politics created random violence when Chief Justice David S. Terry, a candidate for reelection to the California Supreme Court, delivered a strongly worded speech in which he supported the Lecompton Democrats; there was talk of a duel. The speech was a veiled threat against the Tammany Hall Democrats. After Senator Broderick read an account of the speech he called Justice Terry a

"disturbed miserable wretch." Taking offense at Broderick's comments, Terry and Broderick exchanged a series of childish notes. Then Terry challenged Broderick to a duel.

Although the duel was outlawed by state law, this didn't prevent the newspapers from reporting it in great depth. After a number of letters were exchanged between Broderick and Terry, the Lake House ranch in a ravine near the Pacific Ocean was selected as the dueling site. This area was just beyond the San Mateo county line and it guaranteed little law enforcement interest. To most observers it seemed that Broderick had the advantage because the duel rules stated that guns had to be fired at the count of two and not three. This made Justice Terry's backers nervous because Broderick had the reputation as a quick shot. There was no need to worry as Broderick's gun fired prematurely and Terry shot him. Someone in the crowd shouted: "This is murder." There was a controversy over whether or not someone had jammed Broderick's gun.

Broderick's death on the field of honor by a Southern gentleman cast aspersion upon the political process. The duel brought an end to California Democratic politics. The citizenry was disgusted with the political violence and the disregard for state dueling laws. The newspapers began denouncing dueling and condemning those who engaged in it. The **San Francisco Bulletin** editorialized that Terry "should be marked as another Cain." This attitude hastened the destruction of California's Democratic party.

By 1859, Senator Gwin returned to Washington D.C. with the knowledge that his career was over and his party was in shambles. His brief tenure in the

United States Senate was ending. Gwin told close friends that he would not stand for reelection. The coming of the American Civil War and the rise of Union sentiment in the Golden State finally brought an end to Senator Gwin's tumultuous career.

What had Senator Gwin contributed to California history? He had almost single-handedly established the politics of prejudice. The view from the Protestant, white, middle class was one that condemned the ethnic influx, ridiculed the Chinese presence, looked askance at California's Hispanic past and was suspicious of the wrong type of Catholic immigrants. Rather than being quickly forgotten, the political ideas that Gwin championed remained an integral part of California society. In the mid-1870s the Workingmen's Party motto: "The Chinese Must Go" and Gwin's message took on a more popular tone. By 1900, Progressive Republican Hiram W. Johnson based a portion of his politics upon anti Chinese statements and he won two gubernatorial elections. Almost eighty years later, Governor Pete Wilson, in a very sophisticated manner, suggested that immigrants were destroying the fabric of California society. Like Johnson, Wilson was elected to a two term governorship employing the politics of prejudice well into the late 1990s.

It was political demagoguery that was Gwin's main contribution. He was the first in a line long of California politicos who would use the threat of another people, another culture or another viewpoint to rally the American minded behind the politics of prejudice. Politicians found that Californians responded politically to fear, and thus Gwin wrote the book on this political tactic.

Walter and Genie Halland: Enjoying the California Woods, 1990s

WORKSHEET 5: A Tale of Two Political Rivals

1. How did Jessie Benton Fremont create some key myths about California? _____

   _____

2. What did the passengers of the Panama find out about California? _____

   _____

3. Why was corruption so readily accepted as a part of California politics? _____

   _____

   _____

4. William Gwin began his political career in the state of _____ under the political

   tutelage of _____ with a political philosophy that could be defined as _____

5. David Broderick was elected to the political office of _____ in California

   state politics and then he was elected to the _____
6. The Samuel Roberts-Felice Alvarez incident was an indication that California was

   _____

   _____

7. What does Davy Scannal demonstrate about the fanatical nature of some

   Californians? _____

   _____

8. How did Gwin use the Hounds to his own political advantage? _____

   _____

9. Tammany Hall is _____

10. What shaped the political attitudes of William Gwin prior to his California political career? _____

_____

_____

11. Describe how William Gwin developed the politics of prejudice _____

_____

_____

_____

12. What role did William Gwin play in the Constitutional Convention of 1849?

_____

_____

_____

13. What role did William Gwin play in California politics? _____

_____

_____

_____

_____

_____

_____

_____

_____

14. Why was Billy Mulligan typical of California politics? _____

_____

_____

15. How did the Lecompton Compromise influence California politics? _____

_____

_____

16. How did federal improvements or pork barrel influence California politics? _____

_____

17. What was Senator William Gwin's economic vision for California?

_____

_____

_____

The Railroad Era:
The Chinese Question and Monopoly

READINGS: *"THE LABOR AGITATORS AND THE BATTLE FOR BREAD, 1878"* HENRY GEORGE, *"WHAT WILL THE RAILROAD BRING US,"* THE OVERLAND MONTHLY, OCTOBER, 1868 LELAND STANFORD, TESTIMONY BEFORE THE U.S. PACIFIC RAILWAY COMMISSION, MAY 3, 1887 HENRYK SIENKIEWICZ, *"THE CHINESE IN CALIFORNIA: A REPORT BY HENRYK SIENKIEWICZ, 1880"*

On May 10, 1869, the Central and Union Pacific met in Promontory, Utah completing the transcontinental railroad. In a colorful ceremony, one spike of Comstock silver and two of California gold were driven into the ground while a telegraph line attached to one of the spikes beamed the sound of sledgehammer swings into hundreds of American saloons. The birth of the transcontinental railroad inaugurated a commercial, cultural and working class revolution in the Golden State.

California's pioneer era ended with the new railroad system. No longer was the Pacific Coast an isolated entity, suddenly it was open to new settlers, to new businesses and to new ideas. There was also strong market for California goods. The port of San Francisco became a world market and there was a new prosperity. Naturally, Californians congratulated themselves on their bright future.

In San Francisco a local newspaper proudly headlined: "California Annexes the United States." This bit of local nationalism was prophetic, because California ideas influenced national politics guided popular culture and attracted new settlers. Almost single-handedly, in the 1870s, the Golden State influenced Congress of the United States to exclude Chinese immigrants. This was the first in a long line of political directions that Californians took into national politics.

As one of the by-products of the transcontinental railroad, anti Chinese feelings had a dramatic impact upon local politics. In 1871, Newton Booth was elected governor on an anti railroad platform which blamed the Chinese for labor problems. It was as if Governor Booth was prophetic, because midway through his first term California's first major depression occurred. Few political observers had given Booth much of a chance at winning the governor's office. but when he campaigned hard on the dangers of the Chinese and brought in a Mexican American politician, Romualdo Pacheco, as his lieutenant governor, the result was an overwhelming victory. The voters surge toward anti Chinese rhetoric was not lost on other politicians and "the Chinese must Go" became a campaign slogan heard well into the twentieth century.

Foreign trade was one of the most significant changes brought about by the creation of the transcontinental railroad. When the Suez Canal was completed in 1869, it brought Asian and European ships closer to San Francisco harbor. As foreign trade blossomed, the availability of goods increased and the Golden State's purchasing power reached a new high. High wages, the availability of goods and the notion that economic conditions would continue to prosper made it difficult for Californians to accept a general depression.

As depression hit the United States in the 1873, Californians found that their high wages dipped and remained low. Labor unions emerged to point their finger at the Chinese and later in the decade the Workingmen's Party organized to convince voters to support the Constitution of 1879. This document contained specific restrictions to discourage Chinese rights in the marketplace. Why were Californians addicted to anti-Chinese political arguments?

The roots of anti-Chinese sentiment are complex ones. The steady flow of the Chinese into San Francisco caused hostile feelings. By examining California-Chinese history, it is easier to understand how politicians used xenophobic fears to win elections and force exclusionist policies. The key to these fears was the growth of the Chinese. The anti-Chinese politicians painted a historical picture that wasn't flattering.

In 1849 there were less than 500 Chinese in California. The outbreak of the 1851 Taiping Revolution against the Manchu Dynasty led to 15 years of civil war and the rise of poverty. The rumors of easy wealth brought large numbers of Chinese into California. "The Golden Mountain" was the term the Chinese used to describe California. Because of a booming economy, the plentiful job market and the inclination to overlook malevolent labor brokers, the Chinese were welcomed in the 1850s as a source of cheap labor.

The importation of Chinese immigrants through a "credit-ticket" system made it difficult for workers to pay off their passage. It often took an unsuspecting worker as long as twenty years to pay off his passage. The Chinese Six Companies, the chief importer of Asian labor, with offices in San Francisco and China, mercilessly exploited its own people. Using a long established immigration pattern, young men from Canton, Hong Kong and neighboring areas were brought into San Francisco. The Chinese Six Companies negotiated with American businesses to import the cheap labor and the young men went to work, invested their money in California businesses, and became the Golden State's first foreign economic conglomerate.

The nature of the process made the Chinese bitter and created hostility toward them. As one San Franciscan remarked: "they smelled bad and worked hard." This nasty racial remark was typical of the anti-Asian sentiment that dominated California politics for the next century.

By 1852, the influx of more than 25,000 Chinese created tensions in the mines, farming communities and in San Francisco. The Chinese were a tenth of the state's population and in some mining towns the Chinese represented as much as thirty percent of the population. This led to the enactment of a large number of city-county ordinances to control Asian immigrants. San Francisco passed the Pig Tail Ordinance in 1854 to harass the Chinese for minor violations of the law. Since the pig tail was a religious symbol, this was a serious form of punishment. Soon the Chinese Tongs charged that these law violations were more imagined than real. As a result, the Chinese became increasingly political and fought the exclusionists.

The **Alta Californian**, a leading Northern California newspaper, published inflammatory editorials about the Chinese. To speak out against the "Celestial," as the Chinese were known, was a sign of patriotism. But it was in the mining camps of the California gold fields that the earliest and ugliest forms of anti-Chinese sentiment took place.

Throughout the mining camps there were mass meetings and the Foreign Miners' Tax Law of 1850 was imposed upon the Chinese. In this second phase of taxing foreign miners, the $3 to $5 a month tax drove the Chinese from the Sierra Nevada into San Francisco. The Census of 1860 revealed that only 8% of the Chinese resided in San Francisco but by the 1870s the majority of California Chinese lived in the city by the bay.

San Francisco was frightened by the Chinese influx. The Board of Supervisors passed a Cubic Air Ordinance designed to stifle Chinese housing. In 1854 the California Supreme Court ruled in the "People v. Hall" ruled that the Chinese were legally the same as Native Americans. Since the California Indians could not vote or testify in court, the Chinese were denied the benefits of local citizens.

Although the Chinese could not become citizens because of a federal law in 1790 which stated that only "free white persons" could be naturalized, they were still able to gain some influence in California through the Tongs. These organizations negotiated with local officials and worked out some degree of social-economic freedom. The obscure federal provision which prevented citizenship was not overturned until 1952 and California politicians continued to use anti-Chinese rhetoric without fear of an Asian voter backlash.

During the 1860s, the agitation against the Chinese temporarily died down. The nature of Chinese settlement was rural. In the Sierra Nevada mining towns, the Chinese worked on the periphery of the economy. They were needed to fill the low paying positions. In the San Joaquin Valley, the Chinese were not only an excellent source of cheap labor, but they lived quietly outside the mainstream of local life. It was a type of social adjustment that white Americans preferred.

Anti-Chinese sentiment reemerged in 1868 when the Burlingame Treaty allowed free immigration. Without consulting California politicians, the federal government negotiated a treaty to allow the Chinese to come into America in return for economic concessions. Since the majority of Chinese immigrated to California, there was an immediate political reaction. There was also the recently ratified Fourteenth Amendment which forbade states to "deny to any person within its jurisdiction the equal protection of the laws." The Fourteenth Amendment, in effect, gave the Chinese equal rights. The Tongs quickly challenged and won a number of rulings against city and county ordinances that were discriminatory. As the Chinese became civil rights oriented, their opponents were more determined than ever to exclude them from the Golden State.

The federal Civil Rights Act of 1870 continued to increase Chinese rights. It prohibited discrimination in the courts as well as overturning legislation which taxed immigrant groups. This further agitated public opinion. One judge, Justice Stephen J. Fields, of the United States Supreme Court, chided Californians for their racial insensitivity.

The public reaction to the Chinese was based on misconceptions surrounding their culture. The strange gods, exotic foods, bizarre clothing and quiet personalities reinforced long held stereotypes about the Chinese. Since they worked for an unusually low wage, labor leaders argued that the Chinese were dangerous economically. A generation earlier, the Irish-Catholic had faced the same charge. The derogatory use of the term "John Chinaman" in San Francisco newspapers and the rise of anti-Coolie organizations to exclude the Chinese intensified the debate.

The local labor unions joined with Anti-Coolie clubs and Eight Hour Leagues to foment public hostility. In a series of well organized public demonstrations, in the 1870s, the word Coolie became synonymous with cheap labor. From the Los Angeles anti-Chinese riot of October 24, 1871 until the July 23–25, 1877 riots against the Chinese in San Francisco, there was strong hostility toward Asian immigrants.

The prompted Denis Kearney to organize the Workingmen's Party of California. The sole purpose of this San Francisco based third party was to restrict Chinese immigration. The Workingmen's Party demanded an exclusionist law and began approaching federal lawmakers. With Presidential elections often decided by one state in the 1870s, the anti-Chinese issue reached a national audience.

Kearney not only hoped to restrict the Chinese in the Golden State, but he had a specific platform. He became a proponent of rewriting the California Constitution to prohibit the Chinese from exercising full political and economic privileges.

The reasons for Chinese exclusion are varied. A major depression from 1873 to 1877 eroded profits, led to wage cuts and deteriorated working conditions. Who was responsible for this post-Civil War depression? Denis Kearney, the leader of the Workingmen's Party, argued that it was cheap Chinese labor which ruined the thriving California economy. When the railroads cut their wages, Kearney maintained, it was due to the presence of the Chinese. During the winter of 1876–1877, the worst drought in a century cut into agricultural and mineral production. Suddenly large numbers of unemployed workers descended upon San Francisco. The building boom ended, shipping was in decline, and the import-export trade cut into wages and profits. The heinous racial slur, "the Yellow Peril," was bandied about California. Newspaper cartoons featuring grotesque Chinese workers further inflamed public opinion. The editorial cartoons constantly emphasized the themes of the Chinese health hazard, the propensity to produce a large number of children and the willingness to work cheaply.

On July 23, 1877, a mass meeting at San Francisco's City Hall led to the formation of the Workingmen's Party. The anti-Chinese sentiment that had existed for more than two decades burst forth from an angry mob of vigilantes. Initially, the Workingmen's Party was organized to protest wage cuts by the railroad, but it quickly erupted into a political vehicle to attack cheap Chinese labor. Kearney's demagogic speeches were a significant catalyst to the irrational hostility toward the Chinese. The Workingmen's Party leader also charged that the Chinese believed that they were above the law and this charge further heightened the vigilante mentality.

The idea of enforcing vigilante decreed laws was popular. So it was not surprising that mobs ran around San Francisco beating the Chinese indiscriminately and then burning their property. On July 25, 1877, a Workingmen's Party riot led to the burning of the docks of the Pacific Mail Steamship Company and roughly a third of Chinatown. The Pacific Mail Steamship

Company was the primary importer of Chinese labor and it was owned by the Big Four. At San Francisco's City Hall, Kearney stood on a small stage made of empty beer barrel kegs and shouted that the railroad monopoly was a direct result of Chinese labor. It took some time but he created a xenophobic reaction.

This action gave birth to public hysteria against the railroad that reached epic proportions. This helped the Workingmen's Party to achieve some temporary political power and began the final stages of excluding the Chinese. Much of this reaction centered around Denis Kearney. Born in Cork County, Ireland, Kearney had no formal education, but he was one of the most commanding speakers at the San Francisco Lyceum of Self-Culture. This was a night school which taught public speaking and grooming. It was a school for the fledgling middle class. Not only was Kearney one of the most accomplished students but he hit a nerve with his fellow students when he screamed: "The Chinese Must Go." A political demagogue who incited the fury of the anti-Chinese mob, Kearney was not only a guiding light behind the Workingmen's Party, but he was an articulate spokesperson for anti-Chinese arguments. As President of the Workingmen's Party, Kearney harangued large crowds over the wage loss that blue collar workers suffered at the hands of the Chinese. To excite his listeners, Kearney often shouted: "every workingman should have a musket."

Eventually, anti-Chinese sentiment reach a breaking point. On the evening of October 29, 1877, approximately 1,200 workingmen marched to the top of San Francisco's Nob Hill where the Big 4 had built their mansions. Standing in front of Charles Crocker's "spite fence," the workingmen hooted and hollered for their rights. The "spite fence" was built by Crocker to block the area between California and Sacramento street. The fence engulfed one man's home located on a small lot on the same block as Crocker's mansion. The man had refused to sell his home to Crocker and the railroad magnate built the forty foot board fence to demonstrate his power. Then Crocker bragged to the press that he could keep the sunlight from anyone that he desired. This public arrogance infuriated the Workingmen's Party. Kearney called the fence a symbol of the disregard that the railroad had for the common man.

The reaction against the Central Pacific and Southern Pacific railroads grew to epidemic proportions. The years of lobbying for political favors and the outright bribery inherent in railroad politics created a hostile political climate. While the railroad stimulated economic growth, it also created opposition to the "Octopus," or the "Robber Barons."

The critics of the railroad were numerous. Henry George, a well known journalist and popular writer, was the most effective. In the late 1860s George arrived in California to edit the **Oakland Transcript**, a Democratic party newspaper. A polemical writer who simplified the Chinese influence, George urged a speculative tax on railroad profits. Soon he was a well-known popular writer and a leading critic of the Robber Barons. One of the most prestigious national magazine, **The Overland Monthly**, commissioned George to write an article about the Central Pacific's impact upon the Golden State. In the October, 1868 issue of **The Overland Monthly**, George's article "What The Railroads Will Bring Us," expressed the popular notion that as the Central Pacific and Union Pacific race to complete the transcontinental railroad system would have a negative impact upon the Golden State. As George concluded: "The truth is, that the completion of the railroad and the consequent great increase of business and population, will not be a benefit to all of us."

The Big 4, as Leland Stanford, Collis P. Huntington, Charles Crocker and Mark Hopkins were known, were not a retiring lot. They reacted to criticism by strongly defending their role in making the California economy a profitable one. As Central Pacific President, Leland Stanford bellowed: "The prosperity of this state is due to us." But these pronouncements didn't stop the attack on the bribery and general corruption in California. The assault on the honesty of the Big 4 and the business tactics of the Central Pacific and Southern Pacific lasted for twenty years. The object was to create state and federal regulation and to end the monopolistic tendencies of the railroad.

Eventually, the Big 4 fought back. After more than twenty years of criticism the railroad took its fight to the United States Senate. In 1885 Stanford, the railroad president and former California governor, was elected to the United States Senate. His mandate was to defend railroad economic policies. When he entered the U.S. Senate, Stanford vigorously defended railroad business practices. In a hearing before Congress in 1887, Senator Stanford not only described the railroad as the facilitator of prosperity by providing inexpensive transportation for the both the settler and the fledgling business man, but he challenged its critics to prove the corruption charges. Stanford's tactics infuriated anti-railroad foes, and they intensified their attacks on the Chinese.

The hostility to the use of Chinese labor prompted a strong reaction against the railroad. Often the immigrant came to view the Chinese as a threat. In 1876, a small group of Polish immigrants arrived in Anaheim and established a utopian community. This remote Southern California community was an ideal agricultural setting, but the Polish farmers were unable to compete with local Asian laborers. When this experiment in communal living failed, they blamed the Chinese. One of commune leaders, Henryk Sienkiewicz, searched for a reason for their failure. He found it in the low wages and hard work of Chinese immigrants. An amateur historian with a penchant for overstatement, Sienkiewicz used his spare time to write small California history vignettes. During his business ventures he spent some time watching Chinese workers. He praised the Chinese without realizing it by suggesting that they would take any job. After pointing out that the Chinese turned formerly infertile acreage into lush agricultural land, Sienkiewicz wrote: "the Chinese cannot compete with the whites." It is a reaction not only typical of the times but his article highlights the problems of anti-Chinese sentiment.

The next set of readings suggest the intensity of anti railroad feelings. The hostility toward big business was articulated by many groups but none better than Denis Kearney's Workingmen's Party who published a pamphlet, "The Labor Agitators and the Battle For Bread," which articulated the feelings against big business. The hostility toward the Big 4 suggests that the Southern Pacific was an economic Octopus that dominated the Golden State economy. This was a popular notion that the Southern Pacific railroad controlled the economy and prevented legitimate business competition. This idea raised the hackles of voters and allowed reformers to suggest future reforms. Soon demagogues emerged who were reform minded but often used the same loaded language as the Big 4. The best known anti railroad crusader, Henry George, was a journalist who discovered the public's penchant for honest politics.

Henry George book **Progress and Poverty**, published in 1879, continued the assault upon the railroad. By proposing the Single Tax, George continued to blamed the transcontinental railroad for California's problems. George's article in 1868 in **The Overland Monthly** developed a hostility to the railroad which never abated. In defense of the Central Pacific and Southern Pacific, United States Senator Leland Stanford, fights back in 1887 in a remarkably glib testimony before the United States Senate. Stanford argues that California prosperity was the result of the Southern Pacific and the population boom owed its success to the Big 4. What these readings suggest is the intense debate over the role of the railroad, the Chinese and the problems that monopoly created in the Golden State.

The Labor Agitators or the Battle for Bread?
A Workingmen's Party Pamphlet, 1878

In 1877 Denis Kearney burst upon the California political scene as the leader of the Workingmen's Party. He introduced a new type of politics which organized blue-collar workers to push for better wages and working conditions. Kearney's rhetoric charged that the Chinese were the main reason for the depression of the mid-1870s. In this selection from a Workingmen's Party pamphlet there is a strong statement against Chinese labor, the local police and politicians, and the writer suggests that the worker may be the most important force in modern California. What is interesting about this selection is that it provides the Workingmen's Party description of Denis Kearney's arrest, and it generally imparts a spirit of working-class unity. In many respects this pamphlet indicates that political sophistication amongst labor is the wave of the future in the Golden State. The Workingmen's Party offers a strong statement for the rise of blue collar politics.

Denis Kearney: Leader of the Workingmen's Party

The Labor Agitators, Or The Battle For Bread? (San Francisco, 1878)

At last a workingman, a drayman, Denis Kearney, of San Francisco, immortalized himself by these words: "We will have a new party, the Workingman's Party. No great capitalist, no political trickster, no swindler or thief shall enter it. We will fill the offices with honest poor men who will make laws to protect themselves. We will send the Chinese home, distribute the land of the grabber, tax the millionaire, make a law to hang thieves of high as well as low degree, elevate the poor, and once more return to the simple virtue of honest republicanism."

And he added, "When the thieves hear these things they will shake in their boots. They will do all they can to divide and defeat us. They will pervert the law to persecute us. They will try to cheat us, to count us out at the ballot-box, to bribe and corrupt the men we elect. They will provoke us to riot if they can, and set the military upon us. We must arm. We must resolve to fight if need be. We must stand by each other to the death if necessary. We must swear that we will not be defeated. It is life or death. Either we must drive out the Chinese slave, and humble the bloated aristocrat, or we shall soon be slaves ourselves. There is no other solution of the problem. It is death or victory. We conquer or perish. Arm! arm! and let our adversaries see that we are in earnest!"

These words struck the public like electric fire. They listened breathless to what their own hearts had whispered. They said, "We will do it! Lead on and we will follow!" They came to hear him in tens, hundreds, thousands. With one accord they rallied to his support.

The meetings were marked with the strictest order. In no instance was there the slightest approach to riot or tumult.

There was nothing but that calm, settled, solid promise that the people should win and the victory be complete if it had to be fought for. The speakers were vehement, and the applause was genuine, unanimous and vociferous. It was this calm resolution that terrified the enemies of the people. They did not understand it. They dreaded men who held such a reservoir of power under such complete control.

A meeting was called on Nob Hill in mere sport. This is a large hill or nob on which the railroad magnates had built their palaces. It was proposed in jest to invite them to join the workingmen and become officers of the Ward Branch. Two thousand people climbed the hill to enjoy the joke. Two bonfires were made to afford light. Speeches were made, rather in a jocular vein. The applause was hearty. The crowd was full of fun, and when the speaking was over, a thousand men came singing down the hill and dispersed to their homes.

At this meeting a gentleman named Pickett, commonly called Philosopher Pickett, had desired to air his eloquence, and was permitted to do so. He launched out against the railroad magnates with fanatic fury. He proposed to tear down a fence, known as Crocker's fence, which is very obnoxious to a great many people, because it manifested the domineering spirit of a man of millions.

This speech was repudiated by the leaders, and all intention as to the fence abjured. Notwithstanding this the authorities resolved to make it a pretext for arresting the leaders, and not that alone, but for provoking the people into an actual riot as an excuse for shooting them down, and so crushing the movement. Whoever conceived that diabolical plot and moved to its execution meant murder and should be brought to judgment. The miscreants who helped it on will never be forgotten. Those who only obeyed orders are excused. But those who overdid may yet have to answer for a crime.

On the following Saturday night, while speaking to five thousand men Mr. Kearney was arrested. The militia and police were under arms. The excited crowd could have rescued him and torn the police limb from limb. But Kearney, nothing daunted, waved back his followers, bade them be still, and with tears and curses they saw him dragged to jail.

But his place was filled in a moment. Day took the stand. Knight and others followed. The promise of final triumph was again given and received by the people with yells of delight. The meeting adjourned in peace.

On the next day, Sunday, the usual meeting at the Lotta Fountain was forbidden by a notice. It was to have been at 2 o'clock p.m. By noon the streets were filled with people. A large crowd gathered at the Irish-American Hall, which was closed against them. Parties were sent to engage Horticultural Hall on Stockton street, and reporting it secured if the rent, $25, could be paid, the money was collected in a moment. The crowd began to march with fife and drum for Horticultural Hall. It might have been a thousand at the start. It was soon two, three, four. It laughed at opposition, paraded the streets in triumph, and entered the hall amid the entire police force. The authorities had called out the militia, the fire brigade and the vigilantes. All were ready for a murderous onslaught on that peaceful crowd.

Day was the first speaker. He was arrested on a warrant issued the day before. The crowd was fearfully excited. But the tumult was stayed by the leaders, and the people conjured not to break the peace. William Wellock, at that time a new recruit, then spoke for some time, and was permitted to depart unmolested.

By this time the forces of the treacherous officials were all ready. They must have a riot. They must provoke it in any event. H. L. Knight now took the stand, and announced that those who stood ahead of him having gone to prison, the mantle fell upon his shoulders; that he would be worthy of it; that he would still declare that the Chinaman must and shall leave the State of California. Officer Clark, of the police, suddenly sprang at the speaker, and without showing any warrant pushed him off the platform into the hands of the police.

And then and there a tumult arose that it is impossible to describe. Those who had arms felt for them. Fierce men yelled their defiance at the police. But again the leaders calmed the disorder. The prisoner walked between two policemen, untouched. In the hall, five thousand men; in the street, five thousand more; at every door and window, men, women and children; a line of police. Men and women shook hands with the captive as he went down the street. The crowd cheered. The police showed their respect.

This was not the last arrest. Helm, Willey, and Kennedy were collared, too, for some slight disorder. The meeting was again calmed by Bates, who then did good service. There was some other speaking, after which the crowd dispersed.

The city prison is not a nice place to be in. The cell is properly called a "sweatbox." With two persons and a gas light, there is just air enough to live; but not to move, not to eat or drink to any extent. It

An Elderly Chinese Citizen Looking Back (Courtesy of Alan Kirshner)

is truly barbarous to take two men who have been used to the free air and shut them up in such places. The city should be made to pay for it. Monday morning Bates, while on a visit to his friends, was told that he must be locked up too. The prisoners now were Kearney, Day, Knight, Helm, Bates, Willey, Kennedy, Krouse, and O'Donnell, the latter bailed out.

Then came the bailing out. For each offense, a mere misdemeanor, the bail was set at three thousand dollars, in defiance of the constitution, and every principle of law and humanity. The wretch who fixed that bail has placed a mark of infamy on his brow that should follow him to his grave. He should be

impeached and punished. That was not enough. The charges were multiplied, though resting on the same facts and being the same offense—multiplied simply to make bail impossible. No greater villain ever disgraced the Judge's bench than Davis Louderback. It was not ignorance. He knew these were poor men. He knew the law. He had sworn to observe it, and he failed to do it. His reward is sure.

Notwithstanding the heavy bail it was raised for all, though not for ten days. By that time the cases had come on to be heard, and they were dismissed. There was no riot, no conspiracy, nothing said but what any American citizen has a right to say. All the cases were dismissed. Then what was he who signed those warrants? A villain! Yea, a superserviceable villain.

Immediately after the discharge preparations were made for the grand procession on Thanksgiving Day. The different ward branches did nobly. Banners and bands of music were obtained. Several societies joined in the parade. Friends came from outside places, and a more imposing body of workingmen never was seen. Dennis Kearney was the Grand Marshal; William Wellock and H. L. Knight were Deputy Marshals. Each branch had its marshals and aids. A thousand men were appointed to keep the peace. There were at least twelve thousand stalwart men in the procession. On either side of the street twice as many looked on with approval, cheering the line through its whole length. Ladies threw bouquets to the leaders. Chinatown was in terror. The militia and the police were under close orders all day. But no workingman was arrested. There was neither a drunk nor a fight. Never had such order been seen before. The workingmen had been called hoodlums. They had been stigmatized as worthless loafers. Behold, it was all a lie. The eyes of their adversaries were opened. They began to be afraid. They saw numbers, strength, order, sobriety and calm determination and they were afraid. Those who had marshaled that procession were capable. Those who could command that army of men to such profound peace could also move them to deeds of daring.

"Oh," they said, "we cannot frighten these fellows. They are too strong. We will divide. We will sow discord among them." The effort was made. But that too was a failure. The workingmen would not divide. They discerned the purpose of the wily adversary and clung more closely to their leaders. The mischief-makers from Sacramento were scouted. Day had already gone. Bates, O'Donnell and others were expelled for conspiracy, much to the benefit of the organization. And still the ball kept rolling, enlarging, gathering strength, solidarity and determination.

On no occasion have the first words of the leader been retracted, retreated from, or disavowed. The Chinaman must leave the State of California has been and still is the cry, and will be until the end is accomplished. There can be no repose for anybody until this issue is settled. The white freeman with his wife and children cannot live in the same atmosphere as the Coolie slave. One or the other must leave the State, and it must be the Chinaman. The land of the State must be distributed into more hands. The money monopolist must be humiliated and made as amenable for crime as his poor neighbor. These villains have had their own way long enough. The people will now take care of themselves.

They may as well surrender gracefully to the inevitable. It will be better for them. Let the rich who have made their money honestly and use it like gentlemen, come out from among the greedy rascals who have stolen what they have and use it for still further corruption and fraud! Let them join the people! Hasten to take the mark of Cain off your forehead, and leave the thieves to stand alone!

The workingmen of California are not stupid peasants. They are scholars, skilled artisans, soldiers, and know how to live and how to die. They have just woke up to the abominable frauds that have been practiced on them. They see their situation between the aristocrat and the Chinaman, and they will scatter both like chaff before the wind.

Let the newspapers do as they please. Let them help or retard, but they cannot stop this avalanche. California will set the example to the rest of the States. It will have no rich men above the law. It will have no slaves beneath it. An honest middle class who love their country and each are better than all the shoddy aristocrats on earth; and safer for the great Republic.

"What the Railroad Will Bring Us"
by Henry George

*In October, 1868, Henry George, then a relatively obscure California journalist, wrote an article for **The Overland Monthly** expressing skepticism about the future of the railroad. George introduced his article by mentioning the "enormous bounty offered by the government" for completion of this transportation system. The idea that special economic favors from the federal government was the key to the railroads success was an important one. It caused public opinion to turn against the railroad. Journalists like Henry George took advantage of this atmosphere to blame the railroad for California's economic problems. Implicit in George's prose was the notion that the Big 4 were criminals. The railroad had stolen its fortune using cheap Chinese labor, government land grants and vast sums of federal money. As George argued: "land is appreciating-fortunes are being made in a day by day buying and parceling out Spanish ranches. . . ." What the famed journalist argued was that the Central Pacific and Southern Pacific railroads were making a fortune from land sales. He wrote of the need for a speculative tax. Eventually, this was known as the single tax and it would be a political lever to regulate the railroads. George speculated on California's economic growth and agreed that it was substantial. Then he asked: "will she still be the same California?" The resounding answer was "NO." As he concluded his article, the resulting economic and population growth doomed the frontier nature of the Golden State. Perhaps Henry George was right. Big business may have ruined the lush nature of pioneer California. Then again maybe he was wrong. Perhaps it was the railroad which brought modern economic development to Golden State.*

*In 1879 George's book, **Progress and Poverty**, popularized his anti-Chinese and anti-railroad arguments. The corporate form of business that the Central Pacific and Southern Pacific railroads had mastered were not only under attack but they were threatened by a series of state and federal laws. George was not only a leader in this attack, he was considered a visionary. In historical retrospect, the single tax is a weak economic solution and George's writings are little more than demagogic raving. But they did strike a chord with public opinion. The intense political opposition to the railroads established the next stage of California politics. Just after the turn of the twentieth century, as California increased its urban and industrial growth, a group of politicians known as Progressives emerged to attack the Robber Barons. The intensity of anti-railroad politics from the 1880s to the Progressive Era was a tribute to George's journalistic persistence. The following selection sums up his notion that the railroad hindered rather than helped California.*

Henry George, "What the Railroads Will Bring Us," **The Overland Monthly**, Vol. 1 (October 1868), pp. 297–298, 300–302.

Upon the plains this season railroad building is progressing with a rapidity never before known. The two companies, in their struggle for the enormous bounty offered by the Government, are shortening the distance between the lines of rail at the rate of from seven to nine miles a day—almost as fast as the ox teams which furnished the primitive method of conveyance across the continent could travel. Possibly by the middle of next spring, and certainly, we are told, before mid-summer comes again, this "greatest work of the age" will be completed, and an unbroken track stretch from the Atlantic to the Pacific.

Though, as a piece of engineering, the building of this road may not deserve the superlative terms in which, with American proneness to exaggeration, it is frequently spoken of, yet, when the full effects of its completion are considered, it seems the "greatest work of the age," indeed. Even the Suez Canal, which will almost change the front of Europe and divert the course of the commerce of half the world, is, in this view, not to be compared with it. For this railroad will not merely open a new route across the continent; it will be the means of converting a wilderness into a populous empire in less time than many of the cathedrals and palaces of Europe were building, and in unlocking treasure vaults which will flood the world with precious metals. The country west of the longitude of Omaha, all of which will be directly or indirectly affected by the construction of the railroad. (for other roads must soon follow the first) is the largest and richest portion of the United States. Throughout the greater part of this vast domain gold and silver are scattered in inexhaustible profusion, and it contains besides, in limitless quantities, every valuable mineral known to man, and includes every variety of soil and climate. . . .

What is the railroad to do for *us*?—this railroad that we have looked for, hoped for, prayed for so long?

Much as the matter has been thought about and talked about; many as have been the speeches made and the newspaper articles written on the subject, there are probably but a few of us who really comprehend all it will do. We are so used to the California of the stagecoach, widely separated from the rest of the world, that we can hardly realize what the California of the railroad will be—the California netted, with iron tracks, and almost as near in point of time to Chicago and St. Louis, as Virginia City was to San Francisco when the Washoe excitement first commenced, or as Red Bluff is now.

The sharpest sense of Americans—the keen sense of gain, which certainly does not lose its keenness in our bracing air—is the first to realize what is coming with our railroad. All over the State, land is appreciating—fortunes are being made in a day by buying and parceling out Spanish ranches; the Government surveyors and registrars are busy; speculators are grappling the public domain by the hundred of thousand of acres; while for miles in every direction around San Francisco, ground is being laid off into homestead lots. The spirit of speculation, doubles, trebles, quadruples the past growth of the city in its calculations, and then discounts the result, confident that there still remains a margin. And it is not far wrong. The new era will be one of great material prosperity, if material prosperity means more people, more houses, more farms and mines, more factories and ships. . . .

The new era into which our State is about entering—or, perhaps, to speak more correctly, has already entered—is without doubt an era of steady, rapid and substantial growth; of great addition to population and immense increase in the totals of the Assessor's lists. Yet we cannot hope to escape the great law of compensation which exacts some loss for every gain. And as there are but a few of us who, could we retrace our lives, retaining the knowledge we have gained, would pass from childhood into youth, or from youth into manhood, with unmixed feelings, so we imagine that if the genius of California, whom we picture on the shield of our State, were really a sentient being, she would not look forward now entirely without regret. The California of the new era will be greater, richer, more powerful than the California of the past; but will she be still the same California whom her adopted children, gathered from all climes, love better than their own mother lands; from which all who have lived within her bounds are proud to hail; to which all who have known her long to return? She will have more people; but among those people will there be so large a proportion of full, true men? She will have more wealth; but will it be so evenly distributed? She will have more luxury and refinement and culture; but will she have such general comfort, so little squalor and misery; so little of the grinding, hopeless poverty that chills and cramps the souls of men, and converts them into brutes?

Amid all our rejoicing and all our gratulation let us see clearly whither we are tending. Increase in population and in wealth past a certain point means simply an approximation to the condition of older countries—the Eastern States and Europe. Would the average Californian prefer to "take his chances" in New York or Massachusetts, or in California as it is and has been? Is England, with her population of twenty millions to an area not more than one-third that of our State, and a wealth which per inhabitant is six or seven times that of California, a better country than California to live in? Probably, if one were born a duke or a factory lord, or to any place among the upper ten thousand; but if one were born among the lower millions—how then?

And so the California of the future—the California of the new era—will be a better country for some classes than the California of the present; and so too, it must be a worse country for others. . . .

The truth is, that the completion of the railroad and the consequent great increase of business and population, will not be a benefit to all of us, but only to a portion. As a general rule (liable of course to exceptions) those who *have* it will make wealthier; for those who *have not*, it will make it more difficult to get. Those who have lands, mines, established businesses, special abilities of certain kinds, will become richer for it and find increased opportunities; those who have only their own labor will become poorer, and find it harder to get ahead—first, because it will take more capital to buy land or to get into business; and second, because as competition reduces the wages of labor, this capital will be harder for them to obtain.

Leland Stanford, Testimony Before the U.S. Pacific Railway Commission, 1887

By 1887 Leland Stanford had spent almost two years as a United States Senator. In order to support the railroad argument that they were losing money, Senator Stanford testified before a U.S. Senate committee on the role of the Central Pacific and Southern Pacific in the California economy. He used this testimony to argue that the railroad was the chief benefactor for the California economy. Criticism of the railroad was a particularly vexing subject for Stanford. So he did his best to answer the charges that the railroad abused its relationship with the federal government. In an act of monumental poor taste, Stanford not only defended the railroad but he had a public be damned attitude about corruption charges.

Never a retiring individual, Stanford's testimony before the U.S. Pacific Railway Commission suggests his frontier business spirit. He was not only defending the railroad against the "Goo-Goos," as the reformers were known, but he also let everyone know that the Golden State's prosperity was due to railroad business. As one of the founders of the Central Pacific, Stanford was incensed with the heavy criticism of the Big 4 and he was uncomfortable with the term Robber Baron. As he spoke before the Senate, Stanford emphasized that the Pacific Railroad Act of 1862 helped to set the stage for the growth of the railroad empire. It was money well spent by the federal government, Stanford argued, and never did the railroad abuse its financial position. In Stanford's view the Central Pacific railroad "has shown how the national domain can be utilized." Stanford's argument was that prosperity in the Golden State was solely due to the railroad.

Another aspect of Stanford's testimony was that the Central Pacific was a public service bringing the country together. He also concluded that freight and passenger rates were low. The Central Pacific and Southern Pacific transportation facilities, if one could believe Stanford, was little more than a public service. The self serving testimony did little to sway the Big 4's critics and it was long before state and federal regulation ended the railroad's malevolent political and economic practices.

In his testimony Leland Stanford defended a transportation system that offered rebates to large shippers and literally robbed small shippers through high freight rates. The damage had been done, no one believed that the railroad was a public service or deserved more tax breaks or federal funds. So Stanford's testimony turned out to be a countervailing one. Reform and regulation of the railroad was just around the corner and no one could defend railroad practices.

From **U.S. Pacific Railway Commission. Testimony Taken by the United States Pacific Railway Commission Appointed Under the act of Congress Approved March 3, 1887, Entitled "An Act Authorizing an Investigation of the Books, Accounts, and Methods of Railroads Which Have Received Aid from the United States."** Senate Executive Doc. 51, 50th Cong., 1st sess. Washington D.C.: Government Printing Office, 1887, pp. 2465–2466.

The Public Be Damned

The Pacific Railroad has accomplished all the good, both local and national, that was predicted by its most enthusiastic supporters. It has demonstrated the possibility of the construction of a transcontinental road; it has proved to the financial world that the great interior abounds in resources; it has made it possible for the construction of other transcontinental roads, with numerous branches and feeders; it has shown how the national domain can be utilized; it has encouraged the development of the natural resources of California, and shown that its products of fruits and wines can be transported to the Atlantic States by rail. It was the first enterprise anywhere in the world which made possible the habitation of regions of country far remote from navigable waters, and has added untold millions of wealth to the nation. It has performed the public service so faithfully and expeditiously as almost to annihilate the distance between the Pacific and the Atlantic, and bring the whole country into close and intimate political, social, and commercial relations. It has performed the government service in transportation of mails, materials, and supplies, to the complete satisfaction of all Government officers having charge of such business.

While the company has been spending all its energies in furnishing to the Government and the people every possible facility at the lowest possible rate for transportation, Congress has at times, through a misapprehension of the facts, appeared exacting and unjust. . . .

It was supposed when the company accepted the terms [of the Thurman Act of 1878] and entered into the contracts with the Government that the United States would take into consideration the circumstances under which the road was constructed, the difficulties encountered in its construction, and the great benefits accruing to the Government by its increased facilities in mail service and transportation, and allow it a like compensation to that formerly paid for the service when performed by teams and pack animals. The company, instead of receiving four millions per annum, which would have been its reasonable compensation, has, in fact, received not more than one-eighth of that amount.

The Chinese in California

by Henryk Sienkiewicz and the Notion That Chinese Labor Is a Danger to California Society

Henryk Sienkiewicz was a Polish immigrant who settled in Anaheim. In 1876, this small predominantly agricultural area south of Los Angeles had few settlers. It was a sea of orange groves with small farms and it was a haven for Chinese workers. The area also attracted European immigrants who often clashed with the Chinese. Not only was land inexpensive but there was opportunity to grow and sell agricultural goods in a booming economy. Unfortunately, the Polish settlers who bought this land could not compete with the more skilled Chinese labor.

For two years, Sienkiewicz attempted to establish a utopian colony. Unfamiliar with the needs of California agriculture, the Polish were not able to properly market their goods. As a result, this effort at communal agricultural production was not only a disaster but Sienkiewicz found that Chinese workers dominated the market. In a rage, he began writing local history. In his reminiscences, written in Polish, the highly literate Sienkiewicz blames the Chinese for the plight of the white worker. He writes that business had an advantage over the common worker. The Chinese, according to Sienkiewicz' numerous histories provided not only cheap labor but they were manipulated in the job market by unscrupulous labor contractors and monopolistic business interests. The common worker, Sienkiewicz argues, became violently opposed to Chinese labor. This document is an excellent contemporary account of how the common person viewed the Chinese in the late nineteenth century.

Let us now look at the kind of work the Chinese perform in California. A single word describes it accurately: everything. A significant proportion of them has turned to agriculture. The whole of San Francisco is situated on arid dunes and sandy hills, and yet whoever goes to the outskirts of the city will perceive at the ends of unfinished streets, on the hills, valleys, and slopes, on the roadsides, in fact, everywhere, small vegetable gardens encircling the city with one belt of greenness. The ant-like labor of the Chinese has transformed the sterile sand into the most fertile black earth. How and when this was accomplished they alone can tell, but suffice it to say that all the fruits and vegetables, raspberries and strawberries, under the care of Chinese gardeners grow to a fabulous size. I have seen strawberries as large as small pears, heads of cabbage four times the size of European heads, and pumpkins the size of our wash tubs. . . .

[T]he whole of San Francisco lives on the fruits and vegetables bought from the Chinese. Every morning you see their loaded wagons headed toward the markets in the center of town or stopping in front of private homes. It may even be

Henryk Sienkiewicz, "The Chinese in California: A Report," unpublished manuscript written in Polish. Originally appeared in the Warsaw Gazette, Jan 19–29, 1878.

said that in all of California this branch of industry has passed exclusively into the hands of the Chinese. . . .

A large number of Chinese likewise work for white farmers, especially in the orchards. . . . In the vicinity of San Francisco and in Alameda County along the railroad are whole orchards of apple trees, pear trees, peach trees, and almond trees; here and there fields comprising scores of acres are covered with red currant bushes; near Sacramento are extensive hop-gardens. The work on these fields and in these orchards is done almost exclusively by hired Chinese. . . .

In the cultivation of grain in northern California the Chinese cannot compete with the whites. For plowing, harrowing, and harvesting, the white worker, being twice as strong, is much more in demand, for he works faster and with greater energy. Where there are no whites, however, Chinese are used even for these jobs.

In southern California where vineyards abound, there, too, very few Chinese are employed. In this area Mexican and Indian laborers, who are as strong as the Yankees and who work as cheaply as the Chinese, are easily obtainable. . . .

[I]n the cities . . . [t]hey are engaged in business; in the factories they serve as laborers; they are hired by the owners of handicraft shops; in the hotels they perform all the more menial tasks; in private homes they are responsible for orderliness and cleanliness. In restaurants and on the railroads they serve as cooks and waiters. Practically all of the laundries in town are in their hands and it must be admitted that they do the laundry neatly, quickly, and cheaply. They serve as nurses for children. In a private home the Chinaman fulfils [*sic*] all of the duties of a maid; he puts things away, sweeps the floors, makes the beds, cooks the meals, washes the dishes, and does the shopping in town; he is a quiet, sober, industrious, gentle, and obedient servant, and he costs much less than a white servant. Ever since the Chinese have become numerous in California, all prices have declined considerably. Everything from the cigars wrapped by Chinese hands to items of food—everything now costs less because the cost of labor is less. . . .

Taking these things into consideration, one might deem the Chinese a blessing to California were it not for the keen competition they create for the white working-class. . . . A white man . . . requires more food and better living quarters instead of suffocating with a score of others in one hole. Finally, a white worker usually has a family, wife and children, whereas the Chinaman is alone. . . . The result is that if the Chinese are a blessing at all it is only for the wealthy classes who need servants and workers. In the conflict between capital and labor the Chinese have tipped the scales decisively in favor of capital. Even though white workers should offer their services more cheaply, some employers would prefer Chinese . . . as workers who are not fellow citizens but half-slaves, quiet, obedient, and docile . . . and as they become more numerous, they begin to create dangerous competition for small business, small farmers, and small industries.

WORKSHEET 6: The Railroad, The Chinese Question and Monopoly

1. When the transcontinental railroad was completed on May 10, 1869 there were many changes in California. Describe three of them:

    1. _____

    2. _____

    3. _____

2. How did the economic conditions surrounding the completion of the transcontinental

    railroad create anti-Chinese sentiment? _____

    _____

    _____

3. Explain the roots of anti-Chinese sentiment _____

    _____

    _____

4. The "Credit-Ticket" system is _____

5. The chief importer of Chinese labor was _____

6. The **Alta Californian's** attitude toward the Chinese was _____

7. The second phase of the Foreign Miners' Tax Law was directed against _____

8. The People v. Hall in 1854 resulted in _____

9. The 14th amendment was important to the rise of racism in California because it

    _____

    _____

10. The Civil Rights Act of 1870 is important because it _____

_____

11. Denis Kearney was important because he _____

_____

12. The Workingmen's Party was important because it _____

_____

_____

13. The Lyceum of Self Culture helped to further the career of _____

14. Why is July 23, 1877 a major turning point in California history? _____

_____

15. The pamphlet "The Labor Agitators or The Battle For Bread" suggests that _____

_____

16. Henry George's attitude on the completion of the railroad was _____

_____

17. Leland Stanford's testimony emphasized _____

18. Henryk Sienkiewicz's attitude toward the Chinese was _____

_____

19. The Constitution of 1879's attitude toward the Chinese was _____

_____

California Civilization, 1900–1930: Reform or Reaction?

READINGS: RUDOLPH M. LAPP, *"A YOUNG WOMAN OF ADVANCED IDEAS: MABEL CRAFT DEERING"* EARL POMEROY, *"THE CALIFORNIA PROGRESSIVES"* HOWARD A. DEWITT, *"ETHNIC AND ALIEN IMAGES IN CALIFORNIA HISTORY"* CAREY MCWILLIAMS, *"SISTER AIMEE AND THE GREEN RELIGION"*

The California Progressive Movement created the prospect of honest government and highly qualified candidates for public office. By 1910 the Progressives seized control of the Republican party and Hiram Johnson was elected governor. He inaugurated a series of governmental reforms, including the initiative, referendum and recall, and created direct popular democracy.

After consulting with former President Theodore Roosevelt, Johnson delivered an inaugural with an 11 Point legislative program. This prompted the chaplain of the California legislature to remark: "Even Christ only had ten points." This remark illustrates the tension and hostility that the Progressives brought to California politics. Despite their carefully argued programs for reform, the Progressives appeared to have a program that was politically contradictory. They regulated big business, sought more social service money, and talked about honest government. There was also an ugly side to the new governor as Johnson was hostile privately to women's rights, helped push a land law through the State Legislature depriving the Japanese of ownership of farm land and was generally hostile to ethnic minorities. Johnson, like many Progressives, supported labor legislation out of fear. He believed that labor unions might erupt into violence if labor laws were not enacted.

With an iron hand Governor Johnson convinced the California legislature of 1911 to pass legislation regulating the railroad industry, controlling public utilities and implementing more than 150 new laws. In time these devices isolated the Democratic party and prevented serious opposition to the Progressives until the late 1930s. A well organized and finely tuned political machine emerged to crush any changes sought by the Democratic party. The Progressives saw themselves as the guardians of American democracy.

Because of fears of Asian immigrants, Governor Johnson was instrumental in the passage of the Alien Land Law of 1913. He wrote a series of private messages, ghost wrote the bill and generally persuaded politicians to vote for it. When the Alien Land Law passed the California Senate by a vote of 35 to 2 and the Assembly by a 72 to 3 vote, Johnson piously announced that he would sign the bill. He didn't want to frustrate the will of the people. Johnson's subtle racism was not lost on his opponents, and they attempted to demonstrate that the Progressives had an ugly racial side. There were few people who cared about this argument.

In defense of California Progressives, historians point to their model of governmental efficiency. This Progressive program blended scientific government with fiscal conservatism. Since many Progressives were newspapermen they realized that the force of public opinion was a potent political weapon. As a result Progressives manipulated the public by campaigning on a program supporting women's rights. When women were granted the vote in 1911, Governor Johnson appointed Katherine Phillips Edson to the Bureau of Labor Statistics and then to the Industrial Welfare Commission. Privately, Governor Johnson was suspicious of women's rights. As a politician, however, he favored suffrage for women and appointed a number to public office. Johnson's private doubts and public approval of women participating in California political life highlighted a fundamental contradiction in Progressive politics.

Women became a part of California politics in 1907 when a political pressure group, the Lincoln-Roosevelt League, was formed to elect a progressive governor. Katherine Phillips Edson was one of many women in this organization who urged immediate suffrage. Edson campaigned effectively for Johnson in 1910, and she was named to political office. Edson's career continued until her death in 1933 and she was responsible for legislation allowing the Industrial Welfare Commission to investigate working conditions and report on wages paid. Many of the abuses involving women and children in the work place ended due to her persistence. For more than two decades she worked for laws to protect the labor force. She was also an advocate of women's rights. In 1923, when the first Equal Rights Amendment was introduced in the U.S. Congress, Edson was a strong supporter of this constitutional amendment.

Although Katherine Phillips Edson was the best known female political appointee, Mabel Craft Deering was an equally important figure. Not only was

Deering a strong supporter of full political rights for women but she argued that the Colored Women's Clubs should become part of the General Federation of Women's Clubs. As a progressive feminist, Mabel Craft Deering incorporated civil rights concerns with feminist politics. This helped more visible women like Katherine Phillips Edson to make their mark in California politics.

In 1901 the **San Francisco Examiner** called Mabel Clare Craft "a young woman of advanced ideas." Not only was she 29 and single, the **Examiner** observed, but she was a strong advocate of civil rights as well as a respected journalist. In 1899 Craft became the Sunday editor of the **San Francisco Chronicle**. Not only was she the first woman to achieve this position but she attracted attention for her feminist speeches and writings. Craft was in demand as a public speaker because of a messianic female she called Corona. This alter ego allowed Craft to use a fictitious person to develop a feminist approach to political and social issues.

Although her career was a varied and complex one, Mabel Craft Deering's main contribution was in advancing the rights of black women. Professor Rudolph M. Lapp of the College of San Mateo has studied her career in detail and concludes that she was California's earliest feminist civil rights advocate. Although Mrs. Deering didn't possess the political power of Katherine Phillips Edson, she did highlight feminist progressivism and a commitment to social issues. Professor Lapp suggests Mrs. Deering was a political reformer "who also remembered the underdogs in life." An advanced liberal with a penchant for publicity, Mrs. Deering is one of the best examples of Progressivism's social conscience.

There was also a conservative side to Progressivism. In 1911, John F. Neylan was appointed head of a new state government agency, the California Board of Control. The 26 year old Neylan, a **San Francisco Bulletin** reporter, chaired a board which zealously reviewed government spending and inventoried state property. Neylan's conspiratorial mind poisoned state politics and he introduced a heavy handed brand of political conservatism. The investigative skills of Neylan's office led to the indictment of 16 government officials on embezzlement charges. Since Neylan believed in the principles of scientific management, he was a compulsive nit picker. The California State Board of Control was delegated the power to prepare a comprehensive budget and general inventory of state property. This began a tradition of allowing specialists to recommend spending levels and a portion of the politicians power was surrendered to these advocates of scientific government.

Neylan's supporters defended his work as essential. In 1910 the California legislature passed a tax on the gross income of corporations, and the California Board of Control verified the collection of these taxes. For years the railroad had bribed county tax assessors and escaped paying property taxes.

Neylan's agency made sure this did not happen with corporate taxes and for that reason he was a maligned and unpopular figure. Like many Progressives, Neylan had a conservative political side which exposed a jekyl-hyde personality. The domination of big business in the California cities created new opportunities for graft and corruption. So the California Progressive was inordinately concerned with urban influences.

The role of the city was a significant factor in the rise of California reform politics. Professor Earl Pomeroy's seminal study, **The Pacific Slope**, is a pioneering history of the American West which suggests that "urban society" created a politico with education, income and a strong and often hostile feeling toward big business. Hiram Johnson's first political act was to campaign against his fathers bid for reelection to the U.S. House of Representatives. Because his father was a tool of the Southern Pacific railroad, Johnson urged voters to defeat his dad. There was a moralistic tone to Progressivism which transcended loyalty to family, culture and religion. There was a fanatical obsession with condemning the railroad and those who worked for it.

Chester Rowell, the editor of the **Fresno Republican**, suggested that the railroad had taken politicians hostage. For years reformers were frustrated by manipulative corporate activity and, as a result, were overly zealous in their quest for good government. Professor Pomeroy argues that a broad liberal mandate helped California Progressives establish one of the finest reform programs in American politics.

When Governor William D. Stephens succeeded Hiram W. Johnson in March, 1917, anti-radicalism gripped California. Until the onset of the Great Depression, the political climate in the Golden State suffered from right-wing reaction. In an article on ethnic and alien images in California History, Howard A. DeWitt of Ohlone College traces the manner in which politicians used anti-radicalism to frustrate labor unions, political radicals and ideological reformers. The conservatives in State government also passed the Criminal Syndicalism Law of 1919 to control political dissent. This was followed by the rise of right wing organization like the Better America Federation which created an artificial patriotism and squelched political dissent. The Los Angeles Police Department created the Red Squad to chase the politically undesirable out of California and traditional constitutional rights suffered in the Golden State. As DeWitt suggests in his conclusion, images of ethnic and alien forces were used to stifle free speech. Throughout the 1920s, anti-radicalism prevented labor, ethnic workers, Socialists, Communists, and other dissidents from enjoying guaranteed constitutional rights.

Religion wasn't Sister Aimee's only contribution as she became a major Los Angeles political force. But it was McPherson's theatrical flair that inspired a multi-million dollar business empire. She was a genius in using the media and the publicity surrounding her eccentric lifestyle drew millions of followers. Until her death in 1945, Sister Aimee appealed to the handicapped, the alcoholic destitute, the recent Oakie and Arkie migrants, the elderly and those who found it difficult to adjust to Los Angeles life. Carey McWilliams, one of California's finest historians and journalists, offers a brief account of Sister Aimee Semple McPherson's personality. In his description of Sister Aimee, McWilliams analyzes California eccentricity.

A Young Woman of Advanced Ideas:
Mabel Craft Deering

by Rudolph M. Lapp

The Progressive Era in California witnessed the flowering of liberalism and the rise of popular democracy. Women were an integral part of the Progressive dream and they pursued it with zeal. In California Governor Hiram W. Johnson sought political support from women and he brought them into the political mainstream. The selection of Katherine Phillips Edson to head the Industrial Welfare Commission was an example of the Progressives commitment to women.

Professor Rudolph M. Lapp of the College of San Mateo provides an essay, "A Young Woman of Advanced Ideas: Mabel Craft Deering," which highlights the accomplishments of a woman who was in the vanguard of feminist activity. As a professional journalist, Mabel Craft Deering established an enviable reputation as the Sunday editor of the San Francisco Chronicle long before women were in the mainstream of the economy.

In addition to her fame as a working journalist, Mrs. Deering was an advocate of full women's rights. She was a sought after speaker who never failed to entertain and educate her audience. As an advanced feminist speaker, Mabel Craft Deering used a messianic female she labelled Corona to state her feminist ideas. Using this channeling effect, Deering became one of the most sought after speakers in California. Professor Lapp provides a case study of Mabel Craft Deering and suggests her influence paved the way for future feminist triumphs.

When the *San Francisco Examiner* on its front page in 1901 called Mabel Clare Craft ". . . a young woman of advanced ideas . . ." she was twenty-nine and single and had already made her mark. The occasion for the *Examiner's* reference to Mabel Craft was a lengthy article the newspaper ran on the debates within the General Federation of Women's clubs over the question of the admission of "colored" women and "Colored Women's Clubs." On this painfully divisive issue Craft took the courageous position that admission should be supported. But more later on the debate itself.

This article is an attempt to restore for the present generation, the memory of an outstanding progressive feminist and successful career woman of an earlier generation. One may guess that by the middle of this century Mabel Craft Deering's contemporaries were already unaware of her progressive leadership before World War I. Even her son-in-law was unaware of her struggle over the black issue in the women's clubs until this writer approached him.

To flesh out the image of Mabel Craft Deering as a turn-of-the-century progressive, one must go back a number of years.

Rudolph M. Lapp, MABEL CRAFT DEERING: A YOUNG WOMAN OF ADVANCED IDEAS. Reprinted with permission from *California History* magazine, September 1987 issue, Vol. LXVI, No. 3.

Mabel Clare Craft was born in Rochelle, Illinois, and came as a child with her parents to California, eventually settling in Oakland. She entered the University of California in Berkeley and graduated in 1892. It is at this point that one becomes aware of her outstanding ability. Her academic record was the highest in that graduating class but the medal that was awarded to such accomplished graduates was given only to men. In an unusual turn of events the male graduate who was to receive the medal refused it and stated that Mabel Craft should get it. That medal remains unclaimed somewhere on the Berkeley campus. If the papers of Mabel Craft Deering had survived, we might discover how important that incident was in shaping her into a self-conscious feminist.

Although Mabel Craft contemplated a legal career after leaving Berkeley and did graduate from Hastings Law School in 1895, she never practiced law. The field of journalism soon absorbed her talents. As one account has it she approached Michael de Young of the *San Francisco Chronicle* for a job as a reporter and was treated indifferently by him. However, he did (perhaps as whimsy) tell her to talk to his wife. If Mrs. de Young responded well to her, he would hire Craft. Mrs. de Young liked her, and Mabel got the job.

As a *Chronicle* reporter Mabel found herself in a distinguished company of reporters including Will Irwin of later national journalistic fame. From Irwin we get our first personal and flattering description of Craft. He wrote,

Tall, handsome, vital Mabel Clare Craft had taken high honors in scholarship at the University of California, had become an ardent feminist and had deliberately started out to prove her theories by adopting a profession wherein she could compete with men on their own hard terms. In the days of her apprenticeship, a newspaper had only three niches for a woman society, fashions and sobsisterhood. Scorning all three, she made herself a first-class reporter who could match wits with any man in pursuit of a story.

Ishbel Ross, a historian of woman reporters, verified Irwin's claim that Craft could match and exceed male intrepitude in the reporting of an important story. She wrote,

. . . back in the nineties Mabel Craft, of the San Francisco Chronicle, *led a squad of men in a leaky launch through the Golden Gate to meet the ships returning from the Spanish-American War. The* Examiner *crew was already under way in a fine large tug. A storm was raging, they were warned that their launch would sink, but Miss Craft insisted on going ahead. . . . The men called a council and overrode her. Miss Craft took it with grace, conducted her expedition ashore, and hastily chartered a seaworthy tag. They started off again and met the ships. They wrote their stories on the way in, with the tug lurching under them. Their editors were frantic by the time they showed up, waving their copy in their hands. It was the story of the year and they made it by a margin of minutes.*

When Mabel Craft prevented the *Examiner* from scooping the *Chronicle*, she was already recognized as an important journalist. Just previously she had been sent to Hawaii to cover the American annexations. Her articles were published by major newspapers from coast to coast.

They were later published in a book in which she wrote in greater detail about the experience. Her introduction to this small volume makes it clear that anti-imperialism was a part of her progressivism. Recognizing that her sentiments would not be popular with many, she wrote,

> *I do not believe that might necessarily makes right, and I have but reflected the political sentiments of the majority of Hawaiians as I found them during the summer of annexation, when hearts were peculiarly stirred by the culmination of an injustice that amounted to crime.*

She went on,

> *In Hawaii is the old spirit that abides in unhappy Poland, that burns in the breasts of Alsace-Lorraine. The looting of the Hawaiian monarchy by a few Americans was a sort of successful Jameson raid, and not an exploit over which any American need thrill with pride.*

The reference above to "unhappy Poland" brings to mind an incident in Craft's early reporting days. When Ignace Paderewski arrived in San Francisco for his first piano concert just before the turn of the century, Craft was determined to gain an interview with him. He refused to see any reporters but she literally parked herself on his doorstep until he was forced to see her. One can imagine his change of attitude when he saw this strikingly attractive and intelligent young woman. He not only granted her an interview but they became very good friends and remained so for many years. Craft's future husband, Frank Deering, an attorney, served as Paderewski's law-

yer when ever the great pianist needed legal assistance in San Francisco.

By 1899 Mabel Craft became the Sunday editor of the *Chronicle*, the first woman to achieve this status in the country. It was noted in the journalistic world from coast to coast.

The prominence she achieved in the Bay area gave Craft the opportunity to gain a wider audience not only in newspapers but also on the speaking platform and in a variety of publications. The issues of feminism were her persistent themes. But her progressivism was not of a single-issue kind. In 1901 she was invited to speak to the University of California Club of Oakland. Her address was a challenge to the audience whom she asked to imagine that she was speaking in the year 2051, a century and a half later. This futuristic foray "looked back" at the dismal year of 1901. In a Bellamy-esque presentation, Craft spelled out bitter criticisms of that period's progressives. She spoke of the selfishness and materialism of the "earlier" period and how the peacemakers were called traitors. And she spoke of women who could bear sons who could become good citizens but "might never become a citizen herself." The economic system was also part of her eloquent Jeremiad. She said,

> *Commerce was the thing not as we know it, the exchanging of product for product that all men might have their share of what the earth yields, but a fierce and insatiable striving after wealth through trading at the largest possible profit. A nation's welfare was measured by the excess of what it sold over what it bought, and commerce dominated the earth, making its laws and making its wars.*

Craft brought feminism into her speech in a unique manner. The new era that her speech was fantasizing had been initiated by a messianic female she called Corona. From Corona came the inspiration and wisdom of the new age that Craft's audience was asked to pretend they were living in.

By 1902 Mabel Clare Craft, now firmly entrenched in her position as the Sunday editor of the *San Francisco Chronicle*, entered into an unexpected field of controversy. As an active member of the Forum Club of San Francisco (one of the many women's clubs of the city) she became involved in the national debate on the "color question." The women's club movement was fairly new as a national movement and its national conventions marked the first time since the Civil War that northern and southern white women had come together in shared concern over many social, community, and cultural issues affecting white women. The temperance and suffrage organizations were older and also national, but they were single-issue organizations. And, the reader must be reminded, this was a period when many white Americans felt that the issues of the Civil War should be put behind and a "reunion" of North and South should be encouraged, bitterness not revived. Into this setting the divisive issue of "colored" women in the women's clubs emerged.

This "reunion" mood was occurring simultaneously with the better known brace of concerns called Progressivism. Historians have agreed that defining this term has its difficulties because of the great diversity displayed by followers of its tenets from one part of the country to the other. But there is agreement that the least of these concerns was the plight of blacks in this nadir of Afro-American history. Not since the Civil War era had white Californians been concerned with matters that involved Afro-Americans. At that time blacks were struggling for equal rights before the courts and in 1863, during the temporary idealism of the Civil War, they achieved it in California. In 1870 California blacks gained the vote through the Fifteenth Amendment to the Constitution (not through state law), and concerned whites in the state felt that all was done that needed doing for blacks.

In the decades that followed, a small northern black middle class emerged nationally as well as in California and by the beginning of the twentieth century would be pressuring for entry into mainstream white America's institutions. Progressive sensitivity to this need was in short supply. However, there were a few exceptions in a few major metropolitan centers in the north and some breakthroughs were achieved as a result of the valiant efforts of some progressive-minded whites. In California, Mabel Craft was such a progressive white.

The issue of black admission to the white women's club federation emerged in 1900 at the national convention of the General Federation of Women's Clubs in Milwaukee, Wisconsin. The occasion for this question was the presence at the convention of a black woman, Josephine St. Pierre Ruffin, wife of a black Boston judge, who was there as a delegate from both a Boston white women's club and a black women's club that was a member of the state federation of Massachusetts. Southern pressure resulted in the rejection of her delegacy as a member of the black club, but she was accepted as a member of the white club. Under these circumstances Mrs. Ruffin refused to remain at the convention. In the months that followed, the southern clubs presented a proposal initiated by the Georgia federation to include the word "white" in the GFWC constitution as qualification for membership. This was to be presented at the next national convention. In 1902 in Los Angeles the national "color question" debate was on. That was when Mabel Craft entered the picture as a proponent of black admission to membership in the General Federation of Women's Clubs.

The question of black women in the General Federation of Women's Clubs was contested in several steps in California. The first was the individual club debates in the last months of 1901, the second took place at the San Francisco convention of the California clubs in February 1902, and the last was at the national convention of GFWC which was hosted by Los Angeles in May 1902. Incidentally, this was the first GFWC convention in the far West.

Many, perhaps most of the California clubs, appeared to shy away from the subject but in Los Angeles and in San Francisco full-scale debates took place. There were many women who opposed black membership in the GFWC, but a group of articulate and courageous women in the Bay area argued for open membership based on education and cultural level, and Mabel Clare Craft led the way.

The *San Francisco Examiner* ran a front page headline that read "The 'Color Line' Excites the Ladies" with a picture of Craft. The story said of her,

In a spirited debate Wednesday Miss Mabel Craft stood forth as a champion of social equality of colored women.

Calling Craft, ". . . a bright student of sociology . . ." the *Examiner* printed some of her argument which was,

The difference between the negro and the caucasian, was not one of intellect, but rather of climate and the unrelenting rays of the African sun.

On other debates she said,

The color line is drawn by prejudice. I cannot see where the white skinned man or woman is superior to the dark skinned race unless he or she acts in a superior manner. I would rather know a decent, intelligent dark skinned person than know an indecent white.

Further she said,

This color question is one of great interest to women just now throughout the country. Many ladies who are intellectual, sympathetic and lovable have an inherent prejudice against the negro. I can't reconcile this prejudice with twentieth century logic or our boasted progress in civilization.

She also stated that she believed that she shared with President Theodore Roosevelt the opinion that as a citizen of America, Booker T. Washington and others of his race should have "entree into all polite circles—white, black, or yellow." Given the somewhat Victorian flavor of her remarks and even perhaps some naivete about Teddy Roosevelt, Mabel Craft was for that time well ahead of her contemporaries in opposing racism.

The month of November, 1901, was heavy with women's club debates in the Bay area. They seemed to reach a climax at the debate before the Philomath Club.

Although this club had an all-Jewish membership, Mabel Craft was invited there to team with a Philomath member in supporting black admission to the GFWC. The Philomath member was Mrs. Florence Prag Kahn, who several decades later succeeded her husband, Julius Kahn, in the Congress of the United States.

In this debate Craft developed her position and revealed some of the depth of her feeling. She claimed that the South had retarded its own growth by its subjection of Negroes and that the perceptions of the women's clubs should be broad and not narrow. She also said what must have been a shocker to the audience. "... if we cannot find it in our hearts to do what we can to help the colored women, why, we had better break up our Federation."

Craft's team-mate, Mrs. Kahn, took a softer line, saying that she was not making a plea for social recognition but rather as American women the clubs should "... extend a helping hand to women who, in spite of their color, were striving to lift themselves. ...." She added, "They seek admission into our Federation on their own merit and not to be accepted as a gratuity to an inferior race."

Clear-cut club decisions in this controversy do not emerge, but the general impression is that hard decisions were left up in the air or were unsympathetic to admission. The latter becomes more apparent at the state convention in San Francisco.

Mabel Craft's major efforts on this racial justice question appear to have been devoted to the preconvention period. When the state convention took place in February, 1902, much of the behind-the-scenes work had been done, and the re-sult was a compromise position that would not have required the southern state clubs to admit black women. However, it should be noted that a few Bay area women, led by Mrs. Gertrude Haight, continued vainly to make the case for black admission. Perhaps the progressive pragmatist in Mabel Craft was showing through. Even Caroline Severance, the venerated octogenarian club woman of Los Angeles, often called the "Mother of Clubs," a woman of abolitionist roots, decided not to push the matter.

Three months after the state convention, when the national convention of the GFWC took place in Los Angeles, the "color question" was a lively topic in corridor discussion, but it never came to the floor as a divisive issue. The mood of "reunion" was maintained. With this muting of the admission question northern and southern women were left to admit black women or not as they wished in each locality. Mabel Craft, however, had stood out as the foremost California protagonist for black admission before the state convention. One can imagine more contemporary gatherings where such a clearly defined point of view would have resulted in some form of rejection. At the public level this certainly did not happen; in fact Craft received honors at this convention on another matter.

At the national convention session on education Craft presented a paper entitled "The Advantages of Coeducation" that was so well received that it was printed in its entirety in *Club Life*, the California state organ of the women's clubs. It was called the most brilliant paper presented at the convention. In this paper, which must have been as easy to listen to as it is to read, Craft, with with, humor, logic, and irony made her point that coeducation at every level would make for better men and women. She punctured the apprehensions of the illogical and the opposition of the prejudiced. In one of her choice lines she said,

I believe, of course, that it is the normal form of education that boys and girls, since nature was so rash as to plant them side by side in families, are best educated when, in grammar days, in the high school, in the university, and later in the real school of life itself, they are educated side by side.

This lengthy statement was evoked by attempts to roll back some of the gains made by women in the field of coeducation in the universities. At this time, however, the University of California and Stanford were among those that did admit women students.

Craft also stated that much yet needed to be accomplished in the appointment of women to the faculties and governing boards of the systems of higher education. A few years earlier Craft had written a piece for the *University of California Magazine* that illustrates her gentle style of irony when dealing with feminist issues. The occasion for the article was a discussion of a proposal that students raise a fund for a fountain in honor of the first woman regent of the University, Phoebe Apperson Hearst. Concurrently Mrs. Hearst was preparing architectural plans for University expansion that were evidently considered by some to be in the fantasy stage. Craft used this article to say that Mrs. Hearst's plans would not be a vague notion but would become reality since the Senator's wife was a person of her word. But Craft went on with a gentle dig saying,

I noted the other evening when the speakers at the student reception to President Wheeler were alluding politely to the new plans as though they were nebulous dreams, that Mrs. Hearst smiled quietly, much as she smiles when millionare regents wrangle for an hour over a fifty dollar bill for lights. On such occasion the one woman regent quietly remarks, "Gentlemen, allow me to subscribe the amount." Mrs. Hearst is used to cutting gordian knots and practical men of means will be glad to follow her lead.

In November, 1902, Mabel Clare Craft became Mabel Craft Deering. Her husband was Frank P. Deering, a prominent lawyer who for many years served on the Board of Directors of the San Francisco Symphony and at one time was the president of the Bohemian Club. The couple was very much a part of the social and cultural life of the city, however, as newlyweds their first public appearance together might have been at the gathering in January, 1903, of the most liberal elements of the Bay area.

The occasion for this gathering was the presence in California of the already famed black educator, Booker T. Washington. He was in the state on a two-week fundraising tour for the black school, the Tuskegee Institute, which he had founded. One of the events planned for Washington on this tour was an elegantly arranged banquet organized by the women of the Unitarian Club of California. The assemblage was prestigious enough to make the social column of one daily newspaper, and the names mentioned bore out its liberal character. Among them were Frank P. and Mabel Craft Deering.

In 1904, a daughter was born to the Deerings and named Francesca. She would be their only child. For a few years

Mrs. Deering was out of public life, but the suffragist movement would shortly call upon her talents and energies.

Back in 1895 Susan B. Anthony paid a visit to California shortly before her death. She came to the state to give heart to the 1895–96 campaign for women's suffrage which ended in defeat because of the San Francisco and Oakland male vote. While in San Francisco she sat for a picture with seven local activists. Seated with them was Mabel Craft who appeared to be the youngest of the group.

Mabel Craft Deering's re-entry into the suffragist movement a decade after the 1896 defeat is best told in her own words.

Mrs. Austin Sperry, the then president of the California State Suffrage Association, had asked me several times previous to 1906 to take the press chairmanship as I had been a newspaper woman. I had always selfishly refused on the ground that I was too busy.

After the earthquake and fire in San Francisco in 1906 I found myself with more time on my hands than I had ever had before or ever expect to have again. There were no streetcars or telephones in the city; almost everyone I knew had left town for places where more comforts were to be had; I had lived on a little island entirely surrounded by miles of burnt homes; there were no theatres, no parties, no distractions of any kind. Feeling it our duty to remain in the city during the reconstruction period I said to myself, "what can I do for suffrage?" and the press work occurred to me. I told Mrs. Sperry I would undertake it and was at once appointed press chairman for the entire state.

The "little island" Mrs. Deering refers to was her home at the end of Larkin Street which overlooks the Bay and is still standing today.

The above words were taken from Mrs. Deering's post-victory report on press work during the 1911 campaign. As one proceeds through this report it becomes clear that it was not only a narration of the most important details associated with any large scale electoral campaign but was also a readable guide for suffrage campaigners in any state. It should be remembered that in the vast majority of the states of the Union women did not yet have the vote. In her report called "Cooperative Enterprises," a narration of the field work of women campaigners, Mrs. Deering was justifying the use of skilled women campaigners from other states. This was evidently a bone of contention with some of the California women. She commented,

It is true, undoubtedly, that a mediocre local woman can often do more effective work than a brilliant woman who knows nothing of local conditions, but when all is said and done there is always a dearth of workers at the end of a campaign. It is a question of outside workers or none. . . . I shall always feel that California would not have been carried had it not been for the time and money which our Eastern brothers and sisters gave to us so generously during the last two months. We had not the workers, our funds were rapidly exhausted; we had all of us given of time and strength and money to the limit, when this timely aid came. Let us give credit where credit was due.

In the years that followed the successful California suffrage campaign Mrs. Deering appears to have stepped back from involvement in social issues. However, since so many of the men who supported women's suffrage were supporters and members of the Lincoln-Roosevelt League, the progressive wing of the Republican Party, it stands to reason that she voted for them faithfully. While the social circles she and her husband moved in were staunchly Republican, the liberal streak in her makeup appeared in the 1930s during the Great Depression. She supported Democrat Franklin D. Roosevelt for president in 1932 and 1936. It is doubtful that her husband did likewise. When Frank Deering died, Herbert Hoover was an honorary pallbearer.

Travel was another love of Mrs. Deering's life, and according to her son-in-law, Thomas Carr Howe, Mr. and Mrs. Deering and their child traveled for six months every two years. On two of these trips she wrote travel accounts for the *National Geographic*. The first was a boat trip in China in 1927 from Shanghai to Soochow for which she took several of the pictures for the story. The second was in Korea in 1935 during the years of Japanese rule. Korean nationalists were probably not happy about her narrative, because it took a benign view of Japanese occupation and perceived it as a progressive development in Korean economic life. However, she did not fail to note that while Japanese rule modernized agriculture and increased its production, it placed half of the best Korean land in the hands of the Japanese.

According, again, to Mr. Howe, Mrs. Deering's later years were much involved in "society" and cultural activities. He also noted that she was very involved in financial matters. When she died in 1953, she left an estate of nearly a million dollars. Her obituary notice reported that she was on the board of directors of the San Francisco Opera Association and St. Luke's Hospital and was active in the San Francisco and Burlingame Country Clubs.

While Mrs. Deering did not reach the political distinction as a liberal achieved by Katherine Edson, one of her contemporaries, her contributions as a feminist progressive are an important part of the record. She represented not only a breakthrough by an exceptionally strong woman but was also symbolic of her era. This was a time when middle class women's organizations had reached a particularly high level of maturity, considerable numbers, and sophisticated organizational skills. As a role model for assertive women she is hard to match. Perhaps her later immersion in "society" was for the benefit of her daughter and granddaughter. Mrs. Deering was born into economic circumstances that were extremely modest. Her father was a failure in the world of small storekeeping.

There may have been other women of similar humble origins in her time with her ability, education, looks, and iron determination to succeed, but there were not many who also remembered the underdogs in life.

The California Progressive Movement
by Earl Pomeroy

For many years California has been considered one of the most liberal states in the Union. There is a lengthy historiographical dispute over the degree of liberalism in the Golden State. Most historians trace the reform impulse from the Progressive Era. Political reform began in California in 1910 when Progressive-Republicans elected Hiram W. Johnson governor. Professor Earl Pomeroy of the University of California, San Diego, provides an excellent analysis of the contradictions inherent in California Progressivism. He also catalogs the reforms which made the Golden State one of the leaders in honest government.

The origins of the progressive movement in California corresponded closely to the shape and strains of a rapidly growing urban society. Most of its leaders were men of substantial income and education who rebelled at the political and economic consequences of irresponsible corporate power. Dr. John R. Haynes of Los Angeles, who founded the Direct Legislation League (1895) to challenge the railroad's municipal machine, was a physician, a millionaire, a director in several corporations. The two reform mayors of San Francisco in the 1890's—a Populist and a Democrat—also were millionaires: Adolph Sutro, who had built the tunnel draining the Comstock Lode, and James D. Phelan, banker and heir to a great banking fortune. William Kent, who became probably the most progressive member of Congress from the Far West, had made his fortune in real estate in Chicago. Haynes, Phelan, and Rudolph Spreckels, another San Francisco banker and capitalist, contributed heavily to the costs of the progressives' battles for reform in their respective cities.

Such men as these, both wealthy and sensitive to the opportunities and obligations of wealth, may not have suffered much from personal frustrations, economic or social. But neither they nor the men of more moderate means who dominated the progressive movement could ignore the excesses of big business and labor and the strains between them. Progressives in Los Angeles opposed Harrison Gray Otis and the *Los Angeles Times* and also shared some of Otis's fears of organized labor. In San Francisco, labor developed a powerful distrust of reformers when Mayor Phelan's policemen rode with strike-breaking teamsters in 1901. Then the reformers in turn rebelled against Abe Ruef, boss of the Union Labor Party, who installed Eugene Schmitz, a handsome orchestra leader, as mayor to succeed Phelan and who openly collaborated with the Southern Pacific machine. Their most persuasive exhibit was a widely published photograph, captioned "The Shame of California," of the leaders at the Republican state convention at Santa Cruz in 1906: the railroad's choice

Earl Pomeroy, "The Pacific Slope," (University of Washington Press 1965) pp. 200–205. Reprinted by permission of the author.

for the governorship, Representative James N. Gillett, stood in the center with his hand resting on the shoulder of Ruef, who had received $14,000 for supporting him.

The convention that carried out the railroad's orders had hardly adjourned before the scope of misgovernment in San Francisco began to become generally visible, whether because disorders following the earthquake and fire of the preceding April had uncovered it or merely because the appetites of Ruef's minions had extended it. Just after the elections that November, a grand jury filed the first indictments against Ruef and Schmitz. And during the following winter, investigations of graft at San Francisco vied for headlines with the flagrant thievery of the machine's agents and collaborators at Sacramento in the legislature of 1907. The graft trials produced two colorful figures who dramatized the issues of reform: Francis J. Heney, the deputy district attorney, who had already made a reputation by prosecuting Senator Mitchell and others for fraud in Oregon, and Hiram W. Johnson, who became special prosecutor in November 1908, when an ex-convict shot and nearly killed Heney in the courtroom. The trials also produced a victory for the reformers in the municipal election of 1907, at a time when a seven-month-long streetcar strike, one of the most violent in American labor history, aroused labor against one of the corporations with which Ruef and the Union Labor administration had been cooperating. Full of confidence, Heney went on to turn his attention to the bribe-givers, who included President Patrick Calhoun of the United Railroads.

The prosecutors were too effective to achieve lasting reform in San Francisco.

A substantial part of the labor movement had been reluctant from the beginning to accept the charges against Schmitz, perhaps because it feared that employers might make larger uses of the trials or perhaps because it admired the handsome mayor and rejoiced in his rise from the ranks; the Building Trades Council had denounced the prosecution in 1906. (At Stanford, Thorstein Veblen told a colleague that he was not interested in the trials, "that they were a move of the middle class directed against the workers.") Labor's attitude changed for a time as Heney accumulated irrefutable evidence, and union leaders pointed out correctly enough that the Union Labor Party was misnamed, that it had no connection with the Labor Council or its member unions. Then their doubts revived. And when the continuation of the trials became the main issue in the municipal elections of 1909, Heney as candidate of the Good Government League for district attorney lost disastrously to the anti-prosecution candidate of the Union Labor and Republican parties, Charles Fickert, and the successful Union Labor candidate for mayor, P. H. McCarthy, promised a "tolerant" administration that would restore the "get-together spirit" and make San Francisco "the Paris of America." "In San Francisco," Chester Rowell, progressive editor and politician, wrote later, "our class got possession of the government and then the lower class proceeded to combine with the upper class against the middle class in order to take the government from them again." In his view, the collectivists in labor understood the collectivism of capital better than they understood the individualism of reform; perhaps they remembered more clearly than their betters how recently some of their fellows had moved from south of Market Street to Nob Hill and the rich men's clubs. In a state that only a few years earlier, during the gold rush, had seemed to reenact the social contract and approach an ideal democracy, civic virtue seemed limited to the hope that partners in crime would not stand together—not that the classes at the extremes of society would reform, but that government might fall to the one class that cherished the welfare of the commonwealth.

Yet insurgency had tapped broad streams of sentiment and support that converged between 1906 and 1910, in and out of San Francisco. Resistance to the railroad never had quite disappeared since the 1870's; it became formidable in the 1890's, extending into both major parties. Anti-railroad Democratic candidates almost won the governorship twice—in 1902 and again in 1906, when many Republicans resented the methods used in nominating Gillett. That same year, disclosures of the machine's arrogance in Los Angeles prompted a group of business and professional men to present a non-partisan slate in the city election; having elected two thirds of their candidates, they prepared to elect a Good Government candidate as mayor in 1909. When a League of Lincoln-Roosevelt Republican Clubs (generally known as the Lincoln-Roosevelt League) organized at Oakland in August, 1907, it drew on leaders of municipal insurgency in both San Francisco and Los Angeles, includ-

Governor Hiram Johnson (Courtesy of the Bancroft Library)

ing some who had supported the Democratic candidate, Bell, against Gillett in 1906. In San Francisco, leaders of the League backed the Democratic candidate for mayor in 1907 and 1909. And though McCarthy and Fickert turned away from reform locally, the Lincoln-Roosevelt League captured the state Republican organization and found its leader for state-wide reform in the graft trials: it nominated Hiram Johnson for the governorship in 1910. Campaigning throughout the state in a red roadster with a brass bell to draw the crowds at crossroads stops, he attacked the Southern Pacific and its allies as vigorously as he had prosecuted Ruef and Schmitz, and with much broader consequences. His victory that fall changed the course of California politics for half a century or more.

For a time some progressives feared that, having had principles, but uneven success in selling them to the voters, they had found a leader who would not know where to take them. In the campaign, Johnson dwelt on his promise to "kick the Southern Pacific Railroad out of politics" and on the corrupting influences of two newspaper publishers, Otis and William Randolph Hearst, almost to the exclusion of platform promises that leaders of the Lincoln-Roosevelt had written pledging direct legislation, regulation of public utilities, employers' liability for industrial accidents, and protection for the rights of collective bargaining, among other progressive measures. There was little in his record to go on, since he had not held state office. "If you are going to write about me," he once told a reporter, "you won't have to go back of 1910."

Actually, even Johnson's chief supporters, the leaders of the League, had had few occasions to show their hand. Most of them were outsiders denouncing the morals of insiders, and moreover, they were newcomers to politics; those who had served in the legislature had seemed concerned chiefly with ethical and procedural issues, and much of the initiative for the program of economic and social reform in the spirit of Theodore Roosevelt's New Nationalism came from pressure groups such as the State Federation of Labor and from officers of state agencies. Recalling Phelan's strikebreakers in San Francisco and the anti-picketing legislation of Los Angeles, labor could not know what to expect from reformers in Sacramento, though Johnson himself had had congenial enough relations with labor in his private legal practice, serving as counsel for several unions. His attacks on the publishers from the stump were at the least confusing, for to most laboring men Hearst seemed almost as friendly as Otis seemed hostile. Further, Johnson had found his strongest support in southern California, where the leading reformers placed little trust in organized labor. During the campaign, which coincided with the height of the drive for the union shop in southern California, the Los Angeles City Council, elected on a Good Government ticket in 1909, adopted an extreme anti-picketing ordinance; five weeks before election, tension increased with the bombing of the *Times* building. Fear of violence and fear of a Socialist victory in the municipal election of 1911 prompted the Good Government group to cooperate with men who were anathema to labor and even hostile to reform itself.

But if the California progressives seemed intent above all on purifying politics by checking combinations at the extremes of society that threatened to dis-

The San Francisco Earthquake of 1906 (Courtesy of the Bancroft Library)

place government's legal constituency, nevertheless the progressive regime that took power in 1911 soon also took up the larger tasks of the New Nationalism. Meyer Lissner, chairman of the Republican state central committee, had so feared that the new administration would have no program that he appointed committees to plan the work of the legislature. But soon he and other southern Californian progressives were opposing a bill to limit the working day for women to eight hours, which Johnson signed along with bills for a strengthened railroad commission, employers' liability, free textbooks for public schools, conservation, local option, and other measures that Theodore Roosevelt called "the most comprehensive program of constructive legislation ever passed at a single session of any American legislature." Constitutional amendments included provisions for the regulation of public utilities, the initiative, referendum, and recall, and woman suffrage. The legislature of 1913 went still further; it established commissions with jurisdiction over conservation, industrial accidents, industrial welfare, and immigration and housing. In 1915 there followed legislation to encourage cooperative marketing and to establish a commission on colonization and rural credits. No other large state had accepted so boldly, Herbert Croly said in 1914, the whole progressive program of political and economic reform.

Ethnic and Alien Images in California History
by Howard A. DeWitt

The rise of anti-radicalism during and after World War I created a highly conservative political atmosphere in the Golden State. Howard A. DeWitt of Ohlone College presents a brief analysis of the uses of anti-radicalism from 1917 to 1930. His article indicates that modern right wing politics can trace their origins to this period.

In the last decade, the terms crime and violence, law and order, police and pigs, mugging and bugging, riots and commission, have become familiar expressions. The subject of domestic violence in American history has been closely linked with intimidation and outright harrassment of ethnic minorities and political radicals. The passage of recent federal legislation has given the average citizen the right to examine any files maintained on them by government agencies. This legislation is an indication that acts of individual violence are often associated with images of ethnic or labor radicalism, or that government investigative agencies maintain files on potential radicals. As a result of this belief, historians and political scientists are expressing a renewed interest in conflict and violence in American politics. But, reflections of violence in the United States is a relatively recent historiographical phenomena. Only since 1960 has the *Reader's Guide to Periodical Literature* included the separate subject category, "violence" in its main index listing periodical publications.

It is not surprising there has been very little serious study of violence in American politics. Essentially, there are two reasons for this disinterest: First, American political history lacks both an ideological and geographical center. This has prevented the unity and cohesion which radical movements need to develop a recognized political base. Second, we have been too little concerned with the history of violence. A good example is the Tulsa Race Riot of 1921. There is not a single scholarly article or book-length monograph of this incident. Moreover, it is not mentioned in many of the leading Oklahoma history textbooks. In 1967, Senator Fred Harris of Oklahoma described his amazement upon learning of the Tulsa Riot, "It was during my work on the National Advisory Commission on Civil Disorders that I first heard of the Tulsa Race Riot of 1921, despite the fact that I had been a life-long resident of the state of Oklahoma." Senator Harris' experience is not a unique one. The tendency for historians to emphasize a consensus approach to American political history has downplayed violent ethnic or labor riots. It has also helped to exclude discussions of violent outbursts in state or U.S. history surveys. As Richard Hofstadter

Howard A. DeWitt, "Ethnic and Alien Images in California History: A Teaching Proposal," *Community College Social Science Quarterly*, II (Spring, 1978) pp. 40–43. Reprinted by permission of the author and journal.

has suggested, American violence is closely associated with a conservative bias in state governmental power. In other words, violence often results from the policies of a conservative governor. In this paper, I propose to offer some suggestions for including lecture or discussion examples of violence and radicalism in California politics. These suggestions are tentative ones and are drawn heavily from my recently published monograph, *Images of Ethnic and Radical Violence in California Politics. 1917–1930: A Survey*, (San Francisco, 1975).

During World War I, and its aftermath, the first wave of major riots took place in twentieth century America; there were twenty-two major riots from 1915 to 1919. These disturbances, however, were largely inter-racial ones, and they occurred primarily in the Middle West as southern blacks moved into the labor market. The resulting atmosphere was one which created images of possible ethnic and radical violence. In California there was not a single race riot as California's black population was a relatively small and static one, but California politics reflected the "images" of possible violence which permeated American history. As a result of the national hysteria, California politicians used images of ethnic and labor radicalism as a political weapon. It became the rationale for a decade of systematic destruction of political liberalism in the Golden State.

In the second decade of the twentieth century, California political radicalism had been highlighted in violent confrontations between business and labor. The bombing of the Los Angeles Times in 1910, the Wheatland Riot of 1913, and the bombing of San Francisco's Market Street during the 1916 Preparedness Day Parade are the best examples of radical labor activity. Moreover, progressives heightened political tensions by stating that prior to World War I, there were essentially no differences between California Progressivism and Socialism. While this is a highly debatable conclusion, nevertheless, it prompted reactionary Republican politicians, who gained control of California in 1917, to plan to return to a more conservative political orientation. When Hiram Johnson left the California governor's office in March, 1917, the first signs of anti-radical politics formed in state politics.

It was Johnson's successor, William D. Stephens, who initiated anti-radicalism as a political tool. Stephens, was an obscure United States congressman who had been appointed Lieutenant-Governor in 1916 in a political deal in which Southern California Progressive Republicans supported Hiram Johnson's bid for a United States senate seat. Once Stephens ascended to the governor's chair, it was obvious that he was a politician by training and background who would use images of ethnic and radical violence for political gain. Prior to his appointment as Hiram Johnson's Lieutenant-Governor, Stephens had not distinguished himself as a California politician. While he publicly proclaimed his Progressive political leanings, Stephens' background indicated a much different type of political thought.

As a traveling salesman for the M.A. Newmark Wholesale Grocery firm in the 1890's, Stephens witnessed a number of labor strikes which shut down the Los Angeles railroad terminal and caused large quantities of fruits and vegetables to perish. The Socialist led strikes left a deep and lasting impression upon Stephens. When he began his political career in 1910, it was impossible, due to the political atmosphere, for a Republican not to have had Progressive leanings. Whatever liberal political ideas Stephens possessed were erased during the next few years as the Industrial Workers of the World led well-publicized free speech movements in Fresno and San Diego. In sum, by 1917, William D. Stephens had developed very precise ideas about the dangers of labor and ethnic radicalism upon California politics.

The catalyst to Stephens' anti-radicalism was the Industrial Workers of the World. Governor Stephens informed the *Sacramento Bee* that the Wobblies, organized in Chicago in 1905, advocated the abolition of the wage system and of Capitalism in general, and he emphasized that the I.W.W. would use any and all tactics to achieve its desired goals.

In December, 1917, Stephens' dire predictions seemed to come true when the Governor's Mansion was bombed. This bombing was only a small part of a tense and complicated political drama. In the midst of the famous Mooney-Billings case, San Francisco District Attorney, Charles M. Fickert, was the central figure in a recall election. It was well known that Fickert sold political favors, and the widely-held doubts about the handling of cases involving labor radicals prompted a reform political coalition to seek a change in San Francisco politics.

On the night before voters went to the polls in the recall election of San Francisco's District Attorney, Charles Fickert, an explosion rocked the Governor's Mansion. Although the origin and purpose of the bomb was never fully resolved, its impact upon California politics was mo-

mentous. In San Francisco, an unexpected thirty thousand voters from upper income residential areas turned out at the polls to show their support for Fickert's law and order platform. An investigation of the bombing of Governor Stephens' mansion by United States Treasury Department's special agents, E. F. Morse and Dan Rathbun, concluded that Fickert's supporters were responsible for the bombing. This was a logical explanation as the act created a strong mood for law and order; one which aided both Stephens and Fickert. Its end result was to create a strong public demand for a joint federal-state investigation of ethnic and radical violence in California politics.

The *Sacramento Union* was one of the first newspapers to succumb to the anti-radical political hysteria. It charged that a German agent with I.W.W. connections was responsible for the dynamiting of Stephens' residence. Shortly thereafter, 53 I.W.W. members were indicted for violation of the Espionage Act of 1917. The indictments were the result of strong pressures from Sacramento businessmen and Governor Stephens upon federal authorities. The absence of evidence to convict the Wobblies was demonstrated by the fact that they were imprisoned one year before coming to trial. Federal investigators urged that the charges be dropped due to a lack of evidence. However, California authorities convinced the federal attorneys that a Sacramento jury would convict the I.W.W. members. As a result, the rationale for delaying the trial was that a similar trial in Chicago contained evidence which would be used to convict the Sacramento Wobblies.

The full extent to which radical images can be used for political purposes was demonstrated in December, 1918, when

46 of the original 53 I.W.W. members were brought to trial. By this time, they had already been convicted in the court of public opinion. In particular, the *Sacramento Bee* summed up the attitude of most Californians when it editorialized that the Wobblies would be lynched. In the 1918 gubernatorial campaign, William D. Stephens took full advantage of anti-radical politics. This strong stand against the I.W.W. allowed Stephens, who had been known as a weak and ineffective politician, to take a strong public position against radicalism. This was a critical factor in his successful candidacy for governor. In fact, Stephens exerted political pressure upon federal authorities to delay the trial until after the 1918 election. This was only one of many facets of anti-radical politics which hurt the I.W.W.

The pre-trial publicity, the obvious fabricating of evidence by California law enforcement officials, and the death of five Wobblies during the year in jail had a delibitating effect upon the radicals. As a result, the I.W.W. defendants used a "silent defense." When the 46 Wobblies were finally convicted in the Sacramento trial, it was through evidence which had no direct bearing on the case. This evidence included a number of editorials from the *New Solidarity*, an I.W.W. newspaper. There was also testimony by local sheriffs concerning political speeches and anti-war statements. Most observers believed that images of radical political action were enough to convict the Wobblies. As a reporter for the *The Nation* observed, the jury gave, "the impression of men of habit rather than intelligence. To such men, economic dissentients like the I.W.W. would naturally seem like dangerous characters who should be shut away for

the safety of the public." Although the 46 defendants were convicted; the jury debated only 70 minutes to reach its verdict. The obvious conclusion was that the Wobblies were prejudged. Political radicals were quick to point out that the Sacramento Wobblies received less than two minutes each of consideration from the jury. It was clearly the beginning of institutionalized anti-radical politics in California.

During the remainder of Governor Stephens' administration, the intolerant, irresponsible tone of anti-radicalism intensified. From 1919 to 1921, there were three examples of an institutionalized pattern of reactionary politics in the Golden State. First, labor radicals met with violence and intimidation from local law enforcement officials. The I. W. W. strike in 1919 around the San Gabriel, Azusa, Charter Oak and San Dimas citrus groves in Southern California, for example, reflected a zealous attempt by local authorities to prevent I.W.W. organization. The *Pomona Bulletin* headlines the strike, "IWW PLOT TO SPREAD BOLSHEVISM AMONG ORANGE PICKERS OF VALLEY BARED." Images of a "Bolshevik conspiracy" and fears of "outside agitators" prompted the growers and law enforcement officials to attack the so-called "Russian House" which served as I.W.W. strike headquarters. The *Claremont Courier* demanded that "an extralegal vigilante organization . . ." rid the community of Russian agents. Once the strike was settled, its significance became more readily apparent as heightened fears of ethnic and labor radicalism were demonstrated in California newspapers, business organizations, and in the daily rhetoric of politicians.

A second example of intensified anti-radicalism in California politics was the passage of the Criminal Syndicalism Law of 1919. This measure, designed to control the political rhetoric of California radicals, was a bill aimed at implementing a conservative political atmosphere. In essence, the Criminal Syndicalism Law was a means of prosecuting political radicals by making it a felony under California state law to advocate any changes in the political or economic systems. Its intent was to make an example of certain well-known political leftists. The arrest and prosecution of Charlotte Anita Whitney was the most celebrated case evolving around the Criminal Syndicalism Law. On the basis of her statements at a state convention of the Communist Labor Party, Miss Whitney was convicted of the felony of association with a group which advocated, taught, or aided and abetted criminal syndicalism.

The third example of continued anti-radical politics occurred in May, 1920, when the Los Angeles-based Better America Federation was organized to promote one hundred percent Americanism. In reality, the B.A.F. campaigned for a program of controlled public morals and political attitudes. The extreme conservatism of the B.A.F. was shown in its campaign to silence the political opinions of the Young Women's Christian Association. The Los Angeles branch of the YWCA was a liberal political organization supporting the abolition of child labor, an eight hour day, a forty hour work week, and collective bargaining for women. There was also constant pressure from the YWCA for child care centers for working women. The B.A.F. attached the YWCA's argument that women were paid less than men, and often worked at night,

as an example of a radical attempt to reduce the free contract rights of women in the marketplace.

In sum, the Better America Federation represented a form of political control associated with modern day right-wing political ideas. It offers a contrast to present-day movements from either the left or right to implement a restricted ideological approach to American politics. The Better America Federation was also the logical outcome of a decade of ethnic and radical strife in California politics which began with the bombing of the Los Angeles Times in 1910 and continued to dominate California politics in the 1920's.

This discussion has touched only briefly the relatively unexplored terrain of ethnic and class-oriented violence in California in the second and third decade of the twentieth century. It is a subject which warrants further study and a broader application to the history of California, the West, and the nation as a whole. The changes in an industrial society, moving from an economy of scarcity to one of abundance, with shifting centers of social and political power and fierce competition in a labor market, led inevitably to an exploitation of the fear and insecurity that such change generates in the populace. It is instructive that the relationship between the complex causes and the simple, but explosive, responses to images of ethnic and alien violence be carefully examined by scholar and student alike, both for an understanding of that other time, and not the least, for an understanding of our own. The use to which fear and economic insecurity can be put by a shrewd practitioner of politics is, of course, well known in post-Water-gate America. Its employment in our recent past, the residual tensions and its bitter legacies here, among our own, is neither well known nor, quite often, welcome when broached. Nothing within the realm of human activity should lie beyond our intellectural grasp, and no pattern of behavior, individual or collective, should fail to interest and instruct us. We are enriched by the study of the darker part of our social responses and by including examples of images of ethnic and alien violence in history and political science courses, we directly confront the problem in the classroom.

Sister Aimee and the Green Religion
by Carey McWilliams

In the 1920s evangelic Christianity was one of the most profitable ventures in Southern California. The Queen of the revival circuit was Aimee Semple McPherson. Her Four Square Gospel Temple appealed to thousands of lonely and destitute Californians. The late Carey McWilliams, a well-known liberal writer, places Sister Aimee in the mainstream of California's rapidly changing social climate. This selection is an important reflection of the new forces influencing California thought in the 1920s.

Aimee, who was "not so much a woman as a scintillant assault," first appeared in California at San Diego in 1918. There she began to attract attention by scatter- ing religious tracts from an airplane and holding revival meetings in a boxing arena. That Mrs. McPherson's first ap- pearance should have been in San Diego

Aimee Semple McPherson's Hollywood

Carey McWilliams, "Southern California: An Island On The Land," (Boston, 1946), pp. 259–262. Re- printed with the permission of Peregrine Smith, Inc.

is, in itself, highly significant. In San Diego she unquestionably heard of Katherine Tingley, from whom she probably got the idea of founding a new religious movement on the coast and from whom she certainly got many of her ideas about uniforms, pagentry, and showmanship.

Furthermore, San Diego has always been, as Edmund Wilson once said, "a jumping-off place." Since 1911 the suicide rate of San Diego has been the highest in the nation; between 1911 and 1927, over 500 people killed themselves in San Diego. A haven for invalids, the rate of sickness in San Diego in 1931 was 24% of the population, whereas for the whole country the sick rate was only 6%. Chronic invalids have always been advised to go to California, and, once there, they drift to San Diego. From San Diego there is no place else to go; you either jump into the Pacific or disappear into Mexico. Seventy percent of the suicides of San Diego have been put down to "despondency and depression over ill health." Curiously enough, Southern California has always attracted victims of so-called "ideational" diseases like asthma, diseases which are partly psychological and that have, as Wilson pointed out, a tendency to keep their victims moving away from places under the illusion that they are leaving the disease behind. But once they acquire "a place in the sun" in California, they are permanently marooned.

From San Diego, Mrs. McPherson came to Los Angeles in 1922 with her Four Square Gospel: conversion, physical healing, the second coming, and redemption. She arrived in Los Angeles with two minor children, an old battered automobile, and $100 in cash. By the end of 1925, she had collected more than $1,000,000 and owned property worth $250,000. In the early twenties, as Nancy Barr Mavity has pointed out (in an excellent biography of Mrs. McPherson), "Los Angeles was the happy hunting ground for the physically disabled and the mentally inexacting . . . no other large city contains so many transplanted villagers who retain the stamp of their indigenous soil. . . . Most cities absorb the disparate elements that gravitate to them, but Los Angeles remains a city of migrants," a mixture, not a compound.

Here she built Angelus Temple at a cost of $1,500,000. The Temple has an auditorium with 5,000 seats: a $75,000 broadcasting station; the classrooms of a university which once graduated 500 young evangelists a year; and, as Morrow Mayo pointed out, "a brass band bigger and louder than Sousa's, an organ worthy of any movie cathedral, a female choir bigger and more beautiful than the Metropolitan chorus, and a costume wardrobe comparable to Ziegfeld's." Founding a magazine, *The Bridal Call*, Mrs. McPherson established 240 "lighthouses," or local churches, affiliated with Angelus Temple. By 1929 she had a following of 12,000 devoted members in Los Angeles and 30,000 in the outlying communities. From the platform of Angelus Temple, Sister Aimee gave the Angelenos the fanciest theological entertainment they have ever enjoyed. I have seen her drive an ugly Devil around the platform with a pitchfork, enact the drama of Valley Forge in George Washington's uniform, and take the lead in a dramatized sermon called "Sodom and Gomorrah." Adjutants have been praying, night and day, for thirteen years in the Temple. One group has been praying for 118,260 hours. While Mrs. McPherson never contended that she could heal the sick, she was

Los Angeles in the 1920's

always willing to pray for them and she was widely known as a faithhealer. A magnificent sense of showmanship enabled her to give the Angelus Temple throngs a sense of drama, and a feeling of release, that probably did have some therapeutic value. On state occasions, she always appeared in the costume of an admiral-of-the-fleet while the lay members of her entourage wore natty nautical uniforms.

On May 18, 1926, Sister Aimee disappeared. Last seen in a bathing suit on the beach near Ocean Park, she had apparently drowned in the Pacific. While Los Angeles went wild with excitement, thousands of templites gathered on the beach to pray for her deliverance and return. A specially chartered airplane flew over the beach and dropped flowers on the waters. On May 23, an overly enthusiastic disciple drowned in the Pacific while attempting to find her body. A few days later, a great memorial meeting was held for Sister at Angelus Temple, at which $35,000 was collected. Three days later, the mysterious Aimee reappeared at Auga Prieta, across the border from Douglas, Arizona.

Her entrance into Los Angeles was a major triumph. Flooded with requests from all over the world, the local newspapers and wire services filed 95,000 words of copy in a single day. Airplanes showered thousands of blossoms upon the coach that brought Sister back to Los Angeles. Stepping from the train, she walked out of the station on a carpet of roses. A hundred thousand people cheered while she paraded through the streets of the city, accompanied by a white-robed silver band, an escort of twenty cowboys, and squads of policemen. The crowd that greeted her has been estimated to be the largest ever to welcome a public personage in the history of the city. As she stepped on the platform at Angelus Temple, the people in the crowded auditorium were chanting:

Coming back, back, back,
Coming back, back, back,
Our sister in the Lord is coming back.
There is shouting all around,
For our sister has been found;
There is nothing now of joy or peace we lack.

The jubilation, however, did not last long. Working hard on the case, the newspapers soon proved that the kidnaping story, which she had told on her return, was highly fictitious. In sensational stories, they proceeded to trace her movements from the time she disappeared, through a "love cottage" interlude at Carmel with a former radio operator of the Temple, to her reappearance in Arizona. Following these disclosures, she was arrested, charged with having given false information designed to interfere with the orderly processes of the law, and placed on trial. Later the charges against her were dropped. During the trial, thousands of her followers gathered daily in the Temple and shouted:

Identifications may come,
Identifications may go;
Goggles may come,
Goggles may go;
But are we downhearted?
No! No! No!

Sister's trial was really a lynching bee. For she had long been a thorn in the side of the orthodox Protestant clergy who stoked the fires of persecution with memorials, petitions, and resolutions clamoring for her conviction. No one bothered to inquire what crime, if any, she had committed (actually she had not committed any crime). It was the fabulous ability with which she carried off the kidnaping hoax that so infuriated the respectable middle-class residents of Los Angeles. Miss Mavity writes that, in her opinion, it is "improbable that Aimee ever deliberately sought to harm another human being." Although I heard her speak many times, at the Temple and on the radio, I never heard her attack any individual or any group and I am thoroughly convinced that her followers always felt that they had received full value in exchange for their liberal donations. She made migrants feel at home in Los Angeles, she gave them a chance to meet other people, and she exorcised the nameless fears which so many of them had acquired from the fire-and-brimstone theology of the Middle West.

Although she managed to maintain a fairly constant following until her death in 1945 from a overdose of sleeping powder, she never recovered from the vicious campaign that had been directed against her in 1926. The old enthusiasm was gone; the old fervor had vanished. She was no longer "Sister McPherson" in Los Angeles, but merely "Aimee." In many respects, her career parallels that of Katherine Tingley: both were highly gifted women with a great talent for showmanship, both had lived in poverty and obscurity until middle-age, both founded cults, and both were ruined by scandal.

In 1936 the Four Square Gospel had 204 branch organizations and a total membership of 16,000. More than 80% of her followers were city residents, mostly lower-middle-class people—small shopkeepers, barbers, beauty-parlor operators, small-fry realtors, and the owners of hamburger joints. Never appealing to the working class, as such, she had an enormous fascination for the uprooted, unhappy, dispirited *lumpen-proletariat*. Over the years, many of her followers moved into the area around Angelus Temple, where they still reside.

California Congressman Pete Stark Talks to Ohlone College Students

WORKSHEET 7: California Civilization: 1900—1930: Reform or Reaction?

1. What is Aimee Semple McPherson's Green Religion? _____

   _____

2. The Progressive Movement blended what forces to create a governmental

   philosophy? _____

   _____

3. The Lincoln-Roosevelt League was formed to _____

4. Katherine Phillips Edson was _____

   _____

   _____

5. Describe how Mabel Craft Deering blended feminism, Progressive politics and the

   fight for civil rights in her newspaper and political career. _____

   _____

   _____

   _____

   _____

   _____

6. What role on a SF newspaper did Deering play? _____

7. John F. Neylan was _____

   _____

8. Why was the city so important to California Progressives, according to Earl Pomeroy? _____

_____

_____

9. Chester Rowell was important because _____

_____

10. In the DeWitt article analyze what anti-Radicalism is _____

_____

11. What is meant by the term ethnic and alien forces? _____

_____

12. The Better America Federation is an example of _____

_____

13. The Four Square Gospel Temple was _____

14. Name one change Progressivism brought to California _____

_____

15. Who was Corona? _____

_____

Modern California: Poverty Children, The Chinese, 1937–1944, The Mare Island Mutiny, W. Byron Rumford and Helen Gahagan Douglas

READINGS: JERRY STANLEY, *"CHILDREN OF THE GRAPES OF WRATH"* JOHN C. CHEN, *"REVERSAL OF FORTUNE: IMAGES OF AMERICA'S CHINESE, 1937–1944, THE DOMINANCE OF CALIFORNIA"* CHARLES WOLLENBERG *"THE MARE ISLAND MUTINY AND COURT MARTIAL"* INGRID WINTHER SCOBIE, *"HELEN GAHAGAN DOUGLAS: BROADWAY STAR AS CALIFORNIA POLITICIAN"* LAWRENCE CROUCHETT, *"ASSEMBLYMAN W. BYRON RUMFORD: SYMBOL FOR AN AGE"*

Since the 1930s California has been a civilization in transition. There has been constant conflict between liberal and conservative forces in the Golden State. The result of these differences has made the Golden State a laboratory for democracy. By the mid-1990s California was not only the ethnically most diverse state in the union but the richest and most populous.

There is a natural volatility to California society. When Harry Bridges led the fledgling International Longshoreman's Association to victory in the San Francisco strike of 1934 it brought labor power back. By 1938 California elected a Democratic governor, Culbert Olson and inaugurated a New Deal for California. Ironically, this was the year that President Franklin D. Roosevelt announced that the New Deal was dead. California was never in step with the rest of the nation and Olson's New Deal brought unbridled prosperity.

The Great Depression and the Children of the Grapes of Wrath

During the Great Depression the long tradition of conflict between labor and big business reemerged. For years farm workers were underpaid and exploited. Then in 1934 the Filipino Labor Union won a major strike in Salinas. By 1937 the International Longshoreman's and Warehouseman's Union was in control of the San Francisco docks.

In the farms and fields around Bakersfield the Oakie and Arkie migration brought almost 200,000 migrant workers into Kern County. The Dust Bowlers, as they were known, were not welcome in the midst of the depression. They were so much like the characters in John Steinbeck's best selling book, **The Grapes of Wrath,** that the county banned the book from its library.

The local schools were not happy with the influx of Dust Bowl children. Then in 1939 Leo Hart was elected Superintendent of Schools for Kern County, and he introduced a model program for educating the Dust Bowl children. He did this by building schools adjacent to the fields which provided a broad curriculum including music lessons, experienced teachers, nutritious snacks such as hot cocoa and a commitment to educational excellence. Soon Kern County citizens recognized the importance of maintaining such an enriching program for migrant families.

Initially, however, locals appeared frightened by these young people. The children of the Grapes of Wrath were small, appeared malnourished and tugged at the heartstrings of people around Bakersfield. Soon Leo Hart took these children under his wing. He established the school in Arvin for the children of the Grapes of Wrath. When Hart approached the Arvin-Lamont School Board with the idea of declaring an emergency and setting up a special school, he was called a communist.

It didn't take long for the children to make the Arvin school one of the most important educational experiments in modern California. These poor, beggar looking, children soon blossomed into excellent students.

Pete Bancroft, the principal of the Arvin school bought a C-47 airplane from a surplus center and had it brought to the school. Soon the finest mechanics in the area came from the Arvin school.

From 1940 to 1944 approximately 300 migrant children attended the Arvin school, and they changed the mind of locals about the children of the Grapes of Wrath. The success story continued as a number graduated from college, many became small businessmen, and others were skilled labor. Janice Newton became the first female painting contractor in Kern County. Many others achieved professional positions. When the Arvin Federal Emergency School ended its experiment in 1944, there was reason to celebrate. The poorest students in Kern County had achieved a high level of education and broke some of the nastiest stereotypes about the Oakies and Arkies. It was a civil rights tale which few people recognized and it indicated the diverse nature of California society.

Professor Jerry Stanley of California State University, Bakersfield, has written an exciting article on the "Children Of The Grapes of Wrath," and he has demonstrated one of the cardinal tenets of the Great Depression. This tenet is that hard work and perseverance brought success.

World War II and California Racial Problems

During World War II racial tensions exploded in California. The Sleepy Lagoon incident in August, 1942 resulted from the discovery of a body near this germ infested swimming pool. The Los Angeles police quickly arrested 22 members of the 38th Street Gang and charged them with murder. In a highly publicized trial three were convicted of murder and a number of others were convicted of lesser charges. A crusading journalist, Carey McWilliams, uncovered fabrication of evidence by the police, outright fraud in the investigation and a disdain for the local Mexican American community.

In 1943 the Zoot Suit riot saw a ten taxi cab brigade of Marines and Sailors terrorize East Los Angeles. The Los Angeles police couldn't find the culprits and the community was outraged. The birth of modern Mexican American political organizations and the rise of Spanish speaking politicians can be traced to these incidents.

The San Francisco Bay Area believed that it was free of racial prejudice. Afro Americans were employed in Oakland, Richmond and Sausalito in the shipyards. With more than a million black men and women in the armed forces, there was a feeling that racism was on the wane. Yet, black American troops fought in segregated units.

In order to integrate the armed forces, Port Chicago Naval Magazine on the San Francisco bay some thirty-five miles northeast of San Francisco and fifteen miles east of Mare Island was set up to provide black and white soldiers an opportunity to load ammunition ships at Port Chicago.

On July 17, 1944, at about 10:18 P.M., a military ship exploded in Port Chicago killing 320 seamen, 202 of whom were black. This was the worst home-front disaster during World War II with more than 4,600 tons of ammunition spontaneously exploding. When the debris was cleared a crisis ensued, because only African-American soldiers were selected to carry out the hazardous explosives clean up. It was unthinkable in the 1940s for a group of black sailors to ignore a white officer's direct order. Joseph Small, a twenty-three year old sailor, not only refused to clean up explosives which he believed to be dangerous, but he complained about Naval racism. Small was one of many blacks who challenged the institutionalized racial discrimination of the United States Navy by refusing to go back to work.

The two hundred survivors of the Port Chicago blast went on strike and demanded alternate jobs. The strike collapsed under navy pressure and the threat of "death by a firing squad." As the affair was publicized Afro-Americans had a bitter sweet feeling about their level of equality.

The fifty men who refused to return to work were tried for treason. The black naval personnel were convicted and court-martialed for mutiny. They received sentences of from 8 to 15 years. When Thurgood Marshall, later a U.S. Supreme Court Justice, was retained by the National Association for the Advancement of Colored People, to inquire why only blacks were assigned to local ammunition loading areas at Port Chicago without proper training, the Navy refused to answer.

In July, 1946, after a year of constant pressure from civil rights groups, the Navy released the men from prison. The public outcry was strong. There was civil rights' sympathy in California for the black ammunition loaders. In his article, "The Mare Island Mutiny and Court Martial," Professor Charles Wollenberg of Vista College argues that the black sailors struck the first post World War II blow for civil rights in the bay area.

Professor Wollenberg argues that the sailors' refusal to load ships is one of the most significant examples of Afro American political activism in the Golden State. He sees this action as an indication that black Californians would join collectively to fight racism. This may be the incident which began California's modern civil rights impulse.

Professor John C. Chen offers an analysis of the Chinese American experience in his article: "Reversal of Fortune: Images of America's Chinese, 1937–1944, The Dominance of California." His thesis is that there were important changes in how Americans perceived the Chinese in the California experience and the primary reason for this new perception was the Chinese reaction to war. World War II acted as a catalyst to positive images for Chinese Americans. The result, as Professor Chen writes, was "a reversal of fortune," and the beginning of a new chapter in Chinese American history. No longer were the Chinese cast in a sojourner status, now they were permitted to participate at another level in American society.

Political Activism from the 1940s to the 1960s: The Cases of Helen Gahagan Douglas and W. Byron Rumford

The struggle for social justice and racial equality continued after World War II. Helen Gahagan Douglas who served three terms in Congress from 1944 to 1950 emerged as one of the leading liberals in post World War II California.

Mrs. Douglas fought poverty, bigotry, sexism and racism at a time that these forces were not generally challenged. She emerged as an important political figure by working for better conditions for migrant farm labor. She was in the forefront of Afro American civil rights and considered poverty an important issue.

In January, 1949, as the 81st Congress opened, Representative Douglas was a popular politician supported by labor groups, Hollywood money and civil libertarians. When Douglas announced that she would run for the United States Senate, the California right wing attacked her as a Communist sympathizer. She won the Democratic primary easily but the radical label stuck.

The 1950 Senate campaign provided a new low in American politics. A two term Congressman from Whittier, Richard M. Nixon used innuendo, outright trickery and unfair political terms to cast Douglas in a poor light. Nixon continually used the term "the Pink Lady" to describe Mrs. Douglas. When a reporter asked Nixon: "Does this mean that she is a Communist." Nixon smiled and refused to answer. Another time Nixon stated that it was a reference to her pink dress. In frustration Mrs. Douglas referred to Nixon as "Tricky Dick." The label stuck but Mrs. Douglas was easily defeated in the 1950 Senate election.

Although Helen Gahagan Douglas didn't attain power in Congress, nonetheless, she was a major figure in California politics. She took important stands in favor of labor, the poor, ethnic minorities and worked diligently for peace. In time these themes were the main forces of California politics. Like many pioneers, Douglas was a spokesperson ahead of her time. She established the precedents and moral principles that allowed future politicians to write her promises into law.

The selection by Ingrid Winther Scobie "Helen Gahagan Douglas: Broadway Star as California Politician," presents Douglas' career in great depth. Professor Scobie, who teaches at the Texas Woman's University, vividly portrays the reasons for Douglas' political successes. From the time that Helen Gahagan Douglas entered California politics in the Fall of 1938 through her participation in the 1960 Democratic National Convention which nominated John F. Kennedy, she was a critic of the right wing fanatic and a strong supporter of women, ethnic minorities and the general underdog. Her contribution, as Professor Scobie suggests, was one that "forced a durable legacy of political principal." Her political opponent, Richard Nixon, could never make that claim.

W. Byron Rumford was another seminal figure in California's post World War II ethnic explosion. In 1948 Rumford became the first Afro American elected to public office in Northern California. For the next eighteen years, Rumford was a model politician who fought hard against racial discrimination. By the time he left office in 1966, Rumford had secured state legislation making it illegal not to sell a home to Afro Americans or to deny access to them.

But Rumford was only one of many Afro American politicians who changed the nature of California society. Ruth Acty and Carolese Hargrave were black teachers hired in the east bay. Marguerite Johnson, better known as the poet Maya Angelou, was the first black streetcar conductor in San Francisco, and black attorneys Jay Maurice, Thomas L. Berkeley and John C. Henderson were all active in local politics.

However, it was Rumford who was instrumental in the California Assembly in the passage of fair employment legislation, the right to purchase housing legislation and civil rights bills. Although the California legislature quietly condoned segregation, Rumford spoke out and forced the legislature to pass laws which implemented a wide range of educational and employment opportunities as well as civil rights guarantees.

Professor Lawrence Paul Crouchett's article, "W. Byron Rumford: Symbol For An Era," explains the life long interest in politics which made the Berkeley Democrat a force in the racial advances of post World War II California. From the time Rumford entered the Assembly chamber in 1949, he represented a bipartisan coalition to advance civil rights. As Professor Crouchett concludes: "Rumford made his mark in an age when formal political institutions still sanctioned discrimination." This makes Rumford's accomplishments even more remarkable.

Children of the Grapes of Wrath: A Handmade School Saved Okie Kids for a Happy Ending

by Jerry Stanley

During the Great Depression the Okie and Arkie migration to California led to large settlement camps of migrant workers. In Kern County more than 200,000 migrants settled into small, makeshift agricultural camps. These settlements, which were populated by a large number of children, drew public interest and caused the media to publicize the "Dust Bowl children." Professor Jerry Stanley of California State University, Bakersfield, examines the impact of local schools upon these children. By analyzing the role of Leo Hart, the Superintendent of Schools for Kern County, Stanley provides interesting insights into how a model school system was able to turn out future California leaders.

Contrary to public myth, the children of the Grapes of Wrath were often exposed to an enriched educational program and became the next generation's leaders. Not only was Leo Hart a well known educator but he became the godfather to a new era of political and economic leaders, which led to equal opportunity.

In the quiet rural community of Shafter, California, just north of Bakersfield, an old man with a twinkle in his eye sits in a rocking chair. Back in the 1930s townsfolk called him a communist. Today he has their respect and admiration. Wild dogs, dirt roads, abandoned farm machinery, and a flooded field make his isolated cottage nearly inaccessible. Leo Hart doesn't travel much anymore or see many people, but at the age of eighty-nine he has a keen mind, a sharp wit, and a story worth telling.

Remember the Depression and the Dust Bowl Migration? The Joads, *The Grapes of Wrath,* the old jalopies and flatbed trucks loaded down with pots and pans and bedding and desperate-looking people? Leo Hart does. It all happened the way Steinbeck described it, Leo says, except for the children of the Grapes of Wrath. In the book, and in the academy award-winning film, the Joads end up at Weedpatch Camp, broke, without work, and with little hope for the future. Not so. In 1939 Leo Hart was elected Superintendent of Kern County Schools, and he built a school next to Weedpatch Camp just for the children of the Grapes of Wrath. The story of that school, as Leo tells it, is nothing less than amazing.

Nineteen thirty-nine was a hard year for the Dust Bowlers. Drought still gripped the Central Plains and the Southwest, and Route 66, bearing weary migrants from Oklahoma, Texas, and Arkansas to Kern County, California, was still crowded with people wearing baggy

Jerry Stanley, CHILDREN OF THE GRAPES OF WRATH. Reprinted by permission of the author. First published in *American West* magazine, March–April, 1986.

overalls, tattered dresses, and the look of down-and-out poverty. They called themselves "Okies." They were proud of their origins, though nature had struck them a mighty blow. Most of the Okies believed there was work in California; so they joined the caravan of Model A's and ramshackle buses and headed for the Great San Joaquin, and rich agricultural valley where, they heard, pickers were needed. By 1940, some 180,000 migrants had settled in the rural areas of the San Joaquin Valley, and Kern County experienced its greatest population explosion, over 70% between 1935 and 1940. Year after year they came, looking for work, any kind of work.

The reception the Dust Bowlers received was less than hospitable, for most residents of Kern County saw them as an unproductive lot, socially unacceptable. In 1938 irate farmers, armed with pitchforks, guns, bricks, and clubs, attacked the migrants of Weedpatch Camp at night and tried to drive them out. Hundreds of Okies went to jail, but they returned to the camp. In 1940 the County banned *The Grapes of Wrath* from its public libraries. Armed patrols guarded the County's borders, Leo Hart recalls, and the sheriff, goaded on by an outraged citizenry, burned down the migrant camp under the Kern River Bridge because of unsanitary conditions. "They were victims of the greatest economic depression this country has ever experienced," Leo observed, and he remembers seeing the migrants living "on ditch banks, in shacks, in tents, in squalor and filth." Still they came. And perhaps as many as two-thirds of the transients were children who shared the adversity of their parents—and faced additional hostility as well.

The children looked like war-refugees from some distant country, and in a way they were. Their hand-me-down trousers and skirts didn't fit so well as they could have; so, rope and twine were used to hold the clothing up. A soup bowl and a pair of old scissors were used to give Okie haircuts, string to keep ponytails from unraveling. Those who had shoes were lucky if they had socks. All the kids looked undernourished and in need of medical attention. They spoke a different language, they possessed a different culture, they lacked skills in hygiene, in "manners, morals, and etiquette," Hart recollects.

With little or no formal education, the children of the Dust Bowl crowded into Kern County's schools—the results were predictable. Teachers and taxpayers believed the newcomers were "uneducable," and their appearance offended community standards. Swiftly, these children were either banned from the public schools or forced to sit on the floor in the back of crowded classrooms where they felt humiliated. The Parent—Teacher Association excluded migrant parents from its meetings. Teachers ignored the unkempt pupils. Fellow students, using the term disparagingly, called the outcasts "Okies." With their fists they defended themselves, and harsh discipline or dismissal followed.

Enter the new superintendent of public schools, a Western pragmatist if there ever was one. Compassionate, optimistic, energetic in a cause, Hart had earned a Master of Arts degree from the University of Arizona and had served as head counselor in the Kern County High School District before becoming superintendent in 1939. "The big problem for me," Leo said, "was to find out what to do for these children to get them adjusted into society and to take their rightful place." He saw the Dust Bowl children as having special physical, social, and educational needs but he also saw them as "ordinary kids with the same hopes and dreams the rest of us have." With initiative, hard work, and a dose of Western pragmatism—and without aid from federal, state, or local governments—the children of the Grapes of Wrath just might take their rightful place. Hart thought so.

First, Leo tried to place the migrant children in the outlying rural schools, but he met stiff opposition. Said a high-ranking school official in the Arvin-Lamont area (southwest of Bakersfield near Weedpatch Camp): "You're not going to spend our money for these ——. You can't educate these ——. They're going to grow up just like their fathers and mothers. They're a shiftless lot. They've got no brains." Letters and phone calls from parents in the area were equally blunt, and at least two educators called Hart a communist and warned that his job might be in jeopardy, though he had held it only a few months.

So Leo decided the Dust Bowl children should have their own school. Accordingly, he persuaded the Arvin-Lamont School Board to declare that an "emergency" existed and to give him permission to build a school adjacent to Arvin Federal Camp (Weedpatch Camp in *The Grapes of Wrath*). Hart became a close friend of Dewey Russell, who was managing the camp when Steinbeck visited it and wrote about it. With Dewey's help, in 1940 Hart leased a ten-acre site from the federal government for ten dollars and established Arvin Federal Emergency School, which started with no grass, no sidewalks, no playground equipment, no toilets, no water, no books, no teachers. It started, Leo remembers, with two condemned buildings and "fifty poorly clad, undernourished, and skeptical youngsters."

Leo said his goal was to provide the unwanted children "with educational experiences in a broader and richer curriculum than were present in most schools." He did that—and more. Before the school opened in September 1940, Hart visited several colleges and universities in California and sought out "the best teachers . . . teachers whose attitudes indicated that they were really interested in this type of student and wanted to help in this program." Teachers like Jim McPherson, who finished his doctorate from Columbia University while working at Arvin School, then later taught at the University of California at Los Angeles, Drake University, and the University of Indiana before employment with the United States Office of Education. Teachers like Charlene McGhee, who mastered animal husbandry, besides the 3Rs, and taught the care and feeding of livestock. Teachers like Edith Houghman, who used her own paychecks to buy food for the kids and served them hot cocoa every day for months until the school cafeteria was completed. Teachers like Fred Smith, who was hired as a music teacher for one day a week but usually worked on weekends for free. At the end of the year Leo sent Fred his yearly check for $600, and Fred sent it back.

Then Leo became a beggar, a borrower, a scrounger of wood and nails, of books and paper, of whatever he could lay his hands on that might be of some use. "I became a panhandler," he remembers, and why not? It was the Depression. He stumped the County for donations of supplies and materials; his pitch was just what the community wanted to hear: the Dust Bowl kids would be withdrawn from the public schools, they would be set off from the community in a separate school, and the school would not cost the taxpayers "a single cent," as Leo used to say. From the National Youth Authority, he secured 25,000 bricks. From the Sears Roebuck Foundation, an assortment of sheep, pigs, and cows. From local nurseries, plants and vegetables. From local ranchers, farm machinery.

In September 1940, on a barren stretch of land marked by piles of bricks and boards and boxes of whatnot, Leo met with his faculty, introduced them to "fifty skeptical students," and told them all to get to work. They did. Brick by brick, board by board, the children of the Dust Bowl, along with Hart and his staff, built Arvin Federal Emergency School. They laid a one-quarter-inch pipe between Weedpatch Camp and the school; the school had water. Teachers instructed the pupils on hygiene; then the migrants built two "outdoor facilities" and used them. Orange crates and wooden boxes were fashioned into chairs, desks, and tables. Bricks were laid to make three "temporary" classrooms, which could be used only as long as an "emergency" existed. If the migrant children did not "goof-off," if they kept up on their academics, Leo let them dig in their spare time, "dig on the hole" they called it, which eventually became the only public school swimming pool in Kern County. While helping the migrants lay reinforcement rods and concrete for the pool, Leo

wore old overalls, as did his faculty. He sawed lumber, he dug ditches, he painted buildings, but "the children of the Dust Bowl built the school," Leo says. "It was *their* school."

One day a local butcher heard about the "Okie school" and wandered out to the site. His name and whereabouts have been forgotten, but Leo remembers the man spent ten hours at the school that day slaughtering pigs and cows and instructing the children until they learned the basic skills of a butcher. This is what Hart meant by "educational experiences in a broader and richer curriculum." The girls needed a home economics building. No problem. An old railroad car was located and moved to the school where the boys added plumbing, wired the boxcar, and remodeled its interior. They learned carpentry, plastering, masonry, built pens for livestock, dug a basement to store slaughtered cattle, plowed fields for raising school-grown vegetables— they made *their* school completely self-sufficient. They were proud; their parents were proud. "The longer we ran the school," Hart said, "the longer the people stayed. The greater portion of them stayed there and would stay the year round and work so that their kids could stay in this school. It was the first time that they had ever had anything of their own, where all the attention was on them, where they were given the best and they knew everyone was for them. That was something to watch."

Something to watch—quiet moments in heroism. Pete Bancroft, the principal of Arvin Federal, used $200 out of his pay to buy a C-47 airplane from surplus and have it carted to the school. "I taught them aircraft mechanics," he says from his retirement home in San Diego, "and if they maintained a grade of 90% or better in arithmetic, I let them drive the plane down the makeshift runway and back." He put his own son in the school and brought a doctor and nurse out to care for the sickest children. He remembers dispensing cod liver oil and orange juice between meals until the first crops came in and the school cafeteria was built and paid for, in part, with $250 from the first crop of potatos. Teachers Rose Gilger and Beverly Ahrens worked in that cafeteria as well as in the classroom, and like other faculty took the kids into town on Sundays to go to church and to accept donations of food and clothing from local merchants and the Salvation Army. The teachers, Hart says, "went out of their way to help these children and teach them things about themselves and the world that they couldn't learn anywhere else." Leo might have been thinking about Barbara Sabovitch. She taught the young girl pupils how to use toothpaste, face cream, rouge, lipstick, and mascara —and how to make these products in a chemistry lab. Something to watch.

"A miracle," one of Leo's teachers calls it. "The children were very light complected, blond hair, blue eyes, and fragile looking," first-grade teacher Marie Marble says, "and almost all of them needed help in language, in expressing themselves, and they were shy and retiring." Marie describes the school as "a series of bungalows" where "the children had real life experiences which would help them later on." Mariel Hunter agrees. "Everyone pitched in to make it grow. We all worked together like one big happy family, and *grow* we did together. . . . The kids appreciated everything you did for

them because they had so little to light up their lives." Mariel recalls a girl in the eighth grade whose family was about to move away. The girl wanted to stay in the school "so badly" and go on to high school—she planned to marry so she could stay in town. Mariel took the problem to Leo, and Leo found the girl a home where she could live in return for domestic work. Other teachers, Edith Hougham for instance, spent weekends at the school with children who were sick because "they were better off in the nurse's room than at home in their one-room huts." Uniformly, they describe Leo as an "angel," a "saint," a "caring man," as a man who "saved the children."

Altogether, from 1940 to 1944 about 300 migrant children attended Hart's handmade school, and gradually the community began to change its mind about educating the children of the Grapes of Wrath. Arvin Federal became known statewide for its lack of truancy and disciplinary problems. "We left everything lying around," Leo recalls, "and no one ever stole a thing." Members of the California Youth Authority, after visiting the school, wrote Hart commending him on "the finest crime prevention program in the State of California," but, says Leo, there was no crime prevention program. "It was *their* school and they took pride in it." So did the community. After a few years, the once-hostile residents were clamoring to get their children into Arvin Federal Emergency School. They would phone Hart and write letters seeking to transfer their kids to "Weedpatch School." After all, it grew its own food, raised its own livestock, had the best teachers, a swimming pool, a C-47, and "a richer and broader curriculum." With an unmistakable smile on his face, Leo recalls, "The community that had threatened to drive the migrants out, and who resented their presence, came to accept them as part of the community and to work with them on a friendly cooperative basis."

And what of the children of the Grapes of Wrath who attended the school? What became of the ragamuffins in baggy pants and soiled dresses? Willard Melton laid his share of adobe bricks and plowed the fields season after season. Willard Melton is now a college professor. John Rutledge and Robert Faulkner graduated from high school as student body presidents, and John owns his own mining company in Utah, Robert his own business in California. Pete Bancroft's son, Ed, is a high school teacher, Bob Rutledge runs his own business in Bakersfield, Jim Wren teaches at West High School, Wesley Gosch is a dental technician, Bill Johnson owns two supermarkets in Kern County, Tommy Ross and James Peel own construction companies in Hawaii and California, Jim Montgomery owns two restaurants in Boise, Idaho, his brother Bruce is a marketing manager for IBM, Joe Collins is a judge. . . . Janice Newton became the first woman painting contractor in Kern County, her sister Patsy owns a stereo store, Patty Anderson, one of the school's few black pupils, became a schoolteacher in Los Angeles, so did her sister. . . . Others went on to become legal secretaries, postal clerks, engineers, captains in the Kern County Fire Department, consultant investigators for the California Department of Industrial Relations. . . .

Businessman Bob Rutledge speaks for the migrant children. Bob made the trip from Arkansas in '36, and he has contact with nearly thirty of his classmates every month. "We're closely knit as a group," he says, while studying old photos of Arvin Federal. Pointing to a picture of the migrants in a typing class, he reflects: "Look at these people. They're not dumb." He speaks of poverty as being "in the mind" and says "we never accepted poverty." He describes "the Okie attitude" in the Depression: "This is what we are now, but it's not what we're going to be. Give us some time." He received "nothing but kindness from the teachers." He says: "Everybody should have that experience. You have to live it to understand it. I wouldn't trade my place for anybody's place." He talks of a "pervading affection" between the students, the teachers, and Leo Hart, and relates an example of what he means. "The girls, when they got old enough, couldn't wear nylons because their hands were too rough from picking cotton. And they had to pick cotton to buy their dresses for the prom. But we understood," he adds. "It was part of all of us, what we were and where we were going."

Arvin Federal Emergency School ended in 1944. The District Attorney brought Hart an opinion from the Attorney General in Sacramento. The legal ruling stated that an "emergency" cannot last over five years, and therefore, Hart could no longer run his school. Within a matter of months, Arvin Federal was combined with another school in the district, and the two institutions are known today as Sunset School. Immediately, the trustees of Arvin School District petitioned Leo for permission to let their seventh and eighth grade students attend the school in the camp set aside for migrants. Hart complied, and nonmigrant students enrolled by the hundreds, suddenly out numbering the migrants. It was no longer *their* school, but now that was of no importance. For the migrant children had learned remarkable lessons in journeying out of the Dust Bowl era—and so had the community.

The success of Leo's kids contrasts sharply with the bitter, bitter ending in *The Grapes of Wrath.* "It had a happy ending," Leo says, as he rocks back and forth and remembers. He pauses for a moment and points to a photograph of himself and four of his pupils. He is holding one of the children, and she is wearing his hat. "See that girl," he says. "Sometimes, when she wasn't ready to go to school, I had to hold her and walk her around outside until she was ready. She liked to wear my hat." He smiles, then stares out the window across the dirt road and into the field. The smile spreads over his entire face.

Reversal of Fortune: Images of America's Chinese, 1937–1944, The Dominance of California
by John C. Chen

The following article by Professor John C. Chen of the Charles Drew University in Los Angeles is a microcosmic picture of the Chinese American experience prior to and during World War II. The main thrust of Professor Chen's argument is that the changes in how American's viewed the Chinese resulted in improved conditions. Another basic theme to this excellent study is that the Chinese accelerated their journey to middle class respectability. The article concludes that the Chinese American, like the Mexican American and the African American, recognized their need to strive for improved civil rights and some argue that the modern Asian American movement toward equality began in this period.

If theirs is a Chinaman's chance—very well, they'll take it . . . Their optimism and their courage make them true Americans.

> Ernest O. Hauser
> December, 1940

In most respects the Chinese appeared to me to be a good deal like ourselves, an intelligent and industrious people with much of our humor and much of our adaptability.

> John P. Marquand
> July, 1941

I. Introduction and Historical Background

On December 17, 1943, President Franklin D. Roosevelt signed a bill repealing the Chinese Exclusion Act, thus ending a saga which began over sixty years before with the bill's passage in 1882. The repeal of this act was the culminating event in a long process which

began with a transformation in the public images of the Chinese in America and underscored the importance of a minority's racial image in shaping their experiences in the United States. However, while the history of anti-Chinese agitation is fairly well-known, the story of how the Chinese image improved and the changes that this led to is not.

The Chinese Exclusion Act was passed after several decades of vituperative labor agitation and extremely negative public images which led to nationwide support for the bill. For the first time in this nation's history a racial group was specifically excluded. Like the campaign to adopt the Exclusion Act the campaign for its repeal was preceded by several decades of gradually improving public images for the Chinese. This process intensified and reached its apogee during the Second World War when the United States and China became formal allies against Japan. This led not only led to better treatment for the Chinese popula "occupationally, educationally, politically, numerically and residentially," that positive images began to appear and began to compete with the negative ones. One example of a more positive image was the character of Charlie Chan who began appearing in a series of books and movies in the 1920s. Chan was an Americanized Chinese who was genial and wore Western clothes, but who also spoke pigdin English and was prone to spouting Confucian-like aphorisms. Still Chan was a vastly more positive image than his predecessor Fu Manchu who portrayed the Chinese as evil, mysterious and power hungry. Yet though the images were improved, discrimination against the Chinese in America remained the same.

II. Changes in the Images of the Chinese between 1937 and 1944

When the Sino-Japanese war began in 1937 Gallup polls showed that most Americans were largely indifferent to the plight of the Chinese. However, as news stories from East Asia continued pouring in, Chinese interests were seen to coincide increasingly with those of America and the Chinese themselves were viewed as sympathetic victims of a foreign aggressor. Three years later public opinion had swung solidly in favor of the Chinese and against the Japanese as evidenced by polls showing that 77 percent of Americans sympathized with the Chinese whereas only 2 percent favored the Japanese. Increased negativity toward the Japanese now meant increased sympathy for the Chinese.

The release of the movie The Good Earth, which was based on a popular best selling novel by Pearl Buck, also contributed to a more favorable view. Dorothy Jones estimated that this one movie was seen by 23 million people in the United States and by over 42 million throughout the world and changed people's perceptions of the Chinese more than anything else. In contrast to previous Hollywood movies which showed the Chinese as affable but ignorant houseboys and cooks, this one attempted to portray them as ordinary human beings. It also tried to break the stereotype of the Chinese as a mysterious people. To help ensure the movie's success the studio got the approval of the Chinese government for the making of this picture.

Popular literature also showed increased regard for the Chinese by the non-Chinese population in America. In 1937 Life magazine placed a gripping picture of an abandoned baby that had been badly burned in a Japanese attack on Shanghai on its front cover. The picture had a profound impact on Americans. Five years later people still mentioned this picture when they sent funds to the United China Relief Fund for the aid of Chinese children. In 1938 Time magazine named Chiang Kai-shek and his wife as man and woman of the year. John Marquand, a creator of negative stereotypes of the Chinese in his Mr. Moto series, publicly repudiated his previous stance in Asia magazine and also by writing that Fu Manchu was the wrong image of the Chinese because they were really like Americans. In Carl Glick's 'Shake Hands with the Dragon,' Chinese-Americans were praised for solving the problems of child rearing, juvenile delinquency, divorce, social security, and enjoying a leisurely old age. Glick even praised the traditional Chinese custom of arranged marriages.

After the United States entered the war in 1941 positive images of the Chinese reached unprecedented heights. Magazines like the Saturday Evening Post depicted Chinese Americans as honest, clean, generous, loyal, non-litiginous, and reliable. Others reported the American-born Chinese as optimistic and courageous. American salesgirls described visiting Chinese airmen as "cute." Stereotypical Chinese impassivity was reinterpreted as a mask for "sensitive natures" and the Chinese were found to have an "unfailing humor." Even the Chinese American way of fishing came in for a glowing description.

Pearl Buck's novel Dragon Seed, which was published in 1942, reinforced the image of the Chinese peasants as ordinary human beings. Wallace Stegner's story "Chink," despite its offensive title, was actually a sympathetic portrayal by a young Caucasian boy of two Chinese men who lived by themselves in a New England town. Though the story ends tragically, the Chinese are described as human and sympathetic men. Margaret Keim even managed to reinterpret Bret Harte's writings, long seen as one of the major literary sources of hostility to the Chinese, as favorable to them.

In 1942 Helena Kuo published an article in American Mercury that audaciously told American women that femininity had become a lost art among them because big business now decided what it was, marketed it, and turned all American women into carbon copies of one another. Kuo maintained that there were things about femininity that Chinese culture could teach them. The image of Chinese women received an added boost during the war when Madame Chiang Kai-shek's visit to the United States broke the stereotyped image of Chinese women as China dolls. During her visit Madame Chiang gave a speech before the U.S. Congress that was received with a standing ovation.

One social scientist engaged in an experiment with school children to enhance their appreciation for the Chinese. A sixth grade teacher brought in a sixteen year old Chinese girl and had her speak about her life and family in China and America. Afterward the attitudes of four groups of school children were measured. The group having the most contact with the young Chinese girl had the most improved attitudes toward the Chinese which persisted three months later when they were asked about the subject again.

The improved image of the Chinese in public opinion was evident in a poll about national characteristics that was conducted in July, 1942, in which Americans found the Chinese hardworking, honest, brave, religious, and intelligent. These were the very attributes which Americans used to describe themselves.

During the campaign to repeal Chinese Exclusion, testimony given before the House Committee of Immigration and Naturalization attested to the improved perceptions Americans had for their Chinese inhibitants. Chinese Americans were praised for not relying on welfare, a low crime rate, honesty and industry.

In 1942 the Office of War Information pressured Hollywood to make more positive movies involving the Chinese as part of the war effort and even issued a government information manuel on the subject. Since Japanese Americans were in internment camps or fighting in Europe, Chinese American actors were called upon to help make films oftentimes playing the Japanese villains. In fact one actor, Richard Loo, became so notorious for his roles as a sadistic Japanese general that he was reluctant to appear in public for fear of being attacked. However, Caucasians were still chosen to play all of the major roles including ones where the lead character was Chinese, e.g., Dragon Seed, Castle in the Desert.

Sometimes these casting decisions led to some rather odd results. A Hollywood film director's reluctance to put non-proven Asian American actors in leading roles was demonstrated in the casting for the film version of Pearl Buck's novel Dragon Seed. Although the lead parts called for Chinese actors, only Caucasians such as Katherine Hepburn were cast in them. Even though the director did not think the public was ready for a Chinese lead actor, a critic for the San Francisco Chronicle commented somewhat sarcastically about the decision to cast blue-eyed Caucasians in the lead roles, especially since this was one of the major reasons that Hollywood gave for making the film in black and white instead of color. The Chronicle accused the film industry of being too timid and afraid of not casting stars.

Dragon Seed was also significant for the messages it conveyed about the relationship between the Chinese and Americans. By having Caucasians play the lead Chinese roles the movie identified the plight of the Chinese with that of the Americans. The atrocities which the Japanese inflicted on the Chinese were now inflicted on American actors who were playing Chinese roles. A further twist in the casting of this film was the selection of Chinese American actors to play the important Japanese roles. Unfortunately, the psychological ramifications of these variegated racial casting strategies are too complex to be untangled further here.

Chinese American actors also appeared in mainstream movies, e.g., Keys of the Kingdom, Across the Pacific. In many of these war films the Chinese appeared not only as hard-working and loyal people, but also as helpless before Japanese aggression. Also Hollywood producers increased their efforts to make their films with a Chinese theme more accurate. This was especially true during the filming of Keys of the Kingdom, a movie that starred Gregory Peck. Since the studio planned a worldwide distribution of this movie, it was concerned not to irritate the Chinese government which had refused permission to show movies it considered offensive and actually had shut down the Chinese offices of studios that did so. Though the director refused to submit the script of the movie to Chinese government censors, he did consult with a Roman Catholic priest who had served as a missionary in China about the accuracy of the film. Asian American actors were recruited for those leads roles that called for them.

Some Chinese American actors such as Keye Luke, Victor Sen Yung and Benson Fong, who played Charlie Chan's three sons, did not fault Hollywood for not casting an Asian in the lead role. In fact the Charlie Chan series had first been cast with an Asian American lead actor, but the series floundered until Caucasians started playing the role. Benson Fong defended Hollywood's casting of

Caucasian actors in Asian roles because there were no Chinese actors available. Also a Chinese could not be cast as a sheriff or lawyer at that time because none existed and the character would have been unbelievable. He noted that it was difficult for Chinese males to get parts in the movies and develop their talent. To enhance his abilities to play character parts Victor Sen Yung went to film, voice, and drama school to learn more about Chinese culture. Keye Luke observed that it was hard to make a living doing pictures in Hollywood. Victor Sen Yung and Benson Fong found they had to develop side businesses in order to survive economically.

None of these actors believed that they played parts which stereotyped or degraded the Chinese. Victor Yung defended his playing a subservient Chinese character who wore a queue and spoke with an accent as faithful to history. He also denied that there was racial discrimination on the movie sets. Benson Fong said that he deliberately started his restaurant business so that he could turn down roles that demeaned the Chinese. Keye Luke reported that he turned down all roles that used the word "chink" in them.

In contrast to her male counterparts Anna Mae Wong, who more than any other actress created the Hollywood stereotype of the Chinese woman as dragon lady, did not hesitate to criticize the movie industry. Though she defended her roles at first because there were no other ones for her, Ms. Wong came to hate the parts that Hollywood offered her. Eventually she fled America for Europe and then retired from acting.

However, even during the height of American regard for the Chinese, negative portrayals of the Chinese persisted in the Hollywood film industry. For instance in 1941 a Chinese woman was selected to play a dragon lady in Shanghai Gesture. Then in 1943 Fu Manchu reappeared in the Drums of Fu Manchu.

III. Changes in the Chinese American Experience

Although a better public image did not lead to many improvements in the Chinese American experience as measured by job opportunities, military service, and public accommodations between 1937 and 1941, this changed on December 7, 1941, when the United States entered the Second World War as an ally of China. One of the most significant areas of progress for Chinese Americans occurred in the American military. Opportunities for them in the service expanded and sixteen thousand joined. A few went to fight in Europe where 213 were killed in action. Chinese Americans in the navy could now become seamen whereas before they could only serve as messmen or stewards.

While in the service many had a mixture of both positive and negative experiences. Some joined all Chinese American units and were sent as support forces to the China Burma theater. Years later Peter Phan interviewed a number of these Chinese American veterans. A Chinese American unit was made up of recruits from all over the United States. However, over 40 percent of this unit came from California. Some of the Chinese Americans GIs did not want to belong to an all Chinese American unit because they thought this would hamper their military careers. Others liked it for the protection it offered because they could mitigate the impact of racial discrimination by going to town together. Many felt a mixture of pride and rejection. While they found themselves treated better than African Americans, they were still not accepted as equals by whites.

The myth of white superiority broke down for some when they had to teach white recruits who could not read or write. But many of these soldiers still did not consider themselves Americans because they were not white. Furthermore, racial tensions were reported between Chinese American soldiers and whites, especially when the former developed friendships with Caucasian women. Overall a number of men thought the all Chinese unit had gained them respect in America.

While in China many of these soldiers felt marginalized. They were "familiar strangers in both worlds." Chinese soldiers did not accord them the same respect as they did white soldiers. Many Chinese American soldiers were shocked by the poverty, inequality, and corruption in China and felt a new appreciation for America. These troops faced discrimination at home and an ambivalent reception in China too where they were seen as neither Chinese nor Americans. They also found that racial discrimination against them persisted even in China.

After the war ended some of these soldiers visited Shanghai where they observed Japanese prisoners of war sweeping the streets. Harry Lim thought "those could have been us." It "[m]ade you think about the double standards in America and had you wondering how you would be treated when you went home." Richard Gee said, "If we had traded uni-

forms, we could have been mistaken for them. It was deeply disturbing."

A few Chinese American women joined non-combatant service in 1942. Some women like Maggie Gee found that gender stereotypes also accompanied women recruits when the men had trouble admitting that women could fly as well as they could. Chinese American women supported the war effort by forming associations like the Chinese YWCA, Square and Circle Club, and Fidelis Coteri. They were active and proficient at fundraising.

Before the war job discrimination was one of the greatest areas of frustration for Chinese Americans. Even when they had graduate degrees from the finest universities in America, they could not get jobs outside of Chinatown and many wasted their educations by doing menial jobs. As late as 1941 Carey McWilliams noted that there were no jobs for five thousand young Chinese Americans in San Francisco. Though Li Cai's son was the first Chinese American to graduate from the University of Southern California with a civil engineering degree, he could not find any work in his field. Instead Chinese Americans had to work as cooks, dishwashers, laundrymen, domestics, or in jobs that nobody else wanted.

Charles Chinn found out that unions either would not let you in or would not help you find a job. Even within the Chinese American community you had to join a tong or benevolent association or you would not be able to get work. Once employed through the efforts of the benevolent associations, you were required to contribute a portion of your earnings to meet its needs.

Those who dared to set up businesses in San Francisco's white neighborhoods encountered resistance. For instance a Chinese butcher who located his store outside of Chinatown was forced by rocks and pickets to close it. However, a similar attempt to close down a National Dollar Store for hiring Chinese workers failed.

Because they could not get decent jobs here Chinese parents often sent their children to Chinese school in America so they would have the opportunity to work in China. After Victor Sen Yung's mother died, his father was often away on business and he grew up with a Caucasian family where he learned to speak English first. Still his father thought it important enough to enroll him in a Chinese language school where his classmates thought he was Japanese because he did not know any Chinese when he arrived. Some parents like Sam Chang went even further and sent their children back to China to study. Pardee Lowe's father also sent him to China so he could learn Chinese and get a job there because prospects for getting a job in America were so grim. Benson Fong learned to speak no less than three Chinese dialects and later went to college in China for seven years.

The labor demands of the war effort gave many Chinese Americans employment opportunities outside of Chinatown. This was the first important break in the wall of racial discrimination at home for them. This was true especially for the second generation of Chinese Americans. But for those who stayed in Chinatown the exodus of so many workers into the dominant market created a labor shortage which led to many business closures. The Chinese were now asked to join restaurant unions. More importantly, those who switched jobs during the war found no racial discrimination in their new jobs.

After the war ended Beulah Kwoh conducted a sociological study and found that Chinese American college graduates were not returning to the family business to work because they were able to find employment in white enterprises, especially in the fields of science and engineering. However, all fields were not as open to Chinese Americans. For example, since Chinese Americans hired Caucasian lawyers to do their legal work and no white firm would hire them to work at their firm, there was almost no interest among Chinese Americans in pursuing a legal career.34

In her study of Chinese American women Judy Yung reviewed the census records which showed how both Chinese men and women moved into the primary sector of the labor market between 1940 and 1950. Chinese women in particular made significant strides into the primary sector of the market possibly because the labor shortage opened up jobs for these women in Chinatown.

Changing attitudes among members of majoritarian society were shown in polls taken during the war which showed that discrimination against the Chinese as coworkers had diminished considerably. In one done with high school students, laborers, and farmers only 5 or 6 percent reported that they would refuse to work alongside a Chinese person of equal competence. This compared favorably with polls done by Emory Bogardus during the period of 1924 to 1927 where only 27 percent of the whites and 28 percent of African Americans were willing to have Chinese as coworkers.

The war provided employment opportunities and was also a cause of suffering for Chinese Americans. Many were able to enter the mainstream labor force, but the community as a whole had to give money to both the American and Chinese governments to support the war effort. Almost all of them were extremely anxious about the fate of relatives in China.

In public accommodations Chinese Americans continued to experience discrimination during the war. Chinese American soldiers often ate in Chinese American restaurants not only because they liked the food better but also because they would not have been served in white ones. Charles Chinn was part of a white military unit during the war and was refused food service in Los Angeles and Texas. In 1942 a Colorado restaurant posted a "Whites Trade Only" sign in its window and denied service to several Chinese Americans who tried to eat there.

Sometimes service was refused because the Chinese were mistaken for Japanese. Ruth Wong noted that Asians were not served in restaurants so she got an identification card. She also got harassed because people thought she was Japanese. Sometimes Chinese Americans were also harassed and occasionally beaten because of this mistake and took to wearing buttons saying, "I am Chinese."

The legacy of racial discrimination persisted most of all in the housing sector. Before the war most Chinese Americans lived in Chinatown where rents were high and landlords made no repairs because the tenants could not move out of the area. Chinese families often had to live in the red light district of San Francisco. The Chinese were hedged in Chinatown by restrictive covenants which prevented them from buying houses. The result was that living conditions in Chinatown were extremely crowded. Sometimes people slept eight to a room. In 1944 Elizabeth Coleman noted that a Chinese person from Europe could not get his name listed in white areas for places to rent in San Francisco even though he was working for the U.S. government. As a resident in Europe for many years he had never encountered this kind of discrimination.

The persistence of the unpopularity of the Chinese in America as neighbors was reflected in a poll taken of factory workers in November, 1942, which found that they were the third least popular group after African Americans and Jews. A poll done at the same time among high school students noted that 28 percent of them listed a Chinese person as the least desireable roommate. Still the results of these polls indicated some improvement over the results published by Emory Bogardus in the 1920s. In those polls less than 16 percent of whites and 18 percent of blacks were willing to have Chinese as neighbors.

After the war Chinese Americans found they still could not buy property in the Marina and Nob Hill districts of San Francisco. In fact they were not allowed to buy property outside of Chinatown. Chinese American veterans of World War II were disturbed when they found that housing discrimination persisted. Even in a smaller city like Watsonville Duncan Chin observed that Chinese American veterans could not buy houses in the better parts of town. The GI bill did give some Chinese American GIs mobility which many used to develop professional careers and buy homes outside of Chinatown.

IV. The Repeal of the Chinese Exclusion Act

Improved racial images and attitudes towards the Chinese in America by white Americans led to the major legal advance for them during the war. This occurred in

December, 1943, when President Roosevelt signed a bill passed by Congress repealing the sixty-one year old Chinese Exclusion Act. In some ways the new law was still quite restrictive because it allowed only 105 Chinese to immigrate per year and retained many other discriminatory features in allowing that quota. In fact Fong Man Hee pointed out that the repeal law contained a provision which lumped all people of Chinese origin together regardless of their citizenship. Such a provision was an act of discrimination against the Chinese who lived in other countries and was a way of imposing the discriminatory practices of the United States on the Chinese in those countries. However, the bill also contained important language that allowed the Chinese already in America to naturalize as citizens. This ended a policy of racial favoritism toward Caucasians which had existed in American law since 1790.

Fred Riggs in his book, Pressures on Congress: A Study of the Repeal of Chinese Exclusion, detailed the activity of the Citizen's Committee to Repeal Chinese Exclusion. This Committee acted as a catalytic group and was made up of Sinophilic Caucasians, e.g., Richard Walsh and his wife Pearl Buck, Carl Glick, Charles Spinks, and others. It was deliberately made up of non-Chinese American citizens in order to create the impression that white Americans were calling for a change.

Riggs detailed how this group created the impression that a broad, national consensus existed for repeal. It collected endorsements from groups favorable toward repeal such as commercial, religious, and idealistic groups and also from groups who were traditionally hostile toward the Chinese in America such as organized labor, veteran's groups, and western and southern interests. Where negative opinions were expressed, e.g., by the American Federation of Labor and the American Legion, the committee got branches of these organizations to break ranks and openly support repeal. The repeal law itself was carefully crafted to offend the fewest number of people while attracting the greatest possible Congressional support. Finally the Citizens' Committee helped to find key sponsors of the bill who guided the measure carefully through both houses of Congress.

The Committee's Congressional supporters advanced a wide range of arguments for supporting the bill which allowed most Congressmen to support its passage. These arguments included viewing it as a war measure, that it was needed to boost the morale of the Chinese Nationalists and to counter Japanese propaganda, that the Exclusion laws were now superfulous since the passage of the 1924 Immigration Act, that the Chinese should not be treated worse under our immigration laws than the Japanese which was the case under current law, that 105 Chinese would not be a threat to American labor, that it would bolster democracy in China after the war, and that since America had renounced its right to extraterritoriality, it now needed to maintain good relations with China in order to benefit from business ventures after the war.

Despite the efforts of the Citizens' Committee to give the repeal measure the appearance of broad popular support, its position was undercut by a national poll published in the New York Times on November 11, 1943, which showed that supporters of repeal barely outnumbered those opposed to it.

However, on the West Coast, the traditional center of anti-Chinese hostility, sentiment was definitely in favor of the measure. California Congressman Will Rogers, Jr., a strong supporter of the repeal bill, reported that the proposal to repeal the Chinese Exclusion Act had been greeted with "thunderous applause" by all the groups he met with on a trip home. Supporters included "businessmen, professional men, veteran's organizations, women's groups, labor organizations, and service clubs."

The Citizen's Committee was less successful in persuading the other members of California's Congressional delegation to support the repeal. Besides Rogers only two other California Congressmen went on the record as supporting the measure. One representative registered definite opposition and another expressed reservations about the bill. California's senior Senator Hiram Johnson was a long-time foe of Chinese immigration and remained steadfast in his opposition to repeal. However, his influence was blunted because he was ill at the time and away from the capital.

Before the war the effect of tight immigration laws against the Chinese at Angel Island had led to charges of harassment and to complaints by the business community that such practices hurt them economically because people avoided San Francisco. Even Chinese who were American citizens were subject to being closely examined upon reentering the United States. In 1942 Walter Kong published a list of sample questions which were asked of returning Chinese at Angel Island. Often over 150 extremely detailed questions were posed. Some people compared their stay on Angel Island to being in a concentration camp. Unfortunately the passage of the repeal measure had little immediate effect on the practices of the immigration officials as complaints were still being issued about their actions six months after repeal.

The repeal allowed the Chinese in America to become naturalized citizens. This in turn permitted them to vote. It also invalidated the Alien Land laws and permitted them to own land legally. However, the repeal did not effect California's miscegenation laws. When Keye Luke wanted to marry a Caucasian woman, he had to formalize his marriage in another state and the passage of the repeal law did not change this situation.

Fortunately for the supporters of repeal, the exclusion law was changed before the end of the heyday of positive images of the Chinese. In 1944 these images started turning negative as the public learned of General Joseph Stilwell's reports from the China Burma theater along with those of American GI's who were disillusioned with the Chinese military. By the end of 1944 public enthusiasm for the Chinese had declined dramatically.

V. Conclusion

The period between 1937 and 1944 saw many changes in American perceptions of the Chinese and the Chinese in America. This process was accelerated by the Second World War when positive images of the Chinese reached new heights. Ultimately this led to changes in the experiences of Chinese Americans. The war provided opportunities for Chinese Americans in the military and in employment. Changes were less noticeable in the fields of public accommodations and especially in housing where racial discrimination persisted despite the fact that China was now an ally of the United States. Finally the culmination of the changes wrought by improved public images and the wartime alliance was the repeal of the Chinese Exclusion Act. Though intended by many as a wartime measure, the repeal also allowed Chinese nationals in the United States to become naturalized citizens. This ended their sojourner status and permitted them to participate more fully in American life. These legal changes helped the Chinese in America to withstand the public's hostility which occurred with the start of the Korean War and provided a basis for further advances in the rights of all Chinese Americans.

The Mare Island Mutiny and Court Martial
by Charles Wollenberg

In October, 1944, Black soldiers at the Mare Island Naval Depot in northern California refused to load ammunition ships. When fifty Black soldiers were tried for mutiny, public attention was focused on the racial policies of the United States Navy. Professor Charles Wollenberg of Laney College, Oakland, examines the causes and consequences of the Mare Island mutiny and court martial. What is interesting about Wollenberg's essay is that it demonstrates that Blacks could successfully fight back against segregationist policies. In a broader sense the Mare Island incident was the beginning of the modern civil rights movement in the San Francisco bay area. A new consciousness concerning race crept into the public mind, and this began a movement for equality among liberal Californians of all races and creeds. The ugly reaction from naval segregation led to a liberal renaissance in post-war California civilization.

World War II was a crucible in which a new era of race relations was forged in the United States. For the first time more than a million black men and women served in the armed forces, about half of them overseas. The war also accelerated the migration of blacks to northern and western cities and gave them more economic and political clout than ever before. With Adolf Hitler demonstrating the evils of racism, respectable people and publications no longer could openly espouse white supremacist doctrines. Segregation nevertheless persisted in the United States, and nowhere more obviously than in the military itself. World War II was essentially conducted as a Jim Crow operation by the army, navy and marines, with nearly all black personnel assigned to segregated units commanded by white officers.

The inconsistency of fighting Nazism with racially segregated military units was not lost on black Americans. Accordingly, the armed forces became a special target of protest and organizational activity (helping pave the way for the civil rights activism of the post-war era). A number of specific incidents focused attention on wartime military segregation, among them the important Mare Island mutiny court martial trial of September and October, 1944. The refusal by fifty black sailors to load ammunition ships at the Mare Island Naval Depot in northern San Francisco Bay produced the navy's first mutiny court martial of the war and the longest mutiny trial in navy history. It also resulted in protests and pressures that helped bring about a remarkable transformation in the navy's racial policies.

The so-called mutiny at Mare Island had its origins in pre-war navy personnel policies. In 1941 blacks were still excluded from all naval assignments except the

Charles Wollenberg, "Blacks vs. Navy Blue: The Mare Island Mutiny Court Martial," *California History,* Vol. LVIII (Spring 1979) pp. 62–75. Reprinted by permission of the author.

messman's service. Secretary of the Navy Frank Knox argued that to allow black sailors to do other tasks would "provoke discord and demoralization." Admiral Chester W. Nimitz explained that "the policy of now enlisting men of the Colored race for any branch of naval service except the messman's branch was adopted to meet the best interests of general ship efficiency."

For a time after the Japanese attack on Pearl Harbor, the navy tried to maintain its policy of using blacks exclusively as "chambermaids for the braid." When Dorie Miller, a black messman, manned a machine gun and shot down at least four Japanese planes during the Pearl Harbor attack, navy brass initially played down the incident, apparently to prevent attention to the fact that black men could perform well in combat. But under pressure from civil rights groups and President Franklin Roosevelt, Navy Secretary Knox finally announced on April 7, 1942, that black enlistees henceforth would be accepted for "general service." The "messman only" era was at an end.

The navy's new policy was not one of integration, however. A segregated facility for black recruits was established at Great Lakes Naval Training Center in Illinois, with smaller segregated installations set up at Memphis and Hampton Institute in Virginia. Except for messmen, blacks were assigned to shore duty only, primarily as stevedores and seabees in segregated units commanded by whites. In 1943 the navy began accepting black draftees and a very few black officer candidates. In 1944 the secretary of the navy established a unit of black Waves, members of the women's reserve, and assigned black crews to two auxiliary

vessels. Also in 1944 the navy published a "Guide to the Command of Negro Personnel" which proclaimed that "the navy accepts no theories of racial differences in inborn ability" and cautioned officers against referring to blacks as "niggers," "nigras," "boy," "coon," "darkey," or "jig". But the official policy of segregation continued.

One of the first naval installations to receive "general service" black enlistees was the Port Chicago Naval Magazine on San Francisco Bay, a facility about thirty-five miles northeast of San Francisco and fifteen miles east of Mare Island. Following Secretary Knox's "general service" order of 1942, segregated units of black sailors were assigned to load ammunition ships at Port Chicago. On the evening of July 17, 1944, about half of the Port Chicago stevedores were loading the *Quinalt Victory* and *E. A. Bryan* when a massive explosion rocked the entire area. The blast looked like a "flaming doughnut," a "blinding flash that literally filled the sky." After the fire subsided, the place where the men had been working was described as "a scorched earth scene," with both ships and the pier at which they were docked totally destroyed. Most buildings on the naval base and in the town of Port Chicago had been damaged, and windows were shattered in nearby Martinez. Approximately 320 men died in the blast, more than 200 of whom were black sailors who had been loading the ammunition.

In the days following the event, a navy spokesman expressed doubt that the exact cause of the explosion would ever be known, and he commended the surviving black personnel at Port Chicago for their "coolness and bravery." Off-duty and in their barracks at the time of the blast, the men had immediately begun fighting fires and searching for survivors. They were later joined by black sailors from Mare Island, and eventually four of the men who had battled the flames raging among the boxcars loaded with ammunition received decorations. Admiral C. H. Wright, commandant of the Twelfth Naval District, particularly commended the black soldiers who "gave their lives in the service of their country. . . . Their sacrifice could not have been greater had it occurred on a battleship or a beachhead."

On August 9 and 10, some three weeks after the tragedy, the surviving stevedores were reassembled at Mare Island and, for the first time since the explosion, ordered to load ammunition ships. Some 328 men refused to do so, explaining that they feared another blast. After the initial refusal to work, Captain N. H. Goss, commander of the Mare Island depot, instructed his 3 division officers to give individual work orders to each man, and while this apparently was not done in all cases, 70 sailors did subsequently agree to load ammunition. On August 11 Admiral Wright addressed the remaining 258 men. He permitted about 25 men to state their grievances and reported that they did so "freely and respectfully." After Wright's speech, all but 44 of the sailors agreed to work, although 6 more men later refused. The 50 men abstaining were then separated from their units and held in detention.

On August 13 Captain Goss prepared a written memorandum to summarize the oral report he already had given Admiral Wright. The memo not only covered the facts of the incident, but also included Goss's views on the roots of the problem.

Goss stated that ever since blacks had been assigned to Port Chicago and Mare Island, there had been "agitators, ringleaders among these men." He also thought that the sailors had been subjected to "outside propaganda and subversive influence." Goss apparently considered himself an expert on what he called the "normal characteristics of Negroes," and he believed that the Port Chicago men were unusual because they had "a persistent disposition to question orders, to argue, and in effect to attempt to bargain." Another new characteristic which Goss had never observed before among Negroes" was sensitivity about discrimination. This he could not understand, given "the extreme care and patience which has been exercised both at Mare Island and Port Chicago to avoid discrimination." Goss concluded that "concerted action and persistent refusal to obey orders" among the men "indicated a mutinous attitude." He recommended that the 50 hold-outs be charged with mutiny before a general court martial. The 208 who agreed to work after Admiral Wright's speech should be charged with a lesser offense before a summary court martial. The 70 who chose to return to work on August 10 should be free from disciplinary action.

Admiral Wright had already forwarded Goss's oral recommendations to Washington by August 13. Wright himself was not so free with his personal opinions as Goss, but he did note in his report to Washington that he believed that "a considerable portion of the men involved are of a low order of mentality. . . ." Wright urged that ammunition handling was a "logical use" of black personnel but said that "pains must be taken" to avoid the appearance of discrimination. The admiral suggested a rotation system in which the black men would occasionally be given other duties and the assignment of some white units to the task of loading ammunition.

Wright's report was addressed to the new secretary of the navy, James V. Forrestal, who had replaced Frank Knox after the latter's death in the spring of 1944. Forrestal approved Wright's recommendations and on August 28 wrote to President Roosevelt informing him of the situation. The initial draft of the letter to the president simply covered the facts of the case and the disciplinary action planned. But the final draft signed on August 28 included the proposal to rotate black sailors in other jobs and to assign white units to handle ammunition. Forrestal told the president that these measures would "avoid any semblance of discrimination against Negroes."

The mutiny trial of the black sailors began on September 14 at Treasure Island Naval Base in San Francisco Bay. Retired Admiral Hugo S. Osterhaus presided as president of the seven-man trial board. Chief prosecutor and trial judge advocate was Lt. Commander James F. Coakley. Before the war, Coakley had been an assistant district attorney in Alameda County in an office once headed by Earl Warren. (After the war Coakley was elected district attorney, and he gained prominence in the prosecution of Berkeley demonstrators in the 1960s). The five-man defense team at Treasure Island was led by Lt. Gerald E. Veltmann.

The defense lost its most important legal battle before the trial began. Veltmann had submitted a pre-trial brief calling for dismissal of the mutiny charge in which he quoted from *Winthrop's Military Law and Precedents*. *Winthrop's* defined mutiny as "unlawful opposition or resistance to, or defiance of superior military authority with a deliberate attempt to usurp, subvert or override the same." The brief argued that this definition clearly required that men charge with mutiny must intend to seize or overthrow command. At worst, he argued, the Mare Island sailors had simply disobeyed an order with no intent to "usurp, subvert or override" authority.

The prosecution countered with its own quotation from *Winthrop's:* "Collective insubordination or simultaneous disobedience of a lawful order by two or more persons . . . is an endeavor to make a revolt or mutiny." Commander Coakley argued that under this definition, he was not required to prove that the defendants intended to seize command. Instead, "evidence showing a joint, collective and persistent refusal by two or more men to work after a lawful order to do so" could constitute mutiny. Faced with conflicting definitions, the trial board sided with the prosecution and refused to dismiss the charge.

Coakley then had to show that there had been an organized effort or conspiracy to disobey orders among the men. On the second day of the trial his attempt to do so created another major legal battle. The prosecution presented the testimony of officers who said that they heard black sailors encouraging their compatriots not to load ammunition. The sailors reportedly used such phrases as "Don't go to work for the white m—— f—." "Let's all stick together," and "We have the officers by the b—." The problem with this "evidence" was that none of the witnesses could identify the persons who were supposed to have made these remarks. Lt. Ernest Delucchi, for example, testified that he heard the comments while standing in formation with his back to the men. Veltmann argued that this testimony was inadmissible hearsay and that even if the statements had been heard, there was no way of telling if any of the defendants had made them. Again, however, Admiral Osterhaus ruled in Coakley's favor and allowed the testimony to be entered in the record.

Despite these major blows to the defense case, Veltmann and his colleagues waged a spirited legal battle. In cross-examination they forced prosecution witnesses to admit that the defendants had been polite and respectful and had obeyed all orders except those to load ammunition. Lt. P. H. Pembroke, a navy psychiatrist, testified that the Port Chicago explosion could produce such great trauma among the survivors that the men might reasonably refuse to load ammunition out of a "sense of self-protection." He pointed out that the men had received no psychiatric assistance in dealing with this trauma. Chaplain J. M. Flowers testified that when he admitted his own fear to the defendants and urged them to overcome their fear in order to help "the men in the foxholes," one of the sailors had replied, "In the foxholes a man has a chance to fight back."

The heart of the defense case was the testimony of the accused themselves, and all fifty men appeared on their own behalf. Generally, they testified that they had acted out of fear and had no intention of challenging military authority. They denied planning the work stoppage and said that a petition that had circulated among the men had only requested a change of duty, not urged men to refuse to work. None of the defendants admitted making statements encouraging others to disobey orders, and most claimed they never received individual orders to load ammunition. Many of the men said they would have obeyed such orders had they been given.

Occasionally, the defendants' testimony included some unusual facts. Ollie Green had a broken wrist, and John Dunn was seventeen years old and weighed just 104 pounds, yet both men had been ordered to do the heavy work of loading ammunition. Joe Small described the panic that ensued among the defendants when a piece of paper became caught in the fan in the detention barrack and produced a loud, cracking noise. Several men contended that pre-trial statements taken by the judge advocate's staff were inaccurate. Alphonso MacPherson testified that during the pre-trial interview Coakley had told him to "come clean" or "you will probably get shot." Coakley angrily denied MacPherson's charge, accusing Veltmann of "hitting below the belt." A verbal battle ensued until Admiral Osterhaus observed that MacPherson had not been shot and that it was time for lunch. When defendant Frank Henry neglected to say "sir" in answer to one of Coakley's questions, the prosecutor asked "Did you learn to say 'sir' when you talk to an officer. . . . Why don't you say it instead of being so insolent?" Veltmann vehemently objected to Coakley's remark, and this time Osterhaus agreed with the defense.

In spite of their testimony to the contrary, it is likely that the defendants were motivated by more than fear of another explosion, Robert L. Allen, editor of *Black Scholar* magazine, has recently interviewed some of the surviving Mare Island "mutineers," and he concludes that the work stoppage was a legitimate planned protest against general conditions of segregation and discrimination in the navy and specifically against the lack of recreational facilities, safety precautions, and fair treatment at Port Chicago. At the subsequent court martial, Allen persuasively argues, fear of conviction on mutiny charges led the defendants to deny that they had planned the incident.

Although the confidential reports and memoranda of the navy command indicate concern about the "appearance" or "semblance" of discrimination at Port Chicago, the defense lawyers never identified discrimination as an explanation or justification for the Mare Island incident. In this the lawyers were greatly at odds with leaders of the Bay Area's black community. Joseph James, president of the San Francisco branch of the National Association for the Advancement of Colored People (NAACP), said he was "well aware of the pattern of discrimination practiced in the navy and very much concerned about this trial." Mrs. Irma Lewis of Oakland stated, "We mothers want to know why these loading crews are all Negroes." Reverend C. D. Tolliver of San Francisco also felt it was "unfair that Negroes should always be assigned to dangerous tasks," and J. C. Henderson, an Oakland attorney, believed that "the discriminatory policy of the navy and the overall conditions to which the boys on trial have been subjected should be considered." Henderson explained, "Sometimes it becomes hard to turn the other cheek, even though the oppressor is our brother."

By 1944 Bay Area black leaders were struggling to cope with the consequences of a massive increase in the region's black population. Wartime production created thousands of new industrial jobs, and black immigrants from the South were a major new source of manpower. Between 1940 and 1944, San Francisco's black population grew from less than 5,000 to over 12,000. Similar increases occurred in Oakland and Berkeley, and far greater rates of growth were recorded for the shipyard towns of Richmond and Vallejo, adjacent to Mare Island. For the region as a whole, the black population increased by more than 200 percent between 1940 and 1944.

Local NAACP President James noted that before the war, Bay Area black seldom encountered "Jim Crow treatment" and "recognizing their apparent good fortune, generally exercised care lest they attract too much attention." But the population boom, James observed, had resulted in increasing examples of blatant prejudice. Housing discrimination was producing the area's first black ghetto neighborhoods. Over half the new black population worked in the shipyards, and the chief shipyard union, the boilermakers, required blacks to join segregated "auxiliary locals." In 1944, 1700 black workers at Marinship Company in Sausalito refused to pay union dues unless allowed to join the regular boilermaker locals. The Marin County company honored its union contract by firing the rebels, but in January of 1945 the California supreme court ordered their reinstatement. Joseph James observed that by 1944 the local NAACP branch was carrying "the burden of protest and representation for the Negro community."

It was no surprise that the NAACP

became involved in the Mare Island case. In late September, James asked assistance from the organization's New York headquarters. On October 10, Thurgood Marshall, the NAACP chief counsel, flew to San Francisco with special travel priority supplied by Navy Secretary Forrestal to observe the trial. Marshall met with prosecution and defense lawyers and interviewed all fifty defendants. He soon was convinced that the men were being unjustly prosecuted: "They have told me they were willing to go to jail to get a change of duty because of their terrific fear of explosives, but they had no idea that verbal expression of their fear constituted mutiny." Marshall stayed in the Bay Area twelve days, and his presence helped attract national attention to the trial, particularly that of the national black press. Before leaving, Marshall promised that the NAACP would "expose the whole rotten navy setup which led to the Port Chicago explosion and in turn to the so-called 'mutiny' trial." "Negroes in the navy don't mind loading ammunition," he cautioned, "they just want to know why they are the only ones doing the loading."

Meanwhile, the trial at Treasure Island droned on. On October 18, more than a month after the court martial body originally convened, the defense finally finished presentation of its case. Coakley then called several prosecution rebuttal witnesses to counter a number of allegations made by the defense. Division officers, for example, were called to deny defense testimony that crews loading ammunition had sometimes been forced to race against each other. Members of the judge advocate's staff assured the court that no coercion had been used in taking

pre-trial statements and that the statements were accurate, though not always in the defendant's exact words.

On October 23, Lt. Veltmann presented the defense's final argument. He repeated his objection to the mutiny charge and argued that the defendants had taken no overt action to "usurp, subvert or overthrow" authority. Again Veltmann objected to the use of hearsay evidence and questioned whether precise orders had been given to all the men. He contended that the defendants had been motivated by understandable fear rather than a desire to seize authority.

Commander Coakley's final prosecution argument disputed Veltmann on every point. The prosecutor argued that the men had repeatedly disobeyed orders given over a three-day period. He contended that the defendants had discussed the matter among themselves and urged others to join them and that this constituted a "collective refusal" to accept authority. The men who participated in such a refusal had entered into a conspiracy to mutiny "whether they realized it or not," and fear was no defense for such a crime. Coakley concluded that "any man so depraved as to be afraid to load ammunition" deserved no leniency.

Apparently, Coakley's arguments were persuasive. The trial had lasted thirty-three days and produced a transcript of over 1400 pages. Theoretically, there were fifty separate sentences to decide. Yet on October 24 the trial board deliberated just eighty minutes, during which they also managed to eat lunch, and then found all the defendants guilty. The sentences were not immediately announced, but the board had unhesitatingly sentenced each man to fifteen years detention, reduction of rating to apprentice seaman, and dishonorable discharge.

The trial board's decision was only the first step toward final sentencing, however. Admiral Wright would review the decision, and his findings would in turn be reviewed by the advocate general's office in Washington. Finally, Secretary Forrestal would approve the final decision. At each stage, sentences could be reduced but not increased. On November 15 Admiral Wright confirmed the guilty verdicts but reduced the sentences of forty men because of youth or lack of previous misconduct. Five defendants had their confinement reduced to eight years, eleven to ten years, and twenty-four to twelve years. The remaining ten received the full fifteen-year sentences. The men were then taken to Terminal Island Disciplinary Barracks in Southern California to begin serving their time.

Expressing shock and outrage, the November, 1944, issue of the NAACP magazine, *Crisis,* reported that Thurgood Marshall and his staff were preparing a legal brief on behalf of the convicted sailors. The magazine also quoted Marshall as saying that the men were tried "solely because of their race and color." Marshall was more circumspect in his brief. The document, addressed to the advocate general, repeated the defense objections to the mutiny charge and to the admission of hearsay evidence. In addition, it objected to the procedure of a mass trial for all fifty defendants, arguing that this made it difficult to determine degrees of individual guilt and innocence. Marshall condemned the pre-trial publicity surrounding the case, particularly navy press releases and photographs which made it clear that all the defendants were black. Marshall also charged that Coakley had

subtly injected racial prejudice into the proceedings. The prosecutor had questioned defendants from the North about their homes, for example, but not those from the South. Marshall argued that Coakley was attempting to give the impression that the incident was due to northern black ringleaders and trouble-makers.

On April 3, 1945, the NAACP counsel followed up his written brief with a personal appearance at the advocate general's office in Washington, D. C. Marshall discussed his impression of the defendants, describing them as without "group cohesion" and "apart on everything, including intellect, respectfulness, if you please, and capability of making up their own minds." Half were under twenty-one, and a couple were "just plain kids." He again bitterly attacked Coakley's conduct at the trial, charging him with prejudice and unethical behavior. Marshall commented that the defense lawyers did a good job, but he argued that as naval officers they were limited in the issues they could raise at the trial and hinted that discrimination might be one of those issues. Finally, he reminded the advocate general's staff that "the convictions will forever stand as a disgrace to the entire Negro personnel of the United States navy."

Even before Marshall's personal appearance, an advocate-general staff memorandum had raised some of the same legal points as the NAACP brief. The memo also questioned the admittance of hearsay evidence and the loose definition of mutiny accepted by the court. Accordingly, on May 17, 1945, Acting Navy Secretary Ralph A. Bard informed Admiral Wright that Forrestal wished the court martial trial board to reconvene and reconsider the case without using hearsay evidence and in light of a definition of mutiny which required a "deliberate purpose to usurp, subvert or override" authority. In effect, Forrestal was agreeing with the original defense objections, but he was not throwing out the case. He only asked the trial board to reconsider the decision. The board met briefly and on June 12 "respectfully adhered" to its original verdict. One week later Admiral Wright approved the verdict and repeated the same sentence reductions he made the previous November. On July 13 Bard announced that the navy found the proceedings at Treasure Island fair and the sentences legal, but that the secretary of the navy would still consider mitigating factors.

While the Mare Island case made its way through the navy's appeal channels, Forrestal began moving to liberalize the service's racial policies. In September, 1944, he replaced the commander of the black training facility at Great Lakes, and its rigid segregation policies began to change. In June, 1945, the bureau of naval personnel announced the full integration of all its training facilities, and in August the predominantly white members of an integrated Great Lakes training batallion elected a black as their "honor man." In 1944 and 1945, black crews were assigned to some small combat ships, and integrated crews were tried on auxiliary vessels. In December, 1945, Forrestal finally ordered that "in the administration of naval personnel, no differentiation shall be made because of color."

Forrestal's actions were undoubtedly influenced by growing evidence of racial tension and conflict in the navy. In De-cember, 1944, a full-scale riot broke out between black seabees and white marines on Guam. In 1945 black seabees at Port Hueneme, California, staged a hunger strike to protest discrimination. But the Mare Island "mutiny" remained the most publicized incident, and Forrestal was determined that there would be no repetition of the case. In December, 1944, he ordered that the task of ammunition loading henceforth should be given to "a cross-section of recruit-training graduates."

Forrestal's most significant action on racial matters was the appointment of Lester Granger as his "special representative" to study race relations in the navy. Granger, a black graduate of Dartmouth (Forrestal's *alma mater*), had served five years as executive secretary of the Urban League. In the six months following his navy appointment in March, 1945, Granger travelled 50,000 miles and visited sixty-seven naval installations at home and abroad. He consulted hundreds of officers and found many of them "anxious to remove barriers." He also talked to about 10,000 black sailors without their officers present. In these "heart-to-heart" discussions, the men spoke "freely and sometimes bitterly about conditions they faced daily." Granger made periodic reports to Forrestal and claimed to notice "very progressive changes" on a month-to-month basis.

In this changing environment, it is not surprising that the navy brass increasingly viewed the sentences of the Mare Island defendants as unnecessarily harsh. When the war ended in August of 1945, there was no longer the same need to "set an example." On September 8, the chief of naval personnel recommended a reduction of the men's sentences by one year. On October 15, a Captain Stassen wrote a staff memorandum to Forrestal defending the Mare Island verdict and even arguing that a "non-colored" battalion would have received tougher treatment. Nevertheless, Stassen suggested the sentences be reduced to a total of two years for defendants with good conduct records and three years for all others, with credit given for the nearly one year already served.

Forrestal approved Stassen's recommendations on October 17, but that was not to be the secretary's final word on the matter. Granger and perhaps other staff members pressed for full amnesty, and they convinced the secretary to agree to this proposal by the end of December. On January 6, 1946, Granger informed the *New York Times* that the sentences of most of the Mare Island defendants, along with those of thirty-six seabees arrested on Guam, would be "set aside." On January 7, more than fifteen months after the original court martial sentences, the navy officially announced that forty-seven of the fifty Mare Island sailors had been returned to active duty and would be given honorable discharges if they completed their enlistments with good records. Two other defendants in navy hospitals presumably would be returned to active duty when released from treatment. One man was kept in detention because his conduct record "did not warrant consideration." The executive officer at the Terminal Island Disciplinary Barracks informed the NAACP that the men under his care had been released and were "presumably overseas."

Granger also told the *New York Times* that the majority of black naval personnel still were "bitterly convinced that a general policy debarred them from advancing as rapidly as their abilities warranted." But he quite accurately predicted that such policies would soon disappear. On February 27, 1946, the navy issued Circular Letter 46–48 which read: "Effective immediately all restrictions governing types of assignments for which Negro personnel are eligible are hereby lifted. Henceforth they shall be eligible for all types of assignments, in all ratings in all facilities and in all ships . . . in the utilization of housing, messing, and other facilities, no special or unusual provisions will be made for the accommodation of Negroes." Jim Crow no longer wore a navy uniform.

In the four years from early 1942 to early 1946, the navy had moved from having the most restrictive racial policy among the armed forces to the most liberal. The monumental change had been a three-stage process moving from almost complete exclusion of blacks to segregation and then to integration. Of course, reality never fully corresponded to official policy. Racial separation was incomplete in the early war years, and racism and *de facto* segregation persisted in spite of Forrestal's orders to the contrary. In 1946 more blacks were still in the messman's service than any other naval branch. But the navy had taken a substantial step; it had removed its official sanction from segregation and white supremacy. When President Harry Truman ordered the complete integration of all armed forces in July, 1948, only the navy was already in technical if not full compliance.

In the midst of the Mare Island trial, Water A. Gordon, a prominent black

Berkeley attorney, observed that "any policy that brings about segregation based on race is bound to lead to points of conflict." This was the lesson the navy had learned. The change in navy racial policies may have been partially due to manpower needs and the personal convictions of Forrestal and others in the service hierarchy. Pressure from civil rights groups and the black press certainly played a major role. But it was incidents such as the Mare Island "mutiny" that dramatized the ideological and moral inconsistencies of segregation and proved that black sailors would fight back against racism. It demonstrated that a segregated navy meant a disorderly navy. Lester Granger believed that the release of the Mare Island defendants reflected "the anxiety of navy officialdom to justify its racial record." The release of the prisoners also symbolized the navy's realization that it could no longer afford the hypocrisy of segregation.

Helen Gahagan Douglas:
Broadway Star as California Politician

by Ingrid Winther Scobie

During the post World War II period there was a prolonged debate over American loyalties. The spectre of Communism and the reactionary political climate which emerged in the 1940s and 1950s created demagogic politicians like Richard Nixon. There were many figures in California politics who built their careers upon emotional issues. The triumphs and successes of demagogues began in the 1850s, and prompted many politicians to use images of ethnic, racial or political radicalism to gain office.

These traits prompted Congressman Richard Nixon to create an artificial fear of Communism. As the guardian of American political morality and the protector of Californians from radical influences, Nixon became the archtypical post World War II patriot. Few people challenged Nixon's right wing sentiments and bullying political tactics. Finally, Helen Gahagan Douglas, a former Hollywood actress and a three term member of the House of Representatives, opposed Nixon in the 1950 California Senate race. Although Douglas failed to slow Nixon's rise to power and prominence, she did expose his manic desire for power and unethical political tactics.

Professor Ingrid Winther Scobie's article, "Helen Gahagan Douglas: Broadway Star as California Politician," argues that a lengthy commitment to the underdog and a sense of social justice prompted Mrs. Douglas to combat Richard M. Nixon's demagogic politics. Professor Scobie, who teaches at the Texas Women's University in Denton, analyzes Douglas' career in the broader scope of California liberalism. From the late 1930s to the 1960s Douglas represented the Californian who challenged racism, sexism and a double standard in the Golden State. She was a traditional liberal who believed that the California Dream was for everyone.

Helen Gahagan Douglas died of cancer on June 28, 1980, at the age of seventy-nine. Newspapers across the country reminded readers that in 1950 this actress-turned-politician lost her race against Richard M. Nixon for the United States Senate seat in California in perhaps the most celebrated red-smear campaign of the cold war years. The Los Angeles *Times,* which virtually shut Douglas out of its news coverage during her six-year congressional career, commented that Nixon's campaign "was a model of its kind—innuendo piled on innuendo." The paper cited Douglas's political courage as her most significant contribution to American politics. In a letter to the *Times* editor, Stanley Mosk, a prominent San Francisco judge, commented that to lose both the noted California writer Carey McWilliams and Douglas in the same week was "a tragic loss for American

Ingrid Winther Scobie, HELEN GAHAGAN DOUGLAS: BROADWAY STAR AS CALIFORNIA POLITI-CIAN. Reprinted by permission from *California History* magazine, December 1987 issue, Vol. LXVI, No. 4.

democracy" and called for a "requiem for the demise of an era." Former congressman Jerry Voorhis, himself a political loser to Nixon in 1946, predicted that this "noble" woman would live on as a "symbol of the Gallant American Lady." Tenant farm worker organizer H. L. Mitchell called Douglas a "sainted person." United States senators Alan Cranston and Howard Metzenbaum inserted lengthy newspaper obituaries in the *Congressional Record* with preliminary adulatory remarks of their own.

Melvyn Douglas, Helen's husband of forty-nine years, received several hundred letters which revealed in a more private way the esteem and affection both friends and strangers felt for Helen. The son of New Dealer David Lilienthal, Ernest, who knew Helen as a child, wrote that he still had the copy of *Mary Poppins* that Helen had given him as a child, and "very simply, I worshipped her."

Congressman Claude Pepper called her "one of the greatest and loveliest ladies whom our land has known." Motivated by an "overriding purpose" to build a better world, he said, she "contributed enormously to helping people . . . walk on higher ground." One person who wrote had attended college in 1950 and had been profoundly affected by the senate campaign. He said that "among the little people of America there were those who remember Helen's grandeur" and feel a great loss. "I was one of those whose life was illuminated by her leadership and principles."

In 1897, Walter Gahagan, a civil engineer born and raised in Ohio, and his bride Lillian, a teacher who had grown up in Wisconsin, moved to Brooklyn. In the summer of 1900, Lillian, Walter, and their two-year-old twins, Frederick and William, took up temporary residence in Boonton where Walter had a contract to build a large reservoir. On November 20, Lillian gave birth to Helen shortly before the family moved back into their Brooklyn home. Two years later a second girl, Lillian, was born, and the Gahagans moved their growing and active family into an imposing brownstone house in the city's posh Park Slope area adjacent to Brooklyn Park and Grand Army Plaza. In 1910, a fifth child, Walter Jr., added even more bustle to the busy household.

Walter viewed hard work, constant reading, and education as the essentials of a successful life for men and women, but that did not mean that women should pursue careers. He engrained in his children a series of rules stemming from his business principles. One which made a particular impression on Helen was the directive to "make everybody's life and every place you've been better because you've been there." His wife Lillian also believed in education as well as exposure to the arts and a good religious upbringing in the Presbyterian Church. Unlike some of her contemporaries, Lillian disagreed with her husband over careers for women, and had begun a promising singing career in opera which Walter prohibited her from pursuing. Yet when Helen developed an early interest in the theatre, Lillian was as adamant as Walter in opposing it.

Aside from continual friction over her acting ambitions, Helen grew up feeling a close bond to her parents and enjoyed family activities. Walter often took the children to his construction sights. Lillian invited musicians to the house to perform. She took the children down the street to the Brooklyn Art Museum and the public library on Saturdays. Helen went with her mother to the Metropolitan Opera but did not enjoy it. Helen recalled, "I would be so unhappy sitting through long operas and I'd complain, 'They're all so *fat,* Mother.'" When Helen said she wanted to be an actress, her mother responded, "Why do you want to be an actress? 'Why don't you want to be something really worthwhile—a singer?'"

Summers were special times for the Gahagans. They visited family in the Midwest and when the children became teenagers, the family travelled to Europe. In 1914, Walter bought Cliff Mull, a lovely Victorian house on a hill above Lake Morey near Fairlee, Vermont. After that, the family spent at least part of every summer in Vermont. Although the girls had to endure lessons, including piano and poetry reading, they had their afternoons free to play tennis, swim, hike, and read. Helen regularly found a secluded spot where she read and daydreamed. Even in the last year of her life, Helen found Vermont an escape, a critical source of nourishment, beauty, and repose.

It was always a letdown for Helen to return to Brooklyn to begin school. She and her sister attended Berkeley Institute, a private school in the neighborhood designed to prepare young women for college. Helen's perpetual dislike of school began in kindergarten when Berkeley dropped her behind a grade because she could not spell, a problem that continued to plague her as an adult. Helen hated both her academic courses and the rules outlining proper behavior for "young ladies," and she consistently performed poorly. Helen much preferred to spend her time making up stories and acting them out, but theatre had no place at Berkeley until Helen's freshman year

when Elizabeth Grimball, a drama coach by training, joined the faculty. She quickly realized that this academically rebellious teenager had exceptional acting talent and considerable intelligence. Before long, Helen began starring in plays and participating on the debate team. Helen's grades improved in Grimball's class, but deteriorated in others. Much to Grimball's dismay, not to mention Helen's, the irate Gahagans pulled their daughter out of Berkeley and sent her to the Capon School in Northampton, Massachusetts, a similar school which primarily prepared students for admission into Smith College. Against her parents' instructions, Helen immediately involved herself in play productions and did little better academically. She managed to graduate, but it took a summer of tutoring at Dartmouth for her to pass the entrance examinations for Barnard College, the only school Helen was permitted to consider. Her parents wanted her in New York at a woman's college so they could attempt to keep track of their prodigal daughter.

Barnard, a coordinate college with Columbia University, provided a stimulating intellectual environment and prepared women for a wide variety of employment opportunities. Helen never became part of the intellectual swirl of activity, but to her delight, the college had a strong tradition of dramatic activity, quite unusual for colleges and universities at that time. Helen entered in 1920 and soon discovered a place for herself in the students' tradition of Greek games which had become an elaborate annual pageant. She also had opportunities to act and direct in Wigs and Cues, the student organization for play production.

Helen's most rewarding theatrical adventure at Barnard took place in an Irish literature course that she took with close friend Alis De Sola. In 1922 the two dramatized an episode from an Irish epic which eventually became a one-act play, *The Shadow of the Moon.* The girls showed the script to Grimball, Helen's high school mentor, who arranged to have the play produced off-Broadway with Helen in the lead role. This production led to two more off-Broadway plays for Helen. The noted actress Grace George, who had a reputation for finding young actors and actresses, saw her in a performance and insisted that her husband, the crusty, established Broadway producer William Brady, see Helen perform. Brady was so enthusiastic he asked the starry-eyed Helen to play the lead role in *Dreams for Sale,* a new Owen Davis play about to go into rehearsal in August 1922. Brady also offered her, on the eve of opening night, a five-year contract for starring Broadway roles, which Helen accepted. Few actors, no matter how talented, stepped directly from any preparatory environment—stock company, drama school, or college theatre—into a leading role contract with a New York producer. The time could not have been more propitious, since one of the most vibrant decades in the history of American drama was just beginning. Helen paid a personal price for her dizzying success, nevertheless, because her decision enraged her father. Although Brady eventually convinced Walter that his daughter was not entering an "improper" profession for ladies from fine families, Walter was deeply disappointed over Helen's decision to leave school.

Despite poor reviews for *Dreams for Sale,* Gahagan caught critics' attention. In a comment typical of most of his col-leagues, the eminent critic Alexander Woollcott called her an "indisputable talent." When the show closed, Gahagan moved on to starring roles which spanned the next several years, including Leah in C. M. P. McLellan's *Leah Kleshna,* a part originally written for the famed actress Minnie Maddern Fiske. From her debut, critics compared her style to that of Ethel Barrymore. They rarely failed to mention her uncommon beauty—tall at 5'7" and well-proportioned with a regal bearing. After several years, she was often included in the handful of actresses considered Broadway's best. Gahagan, however, never hesitated to turn down a role that did not interest her. Unlike other fledgling stars, she still had financial backing from her family and spent most summers in Europe with her mother. In 1925, Gahagan left Brady for George Tyler, another veteran producer whose gentle personality and innovative productions suited her better. She did several plays with Tyler, including a long tour in 1925–26 with John Van Druten's *Young Woodley* in which she starred with Glenn Hunter. But by 1927 Helen was restless with the stage and, under pressure from her mother to develop her singing, decided to take voice lessons.

Gahagan began instruction with voice coach Sophia Cehanovska, a Russian immigrant, and eventually immersed herself fulltime in her lessons. In 1929 Cehanovska arranged for her hard working student to tour Europe during the summer. Her repertoire included the lead roles in *Tosca, Aida,* and *Cavalleria Rusticana.* Although her reviews were less than superlative, Gahagan had visions of auditioning for the Met and a variety of American engagements. When none of this materialized, she sailed again to Europe in the summer of 1930 with the idea of staying two years.

This plan evaporated several months later when the aging theatre legend David Belasco offered Helen the lead role in a new play by Lili Hatvany entitled *Tonight or Never*. Belasco thought Gahagan ideal to play an opera singer whose agent is convinced she could sing better if she would only have an affair. The agent's predictions prove correct after the diva has a passionate evening with an "unknown gentlemen" who turns out to be a Met scout. With Gahagan's consent Belasco selected an accomplished actor but a relative newcomer to Broadway, Melvyn Douglas, as the irresistible lover. During the rehearsal period, Gahagan and Douglas fell in love, and in April, 1931, near the end of the play's long run, they married.

The newlyweds' lives took an unexpected turn a month later when Hollywood producer Samuel Goldwyn purchased the movie rights to *Tonight or Never* as a means for Gloria Swanson to launch her singing career. The entire cast moved to Hollywood for the filming. The Douglases initially viewed this trip to California as a temporary one, but movie offers continued to come Melvyn's way and Helen had some singing and acting opportunities with theatres in San Francisco and Los Angeles. The couple did two plays together on Broadway but both plays closed early. In general, however, appealing offers came only sporadically for Helen. She had little luck getting into film, making only one movie, *She* with RKO in 1935. The science fiction fantasy failed at the box office. A radio contract also proved disappointing. The Douglases' lives were further complicated by

the birth of two children, Peter in 1933 and Mary Helen in 1938.

In the summer of 1937 Helen looked forward to a European singing tour culminating with a performance at the Salzburg Festival. Rather than operatic roles, she had developed a solid repertoire of songs, including German lieder and the music of Joseph Marx, a popular Austrian composer. Audiences were enthusiastic, although once again the reviews were mixed. Despite the tense political situation resulting from the rapid spread of Nazism, no unpleasant incidents occurred until Helen's stay in Salzburg. There an individual introduced by a friend asked Helen to provide reports on anti-Nazi activity in the United States. Horrified at the request, she cancelled a fall engagement with the Vienna Opera and returned home, determined to involve herself in anti-fascist activities in Hollywood. Helen and Melvyn both joined the five-thousand-member Hollywood Anti-Nazi League.

Helen initially considered her political activity to be of secondary interest, but her career as a performer was fading. Her cousin Walter Pick, who lived with the Douglases in the late 1930s, commented that after Helen returned from Europe she no longer had the "same great drive as before." Part of the explanation lies in diminished opportunities. Chances to sing in the United States had always been limited, and existing European doors were closing fast in 1938 and 1939. Professional theatre opportunities on both coasts continued to decline as the depression wore on. But another part of the explanation involved Melvyn. By the end of the 1930s, he had become one of the highest paid leading men, known for his fine comic timing, his handsome looks, and his ability to play well against Hollywood's female stars. While not all of his films offered him a chance to demonstrate his talent, *Ninotchka,* produced in 1939, certainly eliminated any questions about his talent as a screen actor. Although Helen never resented Melvyn's success, she had always felt their careers should be equally successful. With his star rising and hers on the decline, she was ready to be pulled off in another direction. Within eighteen months after Helen made her first step into the political arena, she had become a leading figure in the California Democratic party with considerable national visibility. Except for a few minor engagements, Helen neither acted nor sang again until the early 1950s. But she did not set aside her theatrical skills. Her rapid political climb was due in large part to her ability to shift her acting skills from the dramatic to the political stage.

The Douglases' heightened awareness coincided with a change in the political atmosphere in Hollywood. In the early 1930s, the movie colony had been a center of political indifference, but by 1937, it had become a hotbed of radical and liberal activity. The political awakening in Hollywood paralleled the awakening around the country.

Helen Douglas's move into politics began unexpectedly in the early fall of 1938. Melvyn, who had become active in the Democratic party and other organizations during the previous year, offered the patio of the Douglases' spacious home to the John Steinbeck Committee to Aid Agricultural Workers for a meeting. Sitting in, Helen found herself fascinated with the problems being discussed. Her initial curiosity soon evolved into a commitment to action, and she organized a Christmas party for migrant children, which attracted thousands. Then she began to tour migrant camps and attend government hearings and meetings of concerned citizens. In early 1939 she became the committee's chair, working hard to publicize the problem, solicit money, and encourage the public to push for labor laws and social security that would include the migrants. She also urged improvements in housing, health services, and food distribution centers. She constantly asked questions, drawing information from experts, particularly Paul Taylor, professor of economics at the University of California, Berkeley. Soon she was on the lecture circuit as her activities made her a sought-after speaker for concerned groups. She eventually drew the attention of migrant experts in Washington, including Arthur Goldschmidt, who worked for the Department of the Interior under Harold Ickes. Goldschmidt described his first encounter with Helen: "I found myself subjected to an intense cross-examination—grilling might not be too strong a word. She accepted no vague generalities. . . . Her questions were not naive; . . . I came away . . . enchanted with a sense of wonder at Helen's display of energy—at the physical, emotional and mental drive of this beautiful and glamorous person.

By mid-1939 Helen had been noticed by Aubrey Williams, head of the National Youth Authority, who frequently told Eleanor Roosevelt about interesting people around the country whom he thought she and FDR would like to meet. In the summer of 1939, Williams wrote to the Roosevelts about the California political activities of the Douglases. He mentioned to FDR that Melvyn could be a political asset for the 1940 campaign and that Helen's information about migrants would be useful to both Roosevelts. Eleanor Roosevelt was quick to respond; she invited the Douglases to dinner and to spend the night at the end of November 1939. The evening proved delightful; the two couples were drawn to each other, and a genuine friendship from which both couples stood to benefit took shape almost immediately.

During the next few days, the Douglases met a large group of high-ranking New Dealers including cabinet members Frances Perkins and Harold Ickes, who were as eager to rub shoulders with the bright, enthusiastic, and glamorous Hollywood couple as the Douglases were to meet Washington's political elite. The Douglases left Washington exhilarated and carrying a standing invitation to stay at the White House when business brought them to Washington. Thereafter, Eleanor Roosevelt began to visit and often stay with her new friends on her trips west. Neither Douglas hesitated to contact the Roosevelts or the cabinet members they had met concerning their political activities. The President appointed both Douglases to various White House boards and remained in close touch with what each was doing. In turn the Douglases became outspoken supporters of Roosevelt's policies.

When the Douglases returned to Los Angeles, Helen turned her attention to planning the Steinbeck Committee's second Christmas party, a massive gathering that attracted over eight thousand migrants. Shortly after the party Helen resigned from the committee because she learned of Communist infiltration into the organization. Before the Soviet-Nazi pact of September 1939 liberals of all persuasions were virtually indistinguishable from each other; they formed a United Front that supported the New Deal and opposed fascism. But after the pact, American Communists began to object to the anti-Fascist stands of liberal organizations. The United Front fell apart quickly as non-Communist liberals dropped their membership. After Helen resigned, she wrote her friend Congressman Jerry Voorhis that she found herself in the "absurd position . . . of most liberals today. The Communists call us reactionaries and the reactionaries call us Communists!" At this juncture, Helen Douglas took her initial steps into the Women's Division of the Democratic Party in a process that brought her closer to Eleanor Roosevelt and also provided an entry into the power structure of Democratic politics. In so doing, she placed herself right in the middle of party feuds between northern and southern California and between the party's liberals and conservatives. In an article for the February 1940 issue of the *Democratic Digest,* the widely read monthly magazine of the national Women's Division office, Helen urged state and local governments to respond to migrant needs and communities to assimilate the migrant and "recognize him for his true worth—a vital and necessary element in the agriculture structure [and] a human being . . . whose welfare affects the country at large." This impelled Dorothy McAllister, national director of the Women's Division, to invite Douglas to speak at the division's first National Institute of Government in Washington, a conference to educate party women about campaign issues and party organization in preparation for the 1940 fall campaign. That spring Mrs.

Roosevelt came to California to visit migrant camps on a trip arranged by Helen and Melvyn.

In July, the Douglases journeyed to Chicago for the party's nominating convention. Melvyn went as a delegate. Helen as an alternate. When it came time to choose California's Democratic Party Committeewoman there were two principal candidates: long-time party worker, head of the Women's Division in California, and conservative Nettie Jones, and Helen Douglas. Despite her novice status in the party, liberals found Douglas's flamboyant style and attractive appearance, her political views, and her friendship with the Roosevelts much more appealing than the prickly conservative Jones's party credentials. When Douglas won, it was not surprising that Jones resented Helen's lack of the traditional credentials required for this position.

Douglas enjoyed the publicity surrounding her appointment, which drew national attention, and felt comfortable mingling with the Democratic power structure. When she and Melvyn returned to California they both plunged into a hectic campaign speaking schedule—Melvyn nationally and Helen throughout California. When Roosevelt took California by a landslide, party officials in Washington singled out the Douglases for their contributions to the victory. Helen's speaking ability surpassed that of more seasoned politicians, and she had proved that she had the power to draw and hold a crowd. Together the Douglases had led the campaign efforts of Hollywood Democrats, persuading many actors to give political speeches and make substantial campaign contributions.

After a week of festivities during the January inauguration, Melvyn plunged back into his studio work while Helen decided to let her political activities absorb her energies. Through state party chairman William Malone she gained two additional Democratic Party positions. She became vice-chair of the state organization and replaced Nettie Jones as head of the Women's Division. Malone claimed to have appointed her to these jobs so that he would not have to deal with more than one woman; in retrospect he admitted that he had underestimated her abilities.

In the first few months of 1941, Douglas spent most of her time strengthening the existing structure of the statewide Women's Division and making new appointments down to the county level. She appointed two women to head the North while she and an assistant took responsibility for the South. Her appointees were bright professional women, many of whom had never before been active in the Women's Division and were not involved in the rampant factionalism within the division. With her structure in place, Douglas turned her attention to the major focus of the national Women's Division office—home-front defense plans and fundraising. She organized, in conjunction with the Washington office, a regional conference held in September 1941 for party women's education. Invitations were extended to men as well as women from the eleven-state area. She added glamor by including such movie stars on the program as Melvyn, Jackie Gleason, and Douglas Fairbanks. National party figures also addressed the three-day conference, and Douglas enjoyed the aftermath of praise for her "efficient organization and showmanship." Gladys Tillett, who had replaced McAllister as head of the Women's Division, wrote that she would have to place Douglas "apart as the standard among National Committee-women toward which others can work."

Although the conference demonstrated Douglas's organizational ability, a more significant test of her political acumen lay ahead, the mobilization of California Democratic women for the 1942 election. Nationally the picture looked gloomy. The congressional coalition between Republicans and conservative Democrats had continued to grow in strength since the 1936 election. After American entry into the war, hostility towards the number of federal courts and the extension of social reforms had intensified and Democrats feared losing their congressional majority.

Douglas was concerned about all the southern California congressional seats but six in particular. She directed the Women's Division to work outside the regular party structure because she thought the women would be more effective this way. They wrote and distributed thousands of fliers, registered voters, raised money, and canvassed precincts. In the final election, despite Governor Culbert Olson's loss to Republican Earl Warren in the gubernatorial race, Democrats won three of the six critical districts and several others as well. Particularly satisfying to Douglas was the ouster of Representative Leland Ford, an arch-conservative who had viciously redbaited Melvyn in the spring of 1942 when he had assumed a volunteer position with the Office of Civilian Defense in Washington. The Washington Democrats were delighted with the southern California victories in an election in which the party had lost 70 of its 318 House seats. Although it is difficult to assess Douglas's role in these victories, many gave her credit. The Sec-

retary of the Democratic National committee wrote: "You, personally, did a magnificent job. At least we could have come out much worse in our Congressional Districts and where we did come out successfully I am sure the results were due to your efforts. I want you to know that all of us in Washington appreciate this immensely."

Douglas's goal in 1943 was to coordinate the women to develop an education program directed primarily to postwar reconversion, a project she considered critical as groundwork for the 1944 election. Meanwhile, the 1942 campaign had given her close ties to the southern California congressional delegation, and Douglas cultivated these and other Washington contacts. She became particularly close to New Dealer Thomas Ford, who represented the fourteenth congressional district in Los Angeles, and his wife Lillian.

Late in 1943 the Fords suggested that Douglas consider running for Tom's seat. He had long planned to retire in 1944, and Douglas seemed to him an excellent replacement. She, however, had mixed feelings. The idea of running seemed at first somewhat overwhelming. Not only was she a woman, but Helen's credentials did not resemble those of other congressional candidates, male or female. In addition, she did not live in the fourteenth district but in the affluent residential hills of the adjacent fifteenth district. She was, in fact, a total stranger to the fourteenth, which encompassed the downtown core of Los Angeles. Furthermore, state assemblyman Augustus Hawkins had waited patiently for Ford's retirement. In many ways, Hawkins, the second black man to be elected to the state legislature, was a logical successor. He had a distinguished record in his fight for labor and civil rights. During the war years, the Los Angeles black population, which concentrated primarily in the assembly district Hawkins represented, grew substantially and Hawkins had become an increasingly powerful voice in the community. But Ford and his political advisers in the district felt Douglas would stand a better chance of winning. Despite her unfamiliarity with the district's problems, Ford believed the majority of his constituents would identify with her enthusiasm for the New Deal and Roosevelt. Furthermore, as he put it, the "people of the 14th are not going to vote for a Negro, however light-colored he may be." In December, 1943, Douglas agreed to run.

Ford's district surrounded the heart of Los Angeles. It was comprised of four state assembly districts, the forty-fourth, fifty-fifth, sixty-second and the sixty-fourth, with constituents ranging from the poorest of minority families to some of the wealthiest individuals in Los Angeles County. Douglas once described the slums in her district as areas where a "chicken coop would be considered a high-priority dwelling—especially if you could have it all to yourself." Over two dozen racial and ethnic communities, including Chinatown, Little Tokyo, and the city's oldest Mexican district, nestled next to each other and in between commercial districts. Two politically conservative, wealthy areas surrounded LaFayette Park and ran along Wilshire Boulevard. A tiny section of Hollywood intersected at the northwest corner. By 1945, 86,000 black people lived in the district and constituted almost twenty-five percent of the district's total population of 346,000.

Ford passed on to Douglas a strong campaign structure. Its principal figures

included Ford's manager Ed Lybeck, his wife Ruth, and secretary Florence Reynolds. Suzie Clifton, an active Democrat in several elections and an astute campaign worker, joined the group when Douglas ran. The team began to get organized when the primary campaign began in March.

Hawkins decided not to run, but Loren Miller, a prominent black lawyer in the district filed, as did several other candidates. Vicious literature from various candidates began circulating immediately. One flier reminded voters that Douglas was married to a Jew and asserted that she was a Communist. After all, twelve years of the "communistic Tom Ford" was enough. The Los Angeles *Times* accused her of Communist ties because the national Congress of Industrial Organizations (CIO) backed her and because of her friendship with Vice-President Henry Wallace. A poster from a Democratic opponent depicted Douglas, labelled "Lady Bountiful," coming down out of the hills of the fifteenth district and asking a passerby, "Where's the Fourteenth District?" None of this criticism bothered Ford. He wrote to a friend that Douglas would "carry on in the tradition of *Stand by the President* [and] put the 14th on the map." Douglas wrote to Eleanor Roosevelt, "Well, I am really in the campaign and I never knew anything could be quite so repulsive."

Douglas concluded an issue-oriented race, championing the New Deal record and emphasizing her confidence in FDR's leadership. In true Women's Division style she went armed with facts, figures, and simple language while refusing to run down her opponents. Although she only hinted that as a member of Congress she would see herself as representing a national constituency, she communicated that what was good for the country was good for her district. Its problems, she argued, mirrored the challenges facing America. She held dozens of meetings in homes, an effort which helped dissipate some of the hostility from housewives who could not envision a woman in Congress. The key to her success lay both in her message and her means of communicating. She knew how to read an audience and emotionally charge a group by using colorful language, vivid analogies, and large dramatic gestures.

Douglas did not let her campaign interrupt her Women's Division work which included campaigning for other congressional candidates. She wrote Mollie Dewson, the first director of the national Women's Division and still a political power, "I feel sometimes that with the weight of the entire state on my shoulders, as well as my personal campaign, that I'm not going to quite last the day or night, and I begin praying for strength." Douglas won the primary even though they "threw everything at me they could get their hands on," she told Alis De Sola. The Fords were jubilant.

After the Democratic nominating convention in July, where she was the principal woman speaker, Douglas began planning the fall campaign. Her strategy was similar to the one she used in the spring although her campaign committee worked harder to target particular groups, particularly the black community. In the primary, she and Miller had split the black vote, and she wanted to win it in the fall election. She went beyond FDR's position on civil rights by urging a permanent Fair Employment Practices Commission and abolition of the poll tax. She also pressed for more

general issues—better housing, job training for wartime workers, respect for the rights of organized labor, full protection for small farmers and small business, government support for the physically handicapped, and veterans' benefits.

The Republicans, like her Democratic opponents in the primary, conducted a redbaiting campaign. They also emphasized the fact that she lived outside the district and pointed out her connections with Hollywood. Nonetheless, with the hard work of the Lybecks and Fords, Douglas pulled off a victory as Roosevelt swept California. But her margin was less than four thousand votes out of approximately 137,500 cast. Although Douglas gained a majority of the black votes, few black leaders had rallied to her support. Not even the liberal black *California Eagle,* which later became her strong advocate, did much for her candidacy. Clearly she had a difficult challenge ahead of her to keep her district.

Douglas arrived in Washington early in January, 1945. Congress and the President faced two major responsibilities—to direct the economic reconversion of wartime America and to formulate policy for the nation in its role as a new world leader. The contours of the critical debates had begun to take shape late in 1943 and 1944. Home-front questions centered on the appropriate role of government in controlling the cost of living, combating the housing shortage, placing unemployed veterans in jobs, and converting factories from the production of wartime goods back to the manufacture of domestic goods. Blacks demanded that a country which fought for freedom abroad with their help should guarantee them equality at home. Many women had developed both a different consciousness of their own abilities as a result of employment in wartime factories and a new sense of independence after long-term separation from their husbands. These women sought the right to economic and personal equality within the legal structure. The demands of labor, blacks, veterans, and women often conflicted, however, with the desire of business to increase rapidly the production of consumer goods with maximum profits.

The United States also faced new responsibilities abroad. Returning to an isolationist position was not an option as it had been after World War I. Assuming a major role in developing an international body to bring countries together to preserve world peace, the American government also accepted an obligation to rebuild its European allies which had emerged from war burdened by weakened economies and massive physical destruction. The United States had to develop guidelines for dealing with the Soviet Union, another new world power whose status as an American ally during the war developed into an adversary relationship once the war had ended. An American attitude of toughness and mistrust of the Russians led to strong anti-Communist sentiment at home and the development of a Cold War between the two countries. Americans also had to decide how to cope with atomic energy, whether it should be controlled by the military or civilians, whether knowledge should be shared with other countries, specifically the Soviet Union, and how this new source of energy should be developed.

In 1945, the Democrats controlled Congress, but the combination of conservative Democrats and Republicans formed a majority. Thus liberals, including Douglas, feared that Congress would not support a program to promise what they believed every American deserved—the right to a decent way of life including employment, adequate housing, food, and health care—while at the same time preventing rampant inflation. In foreign affairs, liberals argued that Americans should guarantee that the idealistic goals for which the country had fought in the war become a reality. Most initially viewed the Soviet Union if not as a friend at least as a country with which the United States had to work in order to ensure world peace.

Douglas discovered quickly that in order to have any impact as a new member of Congress, she would have to play a nontraditional role. She was too impatient to wait the length of time dictated by the conventions of the House for new members wishing to assume a position of power. She did not wish to spend an inordinate amount of time learning the fine points of legislative procedure, and she realized that even time did not guarantee power to women. Furthermore, she had a purist's theoretical notion of representative government. Viewing political issues in terms of right and wrong, she believed that government, run for and by the American people, should be improved by voters who elected legislators to vote for the right programs. This philosophy set her apart from those who believed that legislative success came only with compromise.

Modeling herself after Eleanor Roosevelt, Douglas set out to develop policy for a national and often an international constituency of "ordinary people." She believed the economic interests of the national groups she deemed important, particularly labor and blacks, were identical to those of the key groups in her district. In foreign affairs, she saw herself speaking for every American who wanted peace. What was good for the world, therefore, was good for the country and for the district. She worked hard towards her goals on the floor of Congress, often lecturing her colleagues and inserting articles and speeches in the *Congressional Record*. She took her assignment to the Foreign Affairs Committee seriously. She also spoke before dozens of groups of concerned citizens all over the country urging them to pressure members of Congress.

The outlines of Douglas's liberal philosophy took shape and matured during her first term, the 79th Congress. Initially she had looked to FDR for policy guidelines, and after his death in April, 1945, her ideals came principally from Truman's Fair Deal program. She developed numerous statements including demands for creation of a homeland for the Jews, support for the United Nations, a permanent Fair Employment Practices Commission (FEPC), the end of the poll tax, a full employment bill, extension of social security, construction of low-cost housing, continuation of wartime rent and price controls, additional funds for day care programs and school lunches, more farm loans, an increase in the minimum wage, support for labor's right to strike, and funding for cancer research. She called the economic need of the veterans a national crisis, began a long-term investigation of the problems of water in California's Central Valley, and demanded more attention to the problems of migrant workers. Her principal legislative success was her cosponsorship of the

Atomic Energy Act of 1946, a law which placed the development of atomic energy in civilian rather than military hands. Douglas struck out against those who redbaited her with a statement she entitled "My Democratic Credo" in which she explained that the way to keep communism out of the United States was by building a strong economy, controlling inflation, and providing jobs and affordable housing for all Americans.

Douglas's approach to the issue of civil rights illustrates her political style. She was a civil rights proponent in a manner reflective of Eleanor Roosevelt. In the upper-class Brooklyn society of her childhood, her Republican family did not mix with blacks, and Douglas became responsive to blacks only after she entered politics. Eleanor Roosevelt played a key role in introducing Douglas to black leaders during the war, including Mary McLeod Bethune, head of the National Council of Negro Women (NCNW). In 1942, at the First Lady's request, Douglas called a meeting to discuss the employment and housing problems of Los Angeles blacks. She worked with FEPC investigations in defense industries. Once in Congress, Douglas aligned herself with a small handful of congressmen (including the two black representatives, Adam Clayton Powell and William Dawson) who persistently introduced FEPC, anti-lynching, and anti-poll tax bills, despite continual failure to get bills passed. Douglas not only tried to generate public pressure on Congress to pass civil rights legislation, but she also gave speeches for national and local branches of the NAACP and helped the NCNW raise funds. Blacks throughout the country recognized her contributions. The Scroll of Honor that she received in 1946 from the NCNW acclaimed her "superb statesmanship" in her first term in Congress.

Douglas's attitude toward civil rights was also politically astute. Her black community was an identifiable audience, and she needed to play to it. She and Lybeck made certain that the blacks in her district knew exactly what she was doing. After a speech in June, 1945, on FEPC, for example, she sent copies of the speech out to the black precincts while the issue was "hot." She reprinted tens of thousands of "The Negro Soldier," a series of speeches she made in Congress at the end of 1945 in which she listed many of the war efforts of blacks, and had Lybeck blanket the black precincts with them. She also worked to bring increased services for blacks into her district. For example, she worked with the Los Angeles Committee for Interracial Progress, a coalition of fifty organizations, to direct federal housing funds into Los Angeles County, particularly into the fourteenth district, and she secured funding to expand post office facilities in the heart of the sixty-second assembly district.

Douglas hoped that her civil rights activities would help her credibility in the 1946 campaign. Although she won the primary easily, the fall campaign proved more challenging. Her Republican opponent Frederick W. Roberts, a long-time state assemblyman, was black, and Roberts' candidacy split the black community. Basing his campaign on the argument that blacks should send blacks to Congress, Roberts supported a platform identical to Douglas's even though it varied from his legislative record. The Republican National Committee helped him financially and even sent Joe Louis to the district to campaign. As in 1944, red-

baiting issues surfaced. One group, the 14th District League for the Preservation of the American Way of Life, circulated a flier asking Douglas why she had made a "secret trip to Moscow" the previous year. Douglas could not campaign in person to counter charges against her, because Truman had appointed her to the 1946 General Assembly of the United Nations. Although this added to her prestige it kept her out of her district during the fall. She spoke weekly on the radio but left Lybeck to make all the daily decisions about campaign strategy.

Douglas's liberal stance on issues in general, her work on behalf of blacks nationally, and her careful cultivation of the black community paid off. In the midst of a landslide Republican victory nationwide in which the party took control of both the House and the Senate for the first time in sixteen years, Douglas almost doubled her margin from 1944. She was particularly delighted that she gained the majority of votes in the black precincts and interpreted this to mean that she had won the confidence of blacks that their interests would be more effectively served by a white Democrat with a liberal record than by a black Republican.

When the 80th Congress opened in January, 1947, the Democrats lost control of committee chairs and the House speaker. Frustrated from the start, liberal Democrats became increasingly angry as the 80th Congress progressed. The conservatives refused to pass any of Truman's Fair Deal legislation; furthermore, they passed the anti-labor Taft-Hartley Act over Truman's veto. Republican support for some reform legislation, including the extension of social security, increases in minimum wage, and a housing bill, was not satisfactory to the Democrats, who objected to the diluted versions of these bills which were enacted. In the arena of foreign affairs Congress gave bipartisan support to aid in Greece and Turkey, the Marshall Plan for rebuilding Europe, and the National Security Act.

Liberal groups clamored for Douglas's attention, and she played a leading role in the futile attempts to buck the Republicans. She stepped up her speaking schedule, addressing a wide range of issues in an effort to reduce voter apathy.

Douglas considered inflation to be the most pressing domestic problem and high rents and the lack of inexpensive houses on the market to be its principal cause. She did not, however, ignore other contributing factors. Her most dramatic and memorable speech in the 80th Congress addressed the rising costs of food. In March, 1947, she delivered a carefully prepared speech which she called her "Market Basket" speech. Her staff filled a basket of groceries which Douglas placed over her arm as she strode to the front of the chamber, announcing that she had just come from the "lowest-priced chain store in the city" located only three blocks from Congress. It took $15, she pointed out, to buy the same items that had cost $10 in June, 1946, shortly before the removal of price controls.

Although Douglas viewed her fight for housing and against inflation as the most important contribution she could make to her district, she continued to seek federal funds for other district needs. She also responded to pressure from Bethune, Lybeck, and black district leaders to hire a black secretary. Douglas was enthusiastic about the idea despite the fact that the woman's salary would have to come from Douglas's personal funds. She had used up her staff funding and did not want to replace existing staff. She and Lybeck eventually agreed to hire Juanita Terry, the daughter of active campaign worker Jessie Terry.

During the 80th Congress Douglas became more outspoken on women's issues, attacked the House Un-American Activities Committee (HUAC), and took strong positions on foreign policy issues. She urged the extension of social security to cover more women and supported legislation for equal pay for equal work. She opposed Equal Rights Amendment efforts, as did all pro-labor legislators who feared that such an amendment would kill hard-earned special interest legislation favoring working women. Her opposition to the House Un-American Activities Committee focused on its mode of investigation, particularly its use of contempt citations during its 1947 investigations of Hollywood. In foreign affairs, she deviated from Truman in opposing aid to Greece and Turkey in 1947 (on the grounds that the aid should come from the United Nations), but she regularly spoke out in favor of the Marshall Plan and numerous related issues.

By early 1948, Douglas not only had blacks solidly behind her but labor as well. She had worked more closely with labor union leaders during the 80th Congress and had campaigned against the Taft-Hartley bill. Labor unions and liberal magazines like the *Nation* and the *New Republic* gave her top ratings for her voting record. As labor stepped up efforts to influence the 1948 elections, she stood to benefit from the unions' careful political organization. Nonetheless, Douglas entered the campaign facing two unknown quantities—how hard the Republican National Committee would work to defeat her and how much support Henry

Wallace's newly-organized Independent Progressive Party (IPP) would draw. Neither threat hurt her primary campaign. In September, the IPP candidate withdrew from the race, although Wallace and local IPP supporters gave Douglas only lukewarm support. Campaigners for her Republican opponent, William Braden, once again raised redbaiting issues. "Doctors for Braden," for example, implied that Douglas was part of the left-wing influences in Congress. Braden also played up her fifteenth congressional district residence—referring to her as the Hollywood representative who lived in the "hotsy-totsy area of Hollywood" as compared to the "modest home of our good neighbor and friend" Braden in the fourteenth district. Lybeck responded with widely-distributed speeches and pamphlets tailored to different constituencies. Despite Braden's attacks, Douglas took each assembly district, even the conservative fifty-fifth. Her vote of approximately 88,000 to Braden's 43,000 surprised even Douglas.

In January, 1949, at the opening of the 81st Congress, Douglas enjoyed enormous popularity in the eyes of labor, blacks, Jews and other minority groups, and civil libertarians. Many of her supporters agreed with Douglas's somewhat egotistical evaluation of herself as possibly the most conscientious member of Congress. She saw herself as a "people's representative" fighting for America's working class. She had grown accustomed to letters telling her that she was the only hope left for America. Organizations frequently presented her with laudatory awards and citations, reinforcing her self-image. Local, state, and national Democratic Party organizations as well as liberal special interest groups regard-

ed her as an unusually persuasive public speaker as indicated by the constant stream of speaking invitations that came into her office.

At the same time that she had built herself a national support group, Douglas had gained the confidence of a broad majority of her constituents. The vast majority in her district, low income and poorly housed, agreed with her position on veterans, housing, unemployment, inflation, and civil rights. In addition, her forthright stand in favor of Israel and her willingness to defend the civil liberties of accused Communists attracted local support, both volunteer hours and financial contributions, among the more elite pressure groups including Jewish associations, Hollywood political groups, and university faculty. She also generated loyal and enthusiastic support among her key group of core campaign workers.

When Douglas announced late in 1949 that she intended to run for the United States Senate, she found that many of her supporters were dismayed and concerned. Many who believed she could continue as long as she wished to represent the fourteenth district did not think she had much of a chance to win a statewide race. Lybeck, for example, knew she did not have the statewide political base or the experience to run for the Senate. Further, while her political views suited her district, they did not reflect majority opinion in the state. Another long-term backer took a trip up and down the state in late 1949 to sound out support. He came back discouraged and urged Douglas not to run. But she remained undaunted.

Douglas explained her decision to run by her intense dislike for the aging incumbent, Sheridan Downey. Although

Downey had enjoyed liberal support in the late 1930s and early 1940s, he had become progressively more conservative after the war. Douglas believed Downey's vulnerability lay in his opposition to the 160-acre limitation on water usage, and she justified her entry into the race on this issue alone. As she told Malone, still a political power in the party, the issue was not going to the Senate but prohibiting Downey from destroying "a program that is essential to the well-being of the West Coast." When Douglas entered the race, however, she quickly broadened the issues. She portrayed herself as representing the lower- and lower-middle-income people of California—veterans, small farmers, women, blacks, ethnics and small businessmen—and Downey as favoring the big farmer, private utilities, oil, and big business.

Despite Downey's strong corporate support, Douglas made him nervous. His health was failing as well. At the end of February, rumors circulated that he planned to back out. A month later he formally withdrew, throwing his campaign support behind Manchester Boddy, the editor of the liberal Los Angeles *Daily News* who had provided critical support to Douglas during her first two terms. Boddy took Douglas and many Democrats aback when he not only made clear that his views suddenly reflected Downey's but also turned to redbaiting as the key to his campaign strategy. Although Douglas's reason for entering the race had vanished, her enthusiasm for winning did not.

As she had before, Douglas campaigned strictly on issues. She cited her continuous support for Truman's Fair Deal program. She also pointed out that she believed she had played an instru-

mental role in the refining of foreign policy as the fourth-ranking member of the House Foreign Relations Committee. She insisted that while she opposed HUAC, she hated communism as she had explained in her "Democratic Credo." Douglas also emphasized her support for federal rather than state control of tidelands oil reserves.

Douglas's views cut her off from the major funding sources. The oil industry, big business, and corporate farmers all backed Boddy. Although the Democratic party could not formally take sides during the primary, Boddy enjoyed the informal support of its power structure. None of this bothered Douglas; she had never sought corporate support but had claimed it would compromise her voting. Many union friends offered considerable assistance, although labor could not play a formal role in the spring election. Douglas also got her help throughout the state from ethnic groups, academics, Jews, farmers, blacks, and liberal women's groups. Eleanor Roosevelt conducted a major fundraising effort on her behalf, and many Hollywood friends offered time and money. Conservative Democratic women found Douglas's views, particularly her stand against the Equal Rights Amendment, distasteful.

Despite Boddy's financial edge and his potentially devastating allegations that Douglas had Communist sympathies, Douglas won the primary by a comfortable margin; her 730,000 votes were nearly double Boddy's. She won for several reasons. Boddy did not have as effective a campaign organization as Douglas, who took advantage of her contacts from Women's Division days to set up strong offices in each county. Boddy's late entry in the campaign and sudden conservative turnaround after years of state-wide reputation as the well-respected editor of a liberal paper cost him votes. Nor did he have Douglas's charismatic appeal as a speaker and ability to articulate issues clearly.

But Douglas's victory did not bode well for the fall. Congressman Richard M. Nixon, the leading Republican senatorial candidate, cross-filed on the Democratic ticket with the hope that he might pull conservative Democrats away from Boddy, since their political positions were similar. Nixon and his campaign strategist Murray Chotiner viewed Douglas as a far less threatening candidate than Boddy for the fall campaign. Nixon won more than 300,000 Democratic votes, which boosted his total over the million mark. If he could take most of Boddy's votes in the fall, he had an easy edge over Douglas.

A member of the House since 1946, Nixon had attained significant national visibility as a member of HUAC, particularly in the committee's investigation of Alger Hiss and as the co-sponsor of the Mundt-Nixon Communist control bill. Nixon and Douglas, as members of the southern California congressional delegation, had shared concerns over nonpartisan issues, but Douglas had developed considerable antipathy towards HUAC committee members, particularly Nixon. In 1946 he and Chotiner had conducted what Douglas and many others considered a ruthless redbaiting campaign against New Dealer Jerry Voorhis, Douglas's close friend and colleague.

Over the summer, Nixon and Chotiner decided to follow Boddy's lead and concentrate on Douglas's vulnerability on the issue of "red-blooded Americanism." Both domestic and foreign events fed this decision. Americans were up in arms about the so-called fall of China to communism, blaming it on Truman's incompetence. In early 1950 United States Senator Joseph McCarthy embarked on his search for American Communists. McCarthy's "revelations" heightened irrational fears about internal security and resulted in a bipartisan Congress passing the Internal Security Act over Truman's veto with Douglas one of the few voting against the bill. In June, 1950, the Korean War began when Americans aided the South Koreans in their struggle against invading communist troops from North Korea. All these events made Nixon's dubbing of Douglas as the "Pink Lady" an effective device.

Nixon won the election by a margin of 2,200,000 to 1,500,000. Most commentators credited the victory to what they called a dirty and ruthless "red smear" campaign. Other leading liberals who lost in redbaiting races that year included Senator Claude Pepper in the primary and senators John Carroll and Elbert Thomas, Senate majority leader Scott Lucas, and several other House members in the fall. Even without the "dirty campaign" issue, however, it seems clear that Nixon still had an edge on Douglas. Republicans swept most of the statewide California races—Earl Warren, for example, easily beat Jimmy Roosevelt for governor without raising the cry of "Communist fellow-traveller." Nixon's position on issues such as taxation, government spending, labor, and farm policy more accurately reflected the general sentiment of Californians. Nixon matched Douglas's skill as a speaker; though their styles were different. Nixon could work a crowd as effectively as his opponent. The Republicans also profited from a substantial financial edge, particularly in the Nixon campaign, and from poor Democratic party organization. Nixon also had the luxury of many "Democrats for Nixon" campaign workers, many of whom had initially backed Downey and Boddy. One of the most effective organizers of this group was George Creel, a prominent member of Woodrow Wilson's administrations, who went beyond Nixon in his red-baiting. Finally, the fact that California had not elected a woman to high state-wide or national office for twenty years was cause enough for Douglas's loss.

Although Douglas later denied it, she believed into election night that she would win, despite all evidence to the contrary and the decline of her support around the state. Once the primary ended, her organization tended to melt away because many of those who viewed her as a more attractive alternative than Nixon saw her as a losing candidate and turned away to work for others. Even the numerous Washington luminaries, including Vice-president Alben W. Barkley and cabinet members Charles P. Brannan, J. Howard McGrath, and Oscar Chapman, who came to California principally to support Douglas, could not change what seemed a foregone conclusion.

Douglas had mixed feelings about her Senate loss. Winning would have thrust her into a very unusual spot for a political woman, but she also felt relieved. Although her marriage was still intact, the previous eight years had placed a strain on Helen's relationship with Melvyn and the children. Melvyn had spent three years in India during the war. When he returned, he based himself in Los Angeles, but he also toured with several productions. The children, after several months with Helen in Washington at the beginning of her first term in Congress, attended boarding school in Los Angeles. In 1950 Helen knew it was critical to reassemble the family. She and Melvyn decided to make New York their home base as Melvyn had decided he wanted to leave movie production and return to the theatre. Helen also wanted to begin spending as much time as possible in Vermont at the family home in Fairlee.

Douglas never wielded significant political power in Congress; she could not make or break presidents or legislation. Yet she stood out among her colleagues as an idealist who spoke and stood for goals that more pragmatic politicians hesitated to embrace. She had a magic as a speaker, and her passionate appeals gave hope to the citizens she represented—not only those in her own district but "little people" around the country—that someone cared. It is unlikely that there will ever be a count of those for whom her inspiration tipped the balance between political involvement and apathy at a grassroots level. But the outpouring of expression which marked her death suggests that Helen Gahagan Douglas forged a durable legacy of political principle.

Assemblyman W. Byron Rumford: Symbol for an Era

by Lawrence Paul Crouchett

After World War II the civil rights impulse in California underwent a dramatic transformation. There was a demand for equal rights and the black voter was determined to gain full civil and economic rights. When W. Byron Rumford was elected to the California legislature, he became a leader who challenged the subtle and direct discrimination that Californians placed upon the black population. In Rumford's lengthy political career he fought many battles for equal opportunity.

Although he is best known as the author of the Rumford Fair Housing Act of 1963, W. Byron Rumford was a life long foe of discrimination. Professor Lawrence Crouchett analyzes Rumford as the "Symbol For An Era" and suggests that he spoke out against the forces who hoped to institutionalize racism. When blacks were unable to purchase homes, Rumford's legislation publicized this inequity and led to a law which began the slow but steady progress toward racial equality.

In a pioneer essay, Professor Crouchett points to the energy, commitment and successes of a black, legislative pioneer. He also suggests that Rumford understood the California mind and worked adroitly inside the Democratic party. It was as a legislative innovator and voice of the underdog that Rumford made his mark. He was able to publicize the obvious inequities in California life and create an atmosphere of change.

When in 1948 William Byron Rumford became the first black person to be elected to public office in Northern California, open discrimination on the basis of race was still a way of life, despite increasing signs of change. By the time he left office in 1966, few public officials, employers, or property owners dared to admit using race as a criterion for denying access to anything from a seat on a bus to a house in an exclusive neighborhood. Although racial discrimination persisted, a changed social climate required that it be cloaked in some other justification. Rumford stands as an appropriate symbol for this age of radical transformation in public institutions, both because he played a crucial role in writing legislation to outlaw the most egregious forms of discrimination and because his career reflects the interaction of decades-long political efforts by black community leaders with the demographic and economic transformations brought about by World War II.

The milestone "firsts" registered between 1940 and 1950 give some measure of the barriers minority people faced:

Dr. Fitzroy E. Younge, an obstetrician, was the first black doctor to be given full hospital privileges at a Bay Area hospital (Berkeley General, now Herrick Hospital). Black doctors had been required to turn their patients over to white doctors for treatment when they entered private

Lawrence Paul Crouchett, ASSEMBLYMAN W. BYRON RUMFORD: SYMBOL FOR AN ERA. Reprinted with permission from *California History* magazine, March 1987 issue, Vol. LXVI, No. 1.

hospitals, where minority patients were customarily assigned to a segregated ward or forced to pay for the extra bed in a double room.

*Berkeley hired its first minority teacher, Ruth Acty, a black woman, in 1943. Alameda hired Carolese Hargrave as its first minority teacher in 1950. Oakland had employed only three black teachers before 1940. East Bay colleges and universities had no black faculty members into the 1950s, and the University of California had thirty-five black students in a student body of sixteen thousand in 1950. California legislation authorizing school segregation by race was not removed from the books until 1947. By that time, however, the primary instrument of school segregation was the creation of segregated neighborhoods by restrictions on access to housing.

*Marguerite Johnson (Maya Angelou) became the first black streetcar conductor in San Francisco in 1944, and the Key Route Transit System in the East Bay hired its first black bus driver in 1951. The Yellow Cab Company in San Francisco hired its first minority drivers in 1956.

Ironically, the widespread use of restrictive covenants and screening by real estate agents to exclude blacks and other minorities from many Bay Area neighborhoods created the political base from which Rumford was elected. As real estate interests banded together to "protect housing values" by fashioning and enforcing restrictive covenants in the face of black immigration to the Bay Area during World War II, black newcomers concentrated in what had been the heterogeneous areas of North and West Oakland, making these districts the center of their cultural, political, and social activities. Here they established their fraternal

and denominational organizations, their churches, and their businesses—barbershops, newspapers, printing shops, real estate offices, mortuaries, cafes, cleaning establishments, drugstores, and nightclubs. These areas fell in the Seventeenth Assembly District, and by 1948 black political leaders realized they had the votes to make election of a black candidate feasible if white liberals could be induced to join forces with them.

There had been black candidates in the East Bay before, but they had faced white incumbents and lost in campaigns requiring coalitions of white and black voters. In 1920, Progressive John W. Fowler had lost the race in the Thirty-Ninth Assembly District. In 1938, Republican attorney Jay Maurice lost in the Seventeenth Assembly District primary. In 1940, Thomas L. Berkeley, John C. Henderson, and Jay Maurice, all attorneys, had lost in the primary, and Claude Allen failed in a write-in effort to unseat incumbent Edward J. Carey in the November general election. Carey's decision not to seek reelection in 1948 opened the field, and black leaders began looking for a candidate early in the year.

William Byron Rumford was born on February 2, 1908, in Courtland, Arizona, a small copper-mining camp in southwestern Arizona Territory. He spent his early childhood, along with his mother Margaret Lee, older brother Chauncey, and maternal grandmother Louise Alice Galbreath Johnson, traveling in the territory. Family tradition has it that the grandmother was seeking a place where the children could attend unsegregated schools, a dream that was shattered when Arizona was admitted to statehood in 1912 and allowed to segregate its pupils by race. Despite his grandmother's protest, young Byron attended segregated schools and in 1926 graduated from the "Colored Department" of Phoenix High School, where he excelled in his courses, drama, sports, and music. He then moved to San Francisco to work his way through the University of California School of Pharmacy, earning his pharmacy degree in 1931. Turned down for employment at several white-owned drugstores in San Francisco, Rumford took a part-time position as a pharmacist at Alameda County's Highland Hospital in Oakland, where he was permitted to fill prescriptions only for outpatient clinics. While he was employed at Highland, Rumford moved to Berkeley, where he went to work for black pharmacist William Montgomery, who had opened his own drugstore on Sacramento Street in 1927. Montgomery died in 1943, and Rumford purchased the business.

But Rumford was to be more than a druggist. In the 1930s he was one of a group of black friends who founded the Appomattox Club to exert an influence in Berkeley city politics. The club eventually joined with the United Negro Labor Committee and the Alameda County Democratic Club to support Democratic candidates in municipal, state, and federal elections. By 1942, Democrat Rumford had come to the attention of Republican Governor Earl Warren through a black law school classmate of Warren's who helped the governor identify black candidates for public appointments. Warren named Rumford to the Berkeley Emergency Housing Commission to help mediate between landlords and minority defense workers in need of housing. In 1943 Rumford appeared before the Berkeley City Council to represent the Berkeley Interracial Committee in asking for non-discrimination in the selection of tenants for Cordonices Village, a war emergency housing complex. In 1944 Warren appointed Rumford to the Berkeley and regional rent control boards and then to the State Housing Commission. It was in these capacities that Rumford first gained popular notice and attracted the attention of social reformers and Democratic Party regulars. Many of these people began to talk of sending him to Sacramento.

Meanwhile, Rumford's drugstore had become a popular gathering center for a coterie of black patrons and—to a lesser degree—their white friends who came there to purchase black weekly newspapers and monthly magazines and to talk. Rumford's eloquence in discussions of social and political topics in this context added to the reputation he was establishing in Democratic Party circles.

As the election of 1948 approached without an incumbent running for the Seventeenth Assembly District seat, black Democrats and Republicans agreed to support a single black candidate regardless of party affiliation, remembers political activist Frances Albrier. A public meeting of district residents was held in March, 1948, at the Beebe Memorial African Methodist Episcopal Temple in Oakland to select a single black candidate to enter the Democratic primary in June. A group of Democratic Party regulars and Congress of Industrial Organizations (CIO) union leaders had asked permission to place Rumford's name in nomination, but he went to the meeting to support another candidate. After a series of maneuvers in which that candidate withdrew, Rumford's sister-in-law nominated him for the floor, and—to his own surprise—he was chosen. Having agreed on a black candidate, the meeting issued a call for labor organizations and other groups to make every effort to get out the vote for Rumford, who filed for the Republican primary as well under the cross-filing system then in effect.

Rumford won the Democratic nomination, and Edgar S. Hurley, a white conservative with American Federation of Labor (AFL) backing, won the Republican contest. Since neither had received a majority of the total vote, they faced off for the November general election. The campaign became one of the most dramatic in Alameda County history as it developed into both a racial confrontation and a struggle between liberal and conservative agendas. As old-timers remember it, Hurley pandered to race prejudice and union baiting. They say that his tone was openly anti-black. Rumford attacked Hurley's record during a term in the Assembly in the 1920s, charging his opponent with indifference to blacks and labor and pointing out that Hurley had voted against bills to improve conditions for labor, the elderly, and children and that he had sponsored a poll-tax bill to disenfranchise non-whites.

When the votes were counted, Rumford had won by a memorable margin of 20,387. Blacks and white of both parties had supported him with full knowledge that he would fight against racial injustices and for social reform.

Two black men had been elected to the Assembly before Rumford, but he was the first from Northern California. Frederick M. Roberts, a Republican from an all-black district in Los Angeles, served from 1919 to 1935. Augustus F. Hawkins, a Democrat, succeeded Roberts in 1935 and was still in the Assembly when Rumford was elected. Hawkins is currently a member of the U.S. Congress. Although Hawkins had sponsored a host of civil rights measures, the legislature had rejected all of them. Although they were no longer willing to pass new restrictions on the civil and social rights of blacks and other minorities, the members of the legislature were not yet prepared to risk the controversy that would result from a serious challenge to the status quo. The first move toward legislative activism had come in 1947, when both houses passed the first modern anti-discrimination law in California, a bill sponsored by Assemblyman Glenn M. Anderson (D-Inglewood) to abolish racially segregated public schooling in the state.

Upon his arrival in Sacramento the night before his installation as a member of the Assembly, Rumford was refused a room—which he had reserved without identifying his race—at the William Land Hotel across the street from the State Capitol. To prove that the incident was not a mistake, he left the hotel and placed a call from a public phone booth inquiring about a room. The clerk, assuming the caller was white, assured him that a room was available. Rumford then returned to the hotel and demanded the room he had originally reserved, threatening to bring the matter up on the Assembly floor if he were refused and presenting documents to confirm his status as a legislator. The manager backed down, and Rumford was shown to a room.

On January 3, 1949, Rumford entered the Assembly chamber to take the oath of office for the first time. The galleries were packed with his friends and supporters, both black and white. They represented an emerging bipartisan coalition supported by Governor Earl Warren and committed to enhancing civil rights for minorities. They saw Rumford as a standard bearer. As he recalled, "When the governor ended his speech to the joint session of the legislature, he drew me aside and asked me to come to his office. When we met, he expressed the wish that I push through some civil rights bills, and promised that if they were passed he would surely sign them into law. He specifically urged me to press for legislation to abolish racial discrimination in the state National Guard.

Aided by Augustus Hawkins, who kept a drawer full of civil rights bills, Rumford brought two civil rights measures to the floor in his first month in the Assembly. Following the governor's suggestion, he proposed a riser to a bill sponsored by Richard H. McCollister (D-Sonoma/Marin) petitioning the federal government to return National Guard units to state jurisdiction. The rider called for a ban on racial discrimination in the National Guard once it was returned to the state. McCollister saw the rider as an obstacle to passage of his bill and opposed it, but the hearing committee passed it with only a few Democratic defections. The Democrat-controlled Assembly then passed the bill and rider by a vote of 47 to 17. The Senate amended the bill and the rider so much that Rumford decided they would actually strengthen racial discrimination and opposed them. Looking back, he described the critical factor in his decision as the lack of an enforcement clause in the Senate version of the anti-discrimination legislation. This insistence on enforcement provisions would characterize all of Rumford's legislation. In the end, the Senate Committee on Military and Veterans Affairs voted both the bill and the rider down.

On January 18, Rumford returned to the fight with his own bill (AB 807) to prohibit California National Guard units from segregating or discriminating against members on the basis of race, color, or creed. At that time, all black members of the Guard were assigned to one of two segregated units, one in Los Angeles and one in San Francisco. In other communities black guardsmen trained with their white colleagues, but they were carried as detached servicemen from the two black units. Rumford's bill also banned National Guard units from using race or religion as criteria for discriminating in enlistments, promotions, and commissions. This meant the Guard could not reduce the rank held by black members when they were reassigned or assigned to integrated units. When the bill came before the Assembly Committee on Military and Veterans Affairs, Attorney General Fred N. Howser opposed it on the grounds that it might cause the federal government to withhold funding for the state units. Howser wanted the National Guard returned to California jurisdiction before changes like those advocated by Rumford were made. Rumford pointed out that New Jersey and Connecticut had integrated their National Guard units without losing federal money. In a pattern of white liberal support which became typical for Rumford's successful legislative efforts, Richard J. Dolwig (D-San Mateo) helped persuade the committee to recommend "Do pass" and submit the bill to the full Assembly.

The Assembly passed the bill and sent it to the Senate, where the Committee on Military and Veterans Affairs deliberately delayed hearings by holding them at night when it was difficult to get a quorum. Rumford had to seek out members of the committee himself to urge them to attend the hearings. A brief hearing was finally held on June 27, after much caucusing among Democratic members, and enough "yes" votes were secured to pass the bill on to the full Senate, which voted for it by a small margin on June 30. Governor Warren signed it into law on July 18, 1949.

The second bill Rumford brought into the Assembly, also in January, 1949, reflected the practice he continued throughout his career of going home to his drugstore on weekends to talk politics and problems with his constituents. Many of the bills he brought to the Assembly floor were conceived in drugstore conversations about specific problems faced by individuals as a result of racially discriminatory customs that were nearly invisible except to their victims. Rumford's second bill tackled insurance companies which refused to issue policies covering automobiles owned by blacks and other minority people and sought to make the practice illegal. Insurance company representatives suggested that certain people were bad risks and that each group should carry its own losses, but Rumford argued that since the state required every car owner to carry a public liability policy, it was unconstitutional to refuse insurance solely because of the applicant's race, color, or creed. Moreover, Rumford charged, insurance companies that did grant coverage to black car owners raised the premium by as much as fifteen percent. The bill (AB-32) passed both houses, and the governor signed it with the comment, "It's about time we end these discriminatory practices."

As Rumford established himself in Sacramento, Democratic Party regulars at home began to consider him as a candidate for his district's congressional seat, which would be empty in 1950. Rumford quashed this proposal, however, by announcing that he preferred to remain in the Assembly where he thought he could accomplish more on issues of unemployment, education, and discrimination in employment and housing. In his second general election Rumford ran for his Assembly seat unopposed, and in his second term he successfully shepherded several civil rights bills through the legislature into law.

Employment was a regular theme in Rumford's bills. He co-authored a law to prohibit public school districts from using photographs and letters of reference as part of the process of hiring teachers, because these instruments had been used to identify the race of applicants and exclude blacks and other minorities without considering their qualifications. He fought against a bill sponsored by Assemblyman Thomas A. Maloney (R-San Francisco) to establish a Commission on Political Equality with no funding or enforcement powers. Arguing that Maloney's bill was weak and meaningless—as he had argued against McCollister's National Guard bill—Rumford proposed an alternative which called for a permanent Fair Employment Commission to be appointed by the governor and provided with a paid executive secretary and support staff and which would be able to impose financial penalties ($500) and jail sentences (six months) on employers and labor organizations that discriminated on the basis of race, color, or creed. This measure was denounced by both employer and labor groups as "a step toward nationalization of jobs" which "constitut[ed] an intrusion by the government on the private right of property of employers." Rumford and his supporters suggested that the failure of labor unions to support this bill was due to fear among white officials and members that blacks would compete for well-paid jobs monopolized by white men. In the end, Rumford's bill was defeated in committee by a vote of 15 to 3, but his opposition had also helped defeat Maloney's measure by a 9-to-3 margin. The field was still open for an effective fair employment commission, and Rumford promised to return to the issue.

In the meanwhile, there were limited campaigns to wage for specific results. With backing and lobbying assistance from Governor Warren, Rumford and Edward M. Gaffney (D-San Francisco) pushed through AB 546 to open union membership and apprenticeship programs to all qualified employees regardless of race, color, or creed. When the governor signed this bill into law on June 22, 1951, the practice of restricting apprenticeship positions to relatives and proteges of influential union members or employers, especially prevalent in plumbing and carpentry, was outlawed. Outraged by Armstrong Business College in Berkeley, which accepted Chinese and Japanese applicants but prohibited the enrollment of black students, Rumford and Hawkins proposed a bill to forbid discrimination in enrollment in both public and private vocational, business, and professional schools. The bill passed the House but died in the Senate, and Armstrong did not admit its first black student until a similar bill passed in 1955, a time lapse that allowed its president to soften his

1951 promise to "get out of the business" if Rumford's bill passed.

Rumford's constant awareness of the need to enlist the authority of the state on behalf of the victims of discrimination showed itself in a pair of bills to end free-speech protection of hate literature. The bills—which prohibited the promulgation of propaganda designed to discredit any religious belief and forbade the dissemination of material advocating hatred of any person or group on the basis of race, color, or religion—were Rumford's response to a resurgence of white supremicist activities. This was particularly notable in the Imperial Valley, where the Ku Klux Klan and other hate groups were active.

In his fourth term, which began in 1955, Rumford returned to the fair employment fight. Joined by Hawkins and eighteen other members of the Assembly, Rumford introduced AB 971 to establish a "little" Fair Employment Practices Commission. The bill called for a five-member commission authorized to hold hearings on employment discrimination, and to issue orders to correct the effects of discriminatory practices or to prevent their recurrence. Enforcement would be through District Courts of Appeal, and violations would be treated as misdemeanors. "Of course it fell short of my wishes," remembered Rumford years later, "but it did fit into my overall hope of resolving job discrimination. Since Assemblyman Hawkins had introduced much stronger bills in 1945 and 1947, and had failed to get them passed, I felt this was the only type of legislation I could get passed by this legislature." The bill was passed and became law. Other fourth-term accomplishments were the passage of Rumford bills to provide free polio vaccine to millions of Californians and to prohibit the use of marital status or age as reasons for rejecting applicants for public school teaching positions.

In January, 1959, as Rumford began his sixth term, he and Hawkins found the conditions right for a civil rights campaign that meant "getting to the center of bigotry which prevents real equality of opportunity not only for racial minorities but for other victims of prejudice as well." Once more, he acted on what he called "the democratic assumption that it is the duty of the state to provide and ensure equal protection of the laws to all its citizens." With the Democrats in control of both houses of the legislature and Pat Brown in the governor's mansion, Rumford and Hawkins on January 7 invited members of the legislature to affix their signatures to AB 91 to create a permanent Fair Employment Practices Commission. As proposed, the commission would be able to bring before a hearing panel by subpoena if necessary any person or persons, employers, or organizations who were accused of discriminating on the basis of race, creed, color, or national origin against any person or persons seeking employment. It could also assess a penalty of six months in prison, a $5,000 fine, or both. It would have a paid executive secretary and support stage, and its members would be appointed by the governor. Before presenting his bill in the legislature, Rumford had already enlisted support from the California State Chamber of Commerce, the California Manufacturers' Association, the California Labor Federation, AFL-CIO, and from Governor Pat Brown. Brown had made fair employment legislation a centerpiece of his legislative program, using his inaugural address to

urge lawmakers to "enact legislation to bar discrimination by an employer or labor union on grounds of race, creed, national origin, or age."

The contest went on for three months, with opponents reminding legislators that voters had defeated a fair employment practices initiative by a margin of two to one in 1946. Almost a hundred amendments were added to the original bill before it passed two different committee hearings in the Assembly on February 19, yet there was little debate when the Assembly voted sixty-five to fourteen for the bill and sent it to the Senate. It took until April 8 for the Senate Labor and Finance Committee to bring the bill to the floor, where more amendments were added before the vote was taken. The bill passed the Senate thirty to five. The Assembly accepted the Senate amendments but added a few more, requiring the bill to go to a conference committee which removed age as one of the outlawed bases for discrimination in a final resolution of the differences between the two versions of the bill. On April 10 the Assembly passed Rumford's measure by a clear majority. After fourteen years of legislative efforts, California now had an enforceable fair employment law; it went into effect on September 18, 1959.

The creation of the Fair Employment Practices Commission was the most memorable event of the 1959 legislative session, but two other civil rights bills also made their way into law. The Unruh Civil Rights Act forbade business establishments dealing with the public to deny services on the basis of race. It declared, "all persons within the jurisdiction of the State are free and equal, and entitled to the full and equal accommodation, advantages, facilities, and privileges or services in all business establishments of any kind whatsoever." Hawkins also brought a bill into law which prohibited racial discrimination in the sale of houses financed with mortgages insured or guaranteed by the Federal Housing Administration (FHA) or the Veterans Administration (VA). Although the penalty on sellers who violated the law were slight, it did create a Commission on Discrimination in Housing.

It took four more years to prepare what Rumford hoped would be the crowning legislative measure to end all discrimination and segregation: a fair housing bill. A fair housing measure introduced by Hawkins in the 1961 session of the legislature failed, and experience had taught the anti-discrimination coalition that legislation on housing was the most controversial kind. Attempts to ensure equal access to housing by forbidding property owners to discriminate on racial grounds in selling houses—in effect limiting their right to choose to whom to sell—were guaranteed to stir up widespread and strong held racist feelings. Thus supporters of the legislature had already marshalled backing and votes for fair housing before bringing a measure to the Assembly. On February 13, 1963, Governor Pat Brown called on a joint session of the legislature to "pass legislation to eliminate discrimination in the private housing market in California." On the same day, Rumford announced that he had on his desk a bill supported by the governor and a broad array of civil rights organizations. The bill, AB 1240, was essentially the same as AB 801, the fair housing bill Hawkins had unsuccessfully sponsored two years before. With Democrats in the majority in both houses and with the governor behind the bill, the time seemed ripe for its passage. Many legislators rushed to add their names as sponsors, and those who opposed it assumed evasive postures.

When the bill reached the floor of the Assembly on April 25, Rumford opened the argument for it by asking that California "rid itself of this insidious practice, that of housing discrimination affecting a great number of American citizens in this state." In the hearings that followed, debate ranged endlessly over the right of the state to restrict the right of private property by legislating against discrimination practices in private housing. The California Real Estate Association (CREA) asserted that there was "no widespread discrimination in the state." Charges flew that the measure was unconstitutional, that it was a kind of class legislation which would create "a special privilege for a chosen group while destroying the private rights of others." After days of quibbling, long-winded speeches, and heckling by activist groups, the Assembly finally passed Rumford's bill by a vote of 47 to 25, with Republicans casting all the negative votes.

On the Senate side, the much-amended AB 1240 was assigned to the Committee on Governmental Efficiency and Economy chaired by Luther E. Gibson (D-Solano). Gibson was rumored to be determined not to let the bill pass his committee, whose mostly rural members often voted as a unit against measures concerning housing and employment opportunities for nonwhites. The rumors proved to be correct, as Gibson employed delaying tactic after delaying tactic. After the first two-hour meeting in May, Gibson announced that the committee would vote on May 29—and immediately provoked a demonstration by members of the Congress of Racial Equality (CORE) who vowed to stay in the Capital rotunda mezzanine until AB 1240 was acted upon. They sat there for three weeks. On June 14, Gibson announced at a hearing, "My committee will never approve a bill prohibiting discrimination in private housing" and proposed an amendment that exempted single-unit dwellings not financed by FHA, VA, or CAL-VET loans. When Rumford pointed out that Hawkins's 1959 bill already covered publicly financed housing, Gibson adjourned the hearing without announcing a new meeting time.

Days passed without a new hearing being announced. Rumford and Assembly Speaker Jesse Unruh met to arrange a conference—and a compromise—with Gibson. Gibson then announced a compromise he claimed he had reached with Rumford, but Rumford denounced Gibson's version of their agreement. As the dispute heated up, Gibson again went public with a statement that negotiations were at an impasse and an offer to meet with Rumford again, but Rumford retorted that he "would prefer to discuss the matter with the full committee." Finally Gibson announced that his committee would hold no further hearings on the measure. A breakthrough came at a closed-door meeting convened by Democratic Party leaders at which members of Gibson's committee, Rumford, and Governor Brown agreed to remove certain provisions of the bill while preserving its substance and the enforcement power of the commission.

As it turned out, on June 21, the last day of the legislative session, after literally picking the bill apart and adopting twenty-three amendments, the Committee on Governmental Efficiency and Economy reported the bill out to the full Senate. The Senate adopted the bill and its amendments and referred it to the Senate Finance Committee to determine whether the measure could and should be financed. Standing in the back of the Senate Chamber, the Finance Committee acted quickly early in the evening and returned the bill to Gibson's committee with a "Do Pass" recommendation.

Watching the clock as the last hours of the session approached, Rumford thought he saw evidence that the Gibson committee would use the long calendar of bills awaiting attention as an excuse not to act on the housing bill. Unable to approach Gibson himself because of the anger between them, Rumford sought help from Senators Joseph A. Rattigan (D-Sonoma) and Bruce V. Regan (D-Los Angeles). Both senators were members of the liberal Democratic majority and shared the governor's commitment to seeing the bill through. They persuaded Gibson to bring the bill to the Senate floor, but if the full Senate adopted any further amendments, the clock would run out before the whole bill could be returned to the Assembly and come before the Senate again for a final vote. While Rumford worried that Gibson or one of his allies might introduce some delaying amendment, Governor Brown moved into the political scuffle, lobbying key senators until resistance to the bill crumbled in the Senate—almost as if by prearrangement. Playing parliamentary rules adroitly, Senator Regan moved at 10:40 P.M. "that AB 1240 as amended be taken up as a 'special order of business' at 11:00 P.M." Regan had already gathered solid support from most Senate Democrats for this motion, which effectively cut off deate and prevented any further amendments.

Twenty minutes later, at exactly 11:00 P.M., Lieutenant Governor Glenn M. Anderson upheld from the chair a point of order by Senator Rattigan and cut off Hugh Burns, the president pro tempore of the Senate and a determined foe of the bill, in mid-speech. Rattigan called for an immediate vote on AB 1240 as amended, following Regan's earlier motion. The bill passed by a vote of 22 to 16 and was rushed to the Assembly within minutes for a vote on the Senate's amendments.

Assembly Speaker Jesse Unruh entertained a motion that AB 1240 be made a "special order of business" and it carried. Voting was set for 11:35 P.M. At the appointed hour, floor leader Jerome R. Waldie (D-Contra Costa) rose to a point of order to call for consideration of the bill with the Senate's thirty-five amendments. Voting began at 11:55. The Assembly Chamber, crowded with anxious spectators who did not know which way the decision would go, was hushed as the roll call began. Rumford said he had expected the Democratic vote, but others were less certain. Slowly the tally mounted to 63 for, 15 against. The gallery crowd burst into a loud cheer of approval, and members of the Assembly gave Rumford a standing ovation. Opponents were silent, perhaps already uniting in a massive and deadly opposition. Outside in the rotunda, sit-downers joined hands and sang "We Shall Overcome." AB 1240 was sent, correctly enrolled, to the governor's office on July 2; it was signed into law on July 18.

In its final form, the Fair Housing Act of 1963 made it illegal for anyone selling, renting, or leasing any residence to attempt to restrict its use on account of race, creed, color, or national origin. Thereby it set a standard for equal access to housing for all discriminated-against minorities. Although the passage of this law can be regarded as the completion of Rumford's civil rights program, it would be almost four years before the final word was in on the use of this right.

The opposition did not disappear when the clerk of the Assembly tallied the vote on June 21. State Senator John G. Schmitz (R-Tustin), the California Real Estate Association, and a coalition of apartment building owners soon led the way to a campaign against what they called "forced-housing" legislation. Their claim that the new law was a dangerous infringement on the rights of private property owners was persuasive to people all over California, and the public debate which followed was heavily laced with derogatory images of blacks and other nonwhites. Rumford became the target of personal abuse and villification and even physical threats. In December, 1963, *CREA,* the official magazine of the California Real Estate Association, ran an editorial mocking the Fair Housing Act and promising to restore the right of choice to the property owners of California.

Before the ninety-day waiting period for the act to go into effect was over, its opponents were trying to circumvent or reverse it. They displayed a deep distrust of lawmakers by devising means to bring the matter to a popular vote. An initial campaign to subject the act to a popular referendum was vetoed by the California Real Estate Association, which preferred the initiative proposition route. If the public would vote for a constitutional amendment prohibiting legislation against discrimination in housing, future legislatures would be bound by it, the association reasoned.

By February, 1964, those who opposed fair housing legislation had gathered enough signatures to qualify a state initiative to invalidate the Fair Housing Act. More than six hundred thousand citizens signed the petition to place Proposition 14—which would reverse the 1963 law and bar the state or any locality from adopting fair housing legislation—on the November ballot. Viewing the effect of the proposition as incorporating racial discrimination into the state constitution, the NAACP and a coalition of other civil-rights organizations undertook an unsuccessful court effort to keep the proposition off the ballot. After an unfavorable ruling in *Lewis v. Jordan,* Governor Brown placed the proposition on the ballot for November 3, 1964.

In the meanwhile, the California Committee on Fair Practices joined Rumford in filing an injunction petition with the State Court of Appeals in Sacramento which questioned the constitutionality of the proposition. Presiding Judge Irving H. Perluss declared the plea inappropriate and rejected it. Four-and-a-half million Californians voted for Proposition 14 and 2.4 million against it after a campaign marked by angry rhetoric, extensive door-to-door electioneering, and dramatic appeals to fundamental rights: private property against equal treatment.

Soon after the results were in, the fair housing coalition filed an appeal with the State Supreme Court to set aside Proposition 14 on the grounds that it violated the equal protection of the laws clause of the Fourteenth Amendment. On May 10, 1966, the court decreed Proposition 14

unconstitutional and reinstated the Fair Housing Act. Supporters of Proposition 14 appealed to the U.S. Supreme Court in a case known as *Reitman et al v. Lincoln M. Mulkey,* but the justices upheld the State Supreme Court's decision.

The Fair Housing Act, adopted by the legislature, repudiated by a two-to-one majority of the electorate, and upheld by two high courts, marked the culmination of a generation of civil rights efforts. It also ended Byron Rumford's political career and may have been the decisive factor in Pat Brown's defeat by Ronald Reagan in the gubernatorial race of 1966. In 1966 Rumford ignored the advice of some of his Assembly colleagues and local supporters and gave up his Assembly seat to seek the newly created Eighth (State) Senatorial District seat in Alameda County. With nine successful campaigns for the Assembly and an impressive legislative record behind him, Rumford's decision seemed logical. Yet he was estranged from most of the local white Democratic leadership because of his insistence on seeking the State Senate seat despite their fears that he could not win it. Young black militants looked askance at his growing conservatism in matters not tied to civil rights. The campaign against him castigated Rumford for his role in enacting the Fair Housing Act. He lost the election by 801 votes to Republican Lewis R. Sherman of Berkeley.

Rumford returned to private life in Berkeley. His attempt to regain his old Assembly seat in 1968 failed when he lost by 5,754 votes in the April 4 primary to the new incumbent, black Democrat John J. Miller. Contemporary analysts asserted that Rumford was not liberal enough for the radicals in his district and that he was too liberal to forestall the growing conservatism of California under Governor Ronald Reagan. In the emotional climate created by the Vietnam War and the mass civil rights movement of the mid-1960s, Rumford no longer matched the radical demands placed on elected officials, especially minority ones.

In his last public position, Rumford served the Nixon and Ford administrations for five years as Assistant Director for Consumer Protection and State-Federal Relations of the Federal Trade Commission (FTC). He was appointed by his former Assembly colleague, Secretary of Health, Education, and Welfare Caspar W. Weinberger. Rumford left the FTC in 1976 to return to pharmacy, from which he retired in 1981. His last years were spent in humble illness in his Berkeley home. Byron Rumford died of Parkinson's disease on June 12, 1986.

In eulogizing Rumford, Los Angeles Mayor Tom Bradley wrote, "Mr. Rumford was one of the torchbearers of the equal rights movement in California. He was a universal man who sought to reach the ideal American goal of a nonracial society where all peoples could be respected and treated as individuals, and as equals." Supreme Court Justice Allen E. Broussard added that the effect of Rumford's work in civil rights and of his mentoring of leading citizens in all walks of life constituted a "monument more enduring than bronze, longer than that of many other historical figures."

The principles Rumford stood for and the institutions he helped create are now placed in the service of other discriminated-against classes of people. According to statistics compiled by the State Fair Employment Practices office, discrimination complaints concerning employment are now much more likely to stem from gender bias than from race. In 1966, eighty-one percent of complaints were filed for racial reasons; in 1983, by contrast, thirty-nine percent of the complaints alleged gender discrimination and only twenty-seven percent charged race or color discrimination. In 1982, fifty-nine percent of complaints about housing discrimination involved race, down from ninety percent in 1959. The handicapped and single mothers with children are now using the principles Rumford espoused to gain access to housing and employment.

Rumford made his mark in an age when formal political institutions still sanctioned discrimination. Yet, as he was the first to acknowledge, his effectiveness was due to the sustained efforts of black-and-white civil rights activists over decades. In the continuing struggle to translate laws into social and economic reality, however, individuals do not stand out as clearly, and appropriate and feasible goals are harder to define.

Name: _____   Date: _____

WORKSHEET 8: Modern California

1. What role did the Sleepy Lagoon incident and the Zoot Suit Riot of 1943 play in

   World War II's racial climate in California? _____

   _____

   _____

   _____

   _____

2. Carey McWilliams was _____

3. Harry Bridges brought back _____

4. What did Leo Hart accomplish with the "Children of the Dust Bowl"? _____

   _____

   _____

   _____

   _____

5. What did Peter Bancroft do to help the Arvin school kids? _____

   _____

6. What position did Leo Hart hold? _____

   _____

7. What success rate did the Arvin school kids have (use some examples)? _____

_____

_____

_____

8. Why was the "Mare Island Mutiny and Court Martial" so important in the rise of post-World War II civil rights? _____

_____

_____

_____

_____

9. Thurgood Marshall was _____

_____

10. What black newspaper defended the Mare Island Mutineers and why was this important? _____

_____

_____

_____

11. Helen Gahagan Douglas' background was _____

_____

12. The base of Mrs. Douglas' political support was _____

_____

13. Name three areas of American politics and society that Mrs. Douglas influenced:

1. _____ 2. _____

3. _____

14. What tactics did Nixon use to defeat Mrs. Douglas in the 1950 U.S. Senate race?

_____

_____

15. Briefly analyze the importance of Helen Gahagan Douglas to California politics

and society _____

_____

_____

_____

16. What does Professor John C. Chen mean by "Reversal of Fortune" in his study of

images of America's Chinese? _____

_____

_____

17. Describe some key elements of hostility to Chinese Americans and how they

overcame them, according to Professor Chen? _____

_____

_____